Jazz Places

The publisher and the University of California Press Foundation gratefully acknowledge the generous support of the Ben and A. Jess Shenson Endowment Fund in Visual and Performing Arts, established by a major gift from Fred M. Levin and Nancy Livingston, The Shenson Foundation.

The publisher also gratefully acknowledges the generous support of the AMS 75 PAYS Fund of the American Musicological Society, supported in part by the National Endowment for the Humanities and the Andrew W. Mellon Foundation, in making this book possible.

Jazz Places

How Performance Spaces Shape Jazz History

Kimberly Hannon Teal

UNIVERSITY OF CALIFORNIA PRESS

University of California Press
Oakland, California

© 2021 by Kimberly Hannon Teal

Library of Congress Cataloging-in-Publication Data

    Names: Hannon Teal, Kimberly, 1983– author.
    Title: Jazz places : how performance spaces shape jazz history / Kimberly Hannon Teal.
    Identifiers: LCCN 2020046903 (print) | LCCN 2020046904 (ebook) | ISBN 9780520303706 (cloth) | ISBN 9780520303713 (paperback) | ISBN 9780520972841 (epub)
    Subjects: LCSH: Jazz—History and criticism. | Jazz—Social aspects—United States—History. | Jazz—Instruction and study—United States—History. | Village Vanguard (Nightclub) | Jazz at Lincoln Center (Organization) | SFJAZZ (Organization) | Preservation Hall (New Orleans, La.)
    Classification: LCC ML3508 .H35 2021 (print) | LCC ML3508 (ebook) | DDC 781.650973—dc23
    LC record available at https://lccn.loc.gov/2020046903
    LC ebook record available at https://lccn.loc.gov/2020046904

29 28 27 26 25 24 23 22 21
10 9 8 7 6 5 4 3 2 1

Contents

Acknowledgments   *vii*

    Introduction: Jazz, Place, and Heritage   *1*

1. Jazz Heritage Live at the Village Vanguard   *15*
2. Phantom Partners: Large-Scale Venues on a National Scene   *51*
3. Schools on the Scene   *92*
4. Unearthing The Stone: From Underground to The New School   *120*
5. Reinventing the Recorded at Preservation Hall   *146*

    Epilogue   *173*

Notes   *175*
Bibliography   *193*
Index   *201*

Acknowledgments

The amount of help I've had from wonderful people throughout the process of writing this book has been heartwarming, humbling, and inspiring. There may be too many to thank, but I'd like to make a start on it here. First of all, there are the musicians and listeners who shared their expertise and their time in interviews at various stages in this project: Judy Carmichael, Mickey Collier, Sylvie Courvoisier, Tim Craig, Bill Dobbins, Dave Douglas, Kate Duncan, Katie Ernst, Beverly Frank, Bill Frank, Nick Finzer, Fred Hersh, Dick Hyman, Ethan Iverson, Calvin Johnson, Richard Kessler, Robert Livingston, Pete Madsen, Tommy Poole, Dave Sturmer, and Michael Van Bebber. Without your generosity and insights, this book would not have been possible, and speaking with and writing to you was an enormous pleasure.

This project began as a dissertation at the Eastman School of Music and was shaped in countless ways by the wisdom and support of my advisor, Melina Esse. I would also like to thank Ellen Koskoff, Dariusz Terefenko, Ralph Locke, Clay Jenkins, and the other faculty members in both the Musicology and the Jazz and Contemporary Media Departments who were so helpful in guiding my research process and growth as a scholar. My fellow students in musicology, including Tyler Cassidy-Heacock, Cristina Fava, Naomi Gregory, Lauron Kehrer, Cindy Kim, Amy Kintner, Emily Mills Woodruff, Matt Morrow, and Tanya Sermer, among many others, taught me just as much. I was also fortunate enough to meet Kira Thurman during my first semester of grad school, and I have been benefitting from her unsurpassed skills as a scholar, friend, and academic life coach ever since.

Many people read drafts and parts of this book along the way and helped to make it better. I am grateful to Raina Polivka and Madison Wetzell at the University of California Press and the anonymous reviewers who offered guidance on the project. I would also like to thank my fantastic colleagues at the University of Arkansas, including Micaela Baranello, Alan Gosman, Melody Herr, Justin Hunter, Wing Lau, Lisa Margulis, Matt Mihalka, and Joon Park. Andrew Berish, Darren Mueller, Nate Sloan, Alex Stewart, Emma Tepfer, and my grandfather Donald Ulmer all offered helpful writing advice, as well.

Travelling to the various venues described in this project was some of the best "work" I've ever had the privilege of doing, and the financial support of the Glenn Watkins Fellowship, Elsa T. Johnson Fellowship, and University of Arkansas Humanities Program made it possible. The hospitality of friends, friends of friends, and even strangers who greeted me in New York, New Orleans, and San Francisco was extremely helpful, so thanks are due to Freya Bellin, Rueben Blundell, Jeannie Evers, Charlie Halloran, Chloë Liotta-Jones, and Josh Reed, among others. Finally, Chris Teal, I imagine you know that I would and could have done none of this without you—from your help in choosing the venues for my dissertation proposal at the very beginning to your taking the girls out of the house for long walks to the tree so that I could make final edits—and all the conversations along the way. At risk of adding to my record of mediocre gift-giving, this book is for you.

INTRODUCTION

Jazz, Place, and Heritage

Famous stages from historical jazz venues appeared in MacArthur Fellow Jason Moran's multimedia exhibit for the 2015 Venice Biennale as works of art in themselves. *STAGED*, a project that involves both new music by the pianist and sculptures recreating stages from now-closed New York jazz spaces, has since turned up in several art exhibitions and museums in both Europe and the United States, placing audiences in situations that encourage them to engage aurally not only with the music they hear but also with the ideas evoked by the physical space from which the music is played. One sculpture represents an eighteen-foot-wide slice of Harlem's Savoy Ballroom as it might have looked behind the likes of Chick Webb and Ella Fitzgerald while throngs of Lindy Hoppers moved on the dance floor. Part recreation drawn from old photographs and part Moran's imagination, the stage wraps performers from behind and above with brilliantly reflective golden scallops and rich, intricately patterned fabric, giving an air of opulence to this depression-era escape into music and dancing once accessed via Lenox Avenue for as little as thirty cents. Yet undercutting that feeling of ease and relief are the recordings, piped through speakers built into the sculpture, of the sounds of a chain gang working outside a Louisiana prison—Moran seems to insist that we see the stage as belonging to a more complex story in a broader world. Another sculpture surrounds musicians with two walls and a ceiling representing the close quarters of the Three Deuces, a bebop-era venue on Manhattan's 52nd-Street scene. The small stage pressed in a corner between padded walls mimics the one that used to host Charlie Parker, Max Roach, and other bebop pioneers. Music pours forth from the exhibit's Steinway Spirio, sometimes because Moran and his band are actively playing in the space, and sometimes in its player piano mode that sounds Moran's music without his body. Music, memory, space, and presence are all served up as rich territory for contemplation, threads that overlap to weave contemporary jazz from a mix of history and innovation grounded in the physical spaces of its creation. Stages are more than empty containers to put autonomous musicians in; they are integral to the fabric of jazz. Considering the role venues play in the culture of jazz provides a means of understanding this music that can't be accessed through sound alone. Moreover, these considerations now take place in the high art world of museums and galleries, rather than the sometimes-seedy clubs and juke joints of the 1920s jazz world or even the popular ballrooms or clubs like the Savoy or Three Deuces themselves. What follows is a close look at how the places in which jazz is heard contribute to both the sound of the music and the cultures that surround it through stories told in both historical sources and the voices of contemporary musicians. As Moran's sculptures suggest, jazz venues not only host but also contribute to the creation and interpretation of jazz history.

"Man, if you have to ask, you'll never know." When I first encountered this popular (if unsubstantiated) bit of jazz wisdom, I was full of youthful enthusiasm for challenging, exciting sounds that enchanted me far before I could come close to playing or naming them, and I assumed Louis Armstrong was telling me that I should innately *get* jazz, in my *soul*, as some kind of fundamental moral relationship or ticket to hipness that I either held or didn't. The more time I've spent with this music and the discourses that surround it, the more I've come to take these words from a different angle, as acceptance of the unknowable. The closer I have looked, the more jazz's definition has come to appear as the heart of some kind of wobbly Venn diagram cobbled together from beach balls on a breezy day, constantly rearranged by a combination of inherent traits and external forces while also appearing completely different depending on the spot the viewer chooses to stand. A ball of swing might appear to overlap perfectly in the very center with others holding particular harmonies, improvisation, and one telling of jazz history, but only from one vantage point, and only for a moment. A few steps to the left or right or a little gust of wind lays some defining jazz features aside as others are pushed into alignment. The jazz of Louis Armstrong and the jazz of Pat Metheny can both look like the middle, as can Ornette Coleman's jazz and Nina Simone's and Benny Goodman's. These musics do not have to have any concrete defining features in common to all hold a place in jazz discourses, and the constant shuffling of sounds and ideas that brings each artist's work into and out of the center has come, for me, to look like jazz's only consistency, the constant changes and shifting niche cultures that both define it and make definition elusive.

This changeability and the constant redrawing of jazz's boundaries are nowhere more apparent than in live performances, events that bring the relationship between the physical spaces and historical narratives into focus. While this book will not define jazz once and for all, it will provide five different recent snapshots of the music's ever-shifting structures, taken from different vantage points and in different weather. By looking at a range of contemporary venues in which jazz is played and heard, the borders of the music and its defining traits remain flexible, but an interesting recent shift comes into focus, one that may prove to be as game-changing as jazz's mid-twentieth-century lean away from popular culture and toward the high art world kicked off by the bebop generation. Sociologist Paul Lopes refers to the 1950s and '60s as a "modern jazz renaissance" in which jazz was "firmly secured...as a major American art tradition." By examining the language used to describe jazz from the music's origins through the late twentieth century in trade magazines and eventually broader forms of media, Lopes identifies the late 1950s as the historical moment in which the idea of "a progressive jazz tradition from folk art, to popular art, to modernist high art" came to dominate the discourse.[1] Certainly related to its now well-established art credentials, jazz of the twenty-first century is found in noncommercial spaces with increasing frequency. As live jazz performance has become more closely tied to nonprofit institutions than the commercial speakeasies, ballrooms, and clubs that at various times in the past defined the music's landscape, its relationship to its own heritage has become increasingly important in its public presentation. If presenting jazz in a commercial context can be said to provide a product, the nonprofit world frames jazz as a service, one that offers some sort of social good that goes beyond its monetary value. Though different jazz spaces explain jazz and its heritage in various and sometimes conflicting terms, ties to the past consistently play an important role in defining the present value of the music in all the places this book explores, as imbuing jazz with a noteworthy heritage helps to define and support the social good that makes possible the jazz-as-service framework. With the themes of heritage, preservation, institutionalization, and education in mind, recent performances at the Village Vanguard, Jazz at Lincoln Center, SFJazz Center, university jazz programs, The Stone, and Preservation Hall offer the opportunity to observe the role played by space and place in shaping what we understand to be jazz and its role in contemporary life. A chief aim of this book is to make more transparent the ways in which our presentation of jazz dictates how we understand both its history and its future, and, in particular, to consider how live performances of heritage redefine the past for the purposes of the present. Jazz places and jazz heritage have always been in conversation, but their relationship has become increasingly central to jazz performances as those performances shift to a service-oriented framework.

While it is impossible to name any one musical element that unites jazz as a genre, it is almost equally difficult to avoid hearing the words "heritage" or "tradition" in all varieties of discourse on jazz. They show up in scholarly and popular books, magazines, documentaries, liner and program notes, blogs, and even the 1987 House Concurrent Resolution 57, a document in which the US Congress declares this music, whatever it may be, a "rare and valuable national treasure" that "is important for the youth of America to recognize and understand...as a significant part of their cultural and intellectual heritage."[2] Martin Williams, a major figure in jazz-as-art-music canonization who won a Grammy for his *Smithsonian Collection of Classic Jazz*, titled his best-known book, a 1970 history of jazz, *The Jazz Tradition*, and its 1985 companion *Jazz Heritage*.[3] The major festival celebrating the music's birthplace is the New Orleans Jazz and Heritage Festival, and *In the Tradition* is the title of albums by a number of diverse artists, such as avant-garde saxophonists Anthony Braxton and Arthur Blythe in the 1970s and the Canadian Fraser MacPherson quartet in the 1990s. Trumpeter Doc Cheatham, whose experience with jazz dates back to the 1920s, also recorded an *In the Tradition* album in 1987, and then Cheatham's grandson and fellow trumpet player Theo Croker released one in 2009, a few years after Cheatham's one hundredth birthday. Such references to the past are a regular fixture in how jazz is verbally described and contextualized, and this common practice has a major impact on both the way jazz is framed for contemporary live audiences and the means by which those performances are supported.

As discussions of jazz tradition have crescendoed, the nature of the music's economic support has been in transition. As Scott DeVeaux wrote in his landmark article, "Constructing the Jazz Tradition," "If at one time jazz could be supported by the marketplace, or attributed a nebulous (and idealized) vision of folk creativity, that time has long passed. Only by acquiring the prestige, the 'cultural capital' (in Pierre Bourdieu's phrase) of an artistic tradition can the music hope to be heard, and its practitioners receive the support commensurate with their training and accomplishments."[4] Tradition and heritage are not ideas associated only with jazz in the past; they are pillars that support the music's present cultural and economic value. Yet leaning on these pillars does more than procure spaces and funding to allow live jazz to be heard, it also changes the music that is made and the modes of listening that audiences bring to it. Barbara Kirschenblatt-Gimblett's theorization of the concept of heritage production, originally formulated in the context of museums and tourism, offers a useful way of understanding how choices made in presenting the "traditional" affect the cultural work that performances do. As she points out, "Much is made of the traditions themselves, as if the instruments for presenting them were invisible or inconsequential."[5] She emphasizes that while heritage production bases itself in the past, "the heritage industry is a new mode of cultural production and it produces something new. There is no turning back."[6] By redefining the past, presenting music as heritage carves out a new space for musical practices that no longer inhabit their traditional spaces, and this means that the musical practices themselves are also new in important ways. Kirschenblatt-Gimblett describes this process as the "second life" of those things we claim as heritage, "Heritage organizations ensure that places and practices in danger of disappearing because they are no longer occupied or functioning or valued will survive. It does this by adding the value of pastness, exhibition, difference, and, where possible, indigeneity."[7] Performing heritage makes visible again that which is fading from view and links histories with physical spaces in the process. But as Peggy Phelan cautions in her work on the politics of performance, increased visibility cannot simply be equated to increased power.[8] Highlighting values such as pastness, difference, and indigeneity, which Kirschenblatt-Gimblett argues are central to the notion of heritage, may increase the visibility of jazz, but this process works through an "aesthetics of marginalization" that cordons off the very things it shows from meaningful interaction with mainstream culture.[9] How certain presenters choose to frame the relationship of jazz to the past has a direct impact on the amount of relevance audiences perceive in the music's relationship to the present.

Another central concern that arises when considering live

performances, especially those that explicitly engage with history, is what it means to be "live" at all. A recurring theme that arose in the venues I studied was the place or influence of past recordings in present performances. Philip Auslander's work on liveness and Jason Stanyek's and Benjamin Piekut's exploration of the idea of "deadness" in recording—the resurrection of voices from the past in current music—provide useful insights into how the dead continue to share agency with the living when they are evoked or replayed and how the very notion of the live can only exist with regard to the recorded.[10] Recent work by jazz studies scholars has increasingly drawn attention to the importance of listening contexts in understanding sounds and cultures in jazz history. For example, as Moran draws attention to the physical space of the Savoy Ballroom through his sculpture in *STAGED*, Christi Jay Wells looks back to the physical bodies that moved to the music there in their reading of Chick Webb's work in relation to dancers. Wells considers technical musical features such as tempo and form not as grist for internal analysis of autonomous musical works but as elements of a live performance tradition worked out in real time through dialog between dancers and musicians.[11] An example of the flip side of this heightened awareness of the difference between live and recorded listening can be seen in the writings of Darren Mueller, whose discussions of the long-playing record format and its impact on jazz draw attention to the ways in which recording and listening technologies help shape our understandings of and experiences with this music.[12] Although this book is chiefly concerned with live performance, contemporary live jazz venues are deeply interconnected with jazz's history as a recorded music. Performance spaces and performers interact with jazz's recorded past through the creation of live albums, through live performances of music from famous records, and simply through the unavoidable reality of presenting in person a musical genre whose whole history has unfolded alongside music recording technology, a situation that makes the sounds of the music's "great masters" available on such different terms than the sounds of Bach or Mozart.

Finally, the physical spaces of these venues and their geographical locations play an essential role in framing and defining the music heard within them; when linked with human ideas and values, both individual and shared, the venues become jazz places. In introducing the concept of place, geographer Tim Cresswell writes, "Place is how we make the world meaningful and the way we experience the world. Place, at a basic level, is space invested with meaning in the context of power."[13]

There is a reciprocal relationship between jazz places and jazz practices, and the concepts of heritage and tradition are important linchpins in that relationship. As Cresswell describes, "Place provides a template for practice—an unstable stage for performance. Thinking of place as performed and practiced can help us think of place in radically open and non-essentialized ways, where place is constantly struggled over and reimagined in practical ways. Place is the raw material for the creative production of identity rather than an a priori label of identity. Place provides the conditions of possibility for creative social practice."[14] Just as jazz is performed in venues, venues as places are performed through jazz practices, and these twin processes both draw on and contribute to contemporary understandings of jazz heritage. Following Edward S. Casey's writings on place and space, the analyses in this book come from a perspective of understanding heritage and place as deeply interconnected. Each of the venues discussed here plays a role in defining a jazz tradition by gathering together the physical, cultural, and sonic elements that make such a tradition perceptible. As Casey writes, "Place is the generatrix for the collection, as well as the recollection, of all that occurs in the lives of sentient beings, and even for the trajectories of inanimate things. Its power consists in gathering these lives and things, each with its own space and time, into one arena of common engagement."[15] Casey points out that, in addition to simply gathering together physical things in a location, "Places also gather experiences and histories, even languages and thoughts."[16]

The articulation of ideas about heritage and tradition through live performance in a given jazz place also reflects the power dynamics of that place and the people who invest it with meaning. In these studies of jazz venues in the United States, a music of African American origin in a nation historically defined by racially segregated spaces can show some of the ways in which place is contested or used to develop or alter ideas about race. In *How Racism Takes Place*, George Lipsitz writes that, even in the twenty-first century, "Because of practices that racialize space and spatialize race, whiteness is learned and legitimated, perceived as natural, necessary, and inevitable. Racialized space gives whites privileged access to opportunities for social inclusion and upward mobility. At the same time, it imposes unfair and unjust forms of exploitation and exclusion on aggrieved communities of color. Racialized space shapes nearly every aspect of urban life."[17] Yet, in looking for productive solutions to the injustices of American racialized space, Lipsitz points to African American music, art, and literature, "African

American expressive culture has functioned as both a symptom and a critique of the nexus that links race and space. Its compelling qualities testify to the shameful duration, depth, and dimension of the racialization of space and the spatialization of race."[18] Live performances of jazz both exist within and comment on the systemic forces Lipsitz explains and critiques.

Similarly, the historically fraught gender politics of jazz both shape and are shaped by the places in which jazz is performed and heard. Geographer Doreen Massey describes what she terms the "power geometry" of space and place to get at how gender figures into understandings of these concepts. Massey highlights how place is both changeable—a process rather than a static fixture—and viewed differently by different users and inhabitants depending on their position within the power geometry of a given place at a given point in time. As she explains,

> One of the problems here has been a persistent identification of place with "community." Yet this is a misidentification. On the one hand, communities can exist without being in the same place—from networks of friends with like interests, to major religious, ethnic or political communities. On the other hand, the instances of places housing single "communities" in the sense of coherent social groups are probably—and, I would argue, have for long been—quite rare. Moreover, even where they do exist this in no way implies a single sense of place. For people occupy different positions within any community.[19]

Collectively, jazz places show contested ideas about and varying experiences with what might be considered a large-scale, shared jazz community; individually, each venue holds different benefits, challenges, pathways, and barriers for every performer and listener who accesses music there—and those who can't or don't.

While choices about which artists to feature, what repertoire to perform, and how to approach that repertoire all contribute important elements to how each venue defines jazz, the location of those venues and the nature of the spaces themselves also shape who hears each version of jazz and how it is interpreted. In order to better understand how ideas of heritage and tradition are presented in the venues studied here, I therefore take into account the general nature of the contemporary urban environments in which these venues exist and the specific cities, neighborhood, and buildings in which each is found. These considerations are framed largely by Adams Krims's *Music and Urban Geography*, which unpacks the important relationship of late twentieth-century global capitalism to contemporary urban landscapes and the musical experiences available within twenty-first-century cities, a connection between music, cities, and economies that he sees as reciprocal, with each factor both shaping and shaped by the others. Krims writes of "design intensity" in the post-Fordist city, a term that "refers to the tendency in advanced societies for products and services to owe much of their value to aspects of design and informational content, and for design and informational aspects of products and services to develop rapidly."[20] Within "design-intensive" cities economically rooted in information, service, and tourist industries, music becomes an important aspect of what Krims describes as "integrated aestheticized space," attracting residents and tourists to a given location and also relying on that location to provide an environment that will contain and support the type of listeners to which that music appeals.[21] Were it possible to physically swap the locations of New York's Village Vanguard and New Orleans's Preservation Hall, transporting the music and musicians of each, it would not be possible to ensure their economic and aesthetic viability went with them to their new environments: the appeal and success of each is tied not just to musical sound but also to how that sound fits into shared ideas of place and heritage that extend beyond their walls to the broader neighborhoods and cities they inhabit and the niche markets served by each.

Place commonly plays a significant role in narratives of jazz history. As Andrew Berish writes, "Although not always theorized, jazz scholarship and criticism have from their beginnings been attentive to the places of the music: where it was developed, practiced, recorded, and performed."[22] Contemporary examples continue to describe the music in terms of space and place as well. For example, Scott DeVeaux and Gary Giddins's popular textbook *Jazz* contains the chapter titles "New Orleans" and "New York in the 1920s." In his book *Jazz Matters: Sound, Place, and Time since Bebop,* jazz studies scholar David Ake writes, "Musicians create and listeners are drawn to certain sounds, forms, and grooves because of the identities they celebrate or the ideas or emotions they convey or evoke *at a particular place and time.* A performance that speaks to us in youth (or in winter, or in Berlin, or in the morning, or in a barroom) may not speak to us in old age (or in summer, or in Memphis, or at night, or in a concert hall)."[23] While jazz has long been created and heard around the world, as recent publications like Philip Bohlman and Goffredo Plastino's *Jazz Worlds / World Jazz* and Alex Rodriguez's "Making the Hang in Chile at Thelonious" attest, in the United States, links between music and place have had a particularly strong presence in jazz discourse.²⁴ As Berish writes in his study of place in mid-twentieth-century swing culture, "Tied as it was to the birth of modern American mass-mediated culture, since its beginning jazz has been about the tension between the voice of the local and the expression of the nation."²⁵ By examining the intersections of place and heritage in contemporary venues, the following chapters reexamine questions of jazz, place, and history in a twenty-first-century American context.

Each chapter ventures into a different type of place, exploring some of the many environments in which jazz is now heard. "Liveness" is a word often paired with the first venue in this study, the Village Vanguard. A multitude of well-known albums have been recorded in front of the audiences in this small club, and many of them boast of their creation "live at the Village Vanguard" in titles or otherwise prominently on their covers. Chapter One explores the persistence of this venue through eight decades of change in the surrounding scene leading to its current status as a site that both exists in the present and evokes a jazz world now mostly erased, a world of clubs functioning as independent businesses rather than their charitable projects—Dizzy's Club Coca Cola inside Jazz at Lincoln Center standing as a clear twenty-first-century contrast case. Conversations with pianists Fred Hersch and Ethan Iverson, both regulars at the Vanguard, bring to light the ways in which the long history of the venue now helps to shape the music that is performed there.

In contrast to Hersch and Iverson, the star musicians featured in the concerts discussed in the second chapter's reading of Jazz at Lincoln Center were not alive to perform or witness their music's live presentation in that space, but the weight of their reputations helped to solidify the presence of jazz at large-scale, nationally visible performing arts centers. The Hall of Fame concert series resurrected a handful of historical artists each season, including Fats Waller, Mary Lou Williams, and Bill Evans in 2010, through productions that featured both music and narration to make the work of these musicians part of the venue's bigger story of jazz history. This chapter explores the shared agency of deceased composer-performer-improvisers and contemporary presenters of their music including in the incorporation of artists of diverse races, genders, and musical styles into a unified blues- and swing-based canon. While that canon and its well defined artistic credentials helped to bolster the presence and growth of Jazz at Lincoln Center, similar venues that have taken shape in the wake of its successes have asserted their own identities in part by reacting to rather than replicating artistic director Wynton Marsalis's model. A Miles Davis festival presented by SFJazz offers a strong contrast to the Hall of Fame concerts at Lincoln Center despite being possible in part because of them.

Just as ghosts take to the Jazz at Lincoln Center stage, they haunt the practice rooms, classrooms, and concert halls of the many colleges and universities in the United States that offer jazz as a topic of academic study. As jazz education has shifted away from an older informal apprenticeship system and toward formal collegiate training, the jazz masters who once provided interactive, on-the-job mentorship continue to be held in high regard, but access to them and the type of training they once provided often seems increasingly out of reach. Chapter 3 documents efforts at several universities to connect students to versions of apprenticeship experiences that evoke past practices of informal learning. Through snapshots of student experiences at the University of Nebraska Omaha, Oklahoma State University, Loyola University New Orleans, and the Eastman School of Music, this chapter explores how jazz educators seek and provide real-world opportunities within jazz curricula by drawing on and connecting to institutional resources, local professional scenes, and recordings of jazz greats, remaking bits of formerly common apprenticeship experiences in new guises.

In many ways, John Zorn's experimental music space The Stone is the antithesis of formal jazz education based in a history of great masters taught at major institutions. Existing for twelve years on an inconspicuous corner in Manhattan's Lower East Side in what used to be a Chinese restaurant, The Stone could only be found by listeners with some form of connection to Zorn's musical community. The small, bare-bones venue advertised only through its website had no visible signage beyond some peeling stick-on lettering near the door handle, and even that could only be seen when a security gate was lifted shortly before a performance. This underground approach provided the avant-garde musicians Zorn supports with a safe space to experiment in front of a small but carefully curated audience. The Stone has moved, however, to a new and much more visible location at The New School's College of Performing Arts. In 2018, The Stone completed its transition to its new academic context, bringing contemporary music and musicians into direct contact with students learning jazz in the institutional model. Chapter 4 explores the transition from insider community to educational partnership, bringing The Stone inward from the musical margins while pulling jazz education outward.

The final chapter returns to jazz's mythical beginnings with the practice of reviving and maintaining early jazz styles in the music's birthplace. Preservation Hall opened in New Orleans in 1961, and it is now a major tourist destination that celebrates the heritage of both the music and the city. Paired with its own charitable foundation created in 2011, this space plays an active role in writing contemporary ideas about jazz as an art music with a positive social mission onto the sonic past of the music's origins in popular and vernacular styles, displaying present values through its embrace of the past.

Among the most exciting features of writing about contemporary live performance is the possibility of engaging directly with the practitioners of this music. This book draws heavily on not just the musical contributions of these artists but also their own words and ideas about what they do. Interviews with Judy Carmichael, Sylvie Courvoisier, Tim Craig, Bill Dobbins, Dave Douglas, Kate Duncan, Katie Ernst, Nick Finzer, Fred Hersh, Dick Hyman, Ethan Iverson, Calvin Johnson, Richard Kessler, Pete Madsen, Tommy Poole, Dave Sturmer, and Michael Van Bebber all significantly shaped my thinking on the issues in this study, and I am deeply grateful for both their music and their generosity in sharing their thoughts on it. Their contributions are what makes this book uniquely valuable, as they have allowed me to link scholarship from historical and theoretical writings, my own fieldwork, and the perspectives of working professional musicians. While no single book could create a complete picture of the rich and multifaceted jazz landscape of the contemporary United States, it is my hope that this one contributes to current understandings of the cultural work jazz does in the changing world of twenty-first-century venues. As geographer Patricia Price writes, one approach to understanding place is to treat it as "a layered, shifting reality that is constituted, lived and contested, in part, through narrative."[26] In the following chapters, the stories told by the musicians I interviewed are woven together with my own experiences, historical narratives, and the research of other jazz scholars to create one possible tale of twenty-first-century jazz in the United States. Jazz history is being written in contemporary live performances, through not just the addition of new sounds but also the way they relate to and define what came before them, where they are held, and the culture that surrounds them.

Finally, I must note that these analyses were completed in early 2020, and sending them to the publisher was one of the last things I did in my office before the university where I work was closed due to the coronavirus pandemic. As I edit from home, reflecting on my own smaller and different world, all the present-tense words that felt contemporary in February now, in July, read to me like a time capsule of a historical period that has certainly come to an end, as the live jazz scene in the United States now barely resembles what existed six months ago. The venues in this book all closed for live performances in March and have yet to reopen. As I write this, the Village Vanguard is selling live-stream performances rather than tickets to in-person shows; Jazz at Lincoln Center is maintaining a daily schedule of online classes, workshops, and concerts; SFJazz is offering a digital membership program; universities are scrambling to create online or socially distanced alternatives to regular in-person music instruction, waiting anxiously for the results of studies underway on the potential for spreading the virus by singing or playing wind instruments; and every item on the detailed July calendar for The Stone is followed by the all-caps exclamation "CANCELED!" Preservation Hall released a statement asking patrons with prepaid tickets to consider holding onto them for a later date when reopening would be possible rather than seeking a refund in order to help support struggling musicians who have suddenly found themselves out of work. Most troubling are the lives lost to COVID-19, including jazz greats Ellis Marsalis, Lee Konitz, Bucky Pizzarelli, Onaje Allan Gumbs, Helen Jones Woods, Henry Grimes, and Wallace Roney. The live jazz scene that emerges from this crisis will undoubtedly look and sound different than the one described in the following pages.

CHAPTER 1

Jazz Heritage Live at the Village Vanguard

There's no other place on the planet where so many greats played for so many years, and that's one of those statements that seems like hyperbole, but it's not.... It's really the only quote unquote holy place left in jazz—period.[1]

Loren Schoenberg, artistic director of the National Jazz Museum in Harlem, on the Village Vanguard

The first night I came to New York to go to college, I came to the Village Vanguard. On a Sunday night, I saw Joe Lovano, Tom Harrell, John Abercrombie, Rufus Reid, and Ed Blackwell play. As the first time I'd seen, well, specifically Ed Blackwell, who is really one of my favorite musicians in history, it was so incredible just to be able to walk down and see him be in this place. There were a lot of other musicians here seeing Lovano and Blackwell—I recognized a lot of musicians. And I think that is the jazz tradition in a sense, a place like the Vanguard where all these people have played. I knew that I wanted to try to be a part of that tradition, so I came to the Vanguard.[2]

Ethan Iverson, regular performer at the Village Vanguard

February 2020 marked the eighty-sixth year since the Village Vanguard first opened its doors, a venue that began on the fringes of the jazz world that now, for many, stands at its sacred center. Having long held the title of New York City's oldest nightclub, the small, triangular basement on Seventh Avenue South in Greenwich Village must appear quite unassuming to those unaware of the club's rich history. It holds just 123 closely packed seats amidst a display of black and white photos and an old tuba. Yet to today's jazz musicians, the Vanguard is, as pianist Jason Moran put it, "the place where Moses and Mohammed and Jesus walked!"[3] Everything—including the red awning out front, the cozy stage at the point of the triangle, and the multitude of recordings whose covers proclaim them recorded "live at the Village Vanguard"—comes together to evoke memories of great past artists whose faces stare down from the pictures on the club's walls: Thelonious Monk, Sonny Rollins, Bill Evans, Charles Mingus, and many more.

Commentators often note the consistencies the Vanguard has maintained over the course of the many years it has been open. As Matthew Kassel wrote in a piece for *The Observer* on the venue's eightieth birthday, "not much has changed about the Vanguard, its distinct red awning jutting out into the sidewalk like a beacon of stability in a neighborhood that often feels like a palimpsest of itself."[4] Yet the very stability of the club and its unbroken links with its own past have begun to drastically set it apart from other venues on the current New York City jazz scene and other clubs throughout the country. While the Vanguard itself has remained remarkably consistent, the cultural meanings surrounding it have fundamentally changed over time, and these changes have ultimately altered the functioning of the club itself. During the past eight decades, the Village Vanguard moved from the periphery of the city's jazz culture to its heart as it came increasingly to represent not so much an artistic vanguard of musical experimentation as a symbol of a historically sanctified jazz mainstream. An examination of the way place and history interact with music makes plain the growing role of heritage in defining today's Village Vanguard and its characteristic showcasing of a tradition of small group improvisation with ties, both sonic and philosophical, to bebop and its related subgenres.

The place in which a sound originates shapes our experience of it in a number of ways, both acoustically and culturally, and musicians and audiences have spoken highly of the Vanguard in both regards. In her introduction to the volume *Music, Sound and Space*, Georgina Born identifies three main lineages of thought in the analysis of sound and space, including metaphorical conceptions of musical space drawn from musical notation, the type of physical spatialization of sound associated with, for example, multichannel recording and a broad third entry point for study that conceptualizes space "not in terms of the internal operations of musical form, nor in terms of the perception of evolving musical or sound objects, but as multiple and constellatory."[5] To consider the sounds of the Village Vanguard as multiple and constellatory helps to identify the various meanings that the music of this ostensibly consistent place traverses through ever-shifting contexts of space and time. Rather than functioning as a fixed point in a shifting sea of jazz history, the Vanguard itself also "moves" with currents that shift over time. Drawing on work in geography by Nigel Thrift, Born writes that "rather than think of space as static, unitary and unconnected to time, it should be interpreted as inherently mobile and in motion."[6] To search for what the Village Vanguard means to jazz is to search for a moving target, as musical, cultural, temporal, and geographic forces are always shifting the way in which the space is experienced. As Born argues, "Taking account of all the elements in these multiplicities—music and sound, space and time, subjectivity and sociality—all are immanent in the experience of music and sound, and all are continually involved in the mediation of the other terms. Abstractly, the six elements can be conceived as composing a dynamic matrix in which each term potentially mediates all the others, together forming a constellation of multidirectional, virtual transformations. But this tidy image pins down what is more aptly portrayed as a decentered, mobile and unruly flux of mediations."[7] The various tensions Born describes as shaping the experience of music, sound, and space occur at the Village Vanguard not only for listeners taking in sound but also for musicians creating those sounds through improvisation on stage. The venue is in a dynamic, ever-changing relationship with musicians, listeners, its local geography, and its broader influence that plays out in part through the musical choices of players as they create the Vanguard's present sound in real time.

The present Vanguard, however, is always in dialog with the past. Barbara Kirschenblatt-Gimblett's theorization of heritage production offers a useful way of understanding how past and present now interact in the Village Vanguard. She writes that, "Heritage is created through a process of exhibition (as knowledge, as performance, as museum display). Exhibition endows heritage thus conceived with a second life."[8] The musicians who now play at the Village Vanguard perform the line between Kirschenblatt-Gimblett's second life and what could be called a first life, relying on heritage for cultural weight, but facing the additional challenge that the heritage in question traditionally values individuality, countercultural cache, and the placement of pressure on established norms. Music that manages this elaborate balancing act both supports and is supported by the venue itself as the Vanguard plays its own set of complex local and global changes to hold onto its literal and cultural real estate. This space made famous by the music performed and recorded there has valorized a heritage that now exerts control over what is played on its stage, and, by extension, what is widely considered to be today's most respected subgenre of jazz. The network of people involved with this space, including musicians, listeners in person and through records, and the management of the business both past and present, together create a unique local identity for the Vanguard and a construction of what jazz is and has been that resonates outward beyond the physical limits of its famous red doors.

While its status as a small, privately owned jazz club that has held on since an era in which such places were common in many ways makes it stand out in sharp contrast to today's growing prevalence of large nonprofit jazz institutions; the fact that it now shares a scene with those institutions contributes to the Vanguard's current value as a historic landmark. Especially as tourism has grown in importance in the area surrounding the venue, its role in presenting not just jazz but also jazz heritage has added weight to what happens on the Vanguard's stage. The site simultaneously enacts its specific local nature, shown in the rhetoric about its consistency, and turns that local specificity into a commodity with a broader reach in its more recently acquired status as a tourist destination and recording space. A delicate balance between sameness and change, local and distributed, characterizes today's Village Vanguard, a place that simultaneously operates as the bohemian club it has always been and a sort of shrine to both its own past and the numerous other places from the heyday of jazz nightclubs that it outlived. We embark now on a tour of the Vanguard, beginning with its position in the context of a national scene of small jazz clubs in the United States then continuing to consider the history of the venue, its role as a recording space, transitions in ownership from one member of the Gordon family to the next, and changes in its surrounding scenes, both in terms of its local neighborhood and a more geographically broad community of artists and listeners who have engaged with the space over the years. Finally, the music of two pianists who have been regulars at the Vanguard for the first two decades of the twenty-first century, Fred Hersch and Ethan Iverson, will be explored to show how the specific intersection of place and heritage at this venue is audible in the music performed there.

JAZZ IN SMALL CLUBS

In the months leading up to their stint at the Vanguard in April of 1961, Art Blakey and the Jazz Messengers combined international touring and festival performances with engagements at various clubs in the United States that often lasted for two weeks at a time. While they spent the month of December, 1960, mostly playing one or two nights each in cities in Sweden, France, Germany, and the Netherlands, they spent a week or more of the same year at several domestic clubs like Birdhouse, the Sutherland Lounge, and the Cloister Inn—all in Chicago—and Showboat in Philadelphia. When in New York, they had multiple extended residencies at Birdland throughout the year. At other points in the early 1960s, the Jazz Messengers had extended club gigs at the Renaissance Club and Shelly's Manne Hole in Los Angeles, the Black Hawk and the Jazz Workshop in San Francisco, Minor Key in Detroit, the Jazz Temple in Cleveland, and the Plugged Nickel in Chicago. In the mid-twentieth century, club spaces around the country booked the same artists as the Vanguard for the same multiday or multiweek engagements.[9]

While there are a number of similarities in the touring practices of jazz musicians who play at the Vanguard half a century later, their relationship to small American clubs has changed considerably. Drummer Antonio Sanchez played three other jazz-specific clubs in major US cities in the months leading up to his 2019 Vanguard appearance, but he performed only one night each at Yoshi's in Oakland and the 1905 in Portland, Oregon, and two nights at Dimitriou's Jazz Alley in Seattle. Likewise, saxophonist Mark Turner, who performed weeks with two different groups at the Vanguard that year, toured a number of US jazz clubs around the time of the release of his album *Lathe of Heaven*, including Boston's Regattabar, Chicago's Constellation, Kuumbwa Jazz in Santa Cruz, and Dazzle Jazz in Denver, and he played only one show at each venue. Many contemporary performers at the Vanguard can be more predictably found playing internationally than in other US cities around when they appear in New York. Brad Mehldau's June 2019 Vanguard stint followed tour dates in eight European countries, South Korea, Hong Kong, and Japan. Others, like Joe Lovano and Renee Rosnes, who both performed elsewhere in the United States around the time of their Vanguard dates, appeared at large concert halls rather than clubs, Lovano at theatres in Seattle, Hollywood, Boulder, and Detroit and Rosnes at the Kennedy Center in Washington, D.C. While these contemporary artists appear for one-off performances at festivals and large theatres, just as Blakey's band did in the 1960s, they rarely have extended club engagements outside New York. When they do play clubs, they appear more frequently in Europe than in the United States.[10]

Although touring jazz musicians can no longer count on working in major cities for weeks or even multiple days at a time, those cities tend to have at least one performance venue operating as or styled as a privately owned jazz club like those that thrived during the mid-twentieth century. Many of the longer standing and more successful and prominent of these venues have developed structures and practices different from those at work in the Vanguard to attain stability within their own local scenes. Some, like Yoshi's in Oakland, California, have been running for decades and regularly feature nationally and internationally touring acts that might also appear at the Vanguard, but often for only one or two nights at a time. Others, like Snug Harbor in New Orleans, tend to feature mostly performers with strong ties to the local jazz scene—the surname "Marsalis" is reliably peppered throughout the monthly schedule, for example. The Ferring Jazz Bistro in St. Louis demonstrates how the small jazz club format has been incorporated into some jazz spaces operated by nonprofit organizations with explicitly educational and preservational missions. Jazz St. Louis, the nonprofit that owns the Bistro, runs this cabaret-style jazz club alongside programs like WeBop and Essentially Ellington, two youth jazz education initiatives connected to Jazz at Lincoln Center, and it offers ticketing options for the club spaces that parallel concert hall experiences in the form of season subscriptions. For spaces without nonprofit support, the strategy of blending jazz programming with other types of music or events is sometimes used to broaden appeal. As the Yoshi's website proclaims, "Under the guidance of current Artistic Director Daniel Grujic, the venue has expanded its focus to include broader genres suitable to a variety of musical tastes."[11] In addition to more expansive missions or musical programming in comparison to the Vanguard, many of these spaces are also more physically expansive. Yoshi's holds more than twice as many listeners with its capacity of 310; the Dakota in Minneapolis can hold an even larger audience of 350; the Ferring Bistro was expanded to seat 220 during a 2014 renovation; and a series of moves and renovations for Dimitriou's Jazz Alley has added over one hundred seats, bringing its total capacity well over two hundred.[12] The majority of jazz clubs in major US cities also differ from the Vanguard in that they serve a dual function as restaurants. For example, Nighttown in Cleveland has a "tiny stage in a crowded room evoking now-gone Short

Vincent in Cleveland or other intimate venues in Manhattan" for jazz performances embedded in what it advertises as "perhaps the largest restaurant in Greater Cleveland, based on seating capacity."[13] The Dakota reserves the seats with the clearest sightlines to the stage for people who also order dinner, and those dining in the restaurant adjoining the performance space at Yoshi's can have the best available seats for a show held for them while enjoying a meal. It has been decades since the tiny kitchen at the Vanguard served food; its more recent usage has been closer to that of a green room and office for musicians and staff. In part, what has allowed the Vanguard to continue to operate as a no-frills jazz club featuring well-known players for a week at a time has been the way in which the local and national scenes in which it is embedded have departed from the model the Vanguard represents. Gradually, it has become one of a kind.

FROM EXPERIMENT TO LANDMARK

In an article celebrating the seventieth anniversary of the Vanguard, jazz writer Ashley Kahn begins by suggesting that the very words "Village Vanguard" sound like jazz, "Try repeating it out loud: VIL-lage VAN-guard, VIL-lage VAN-guard. For seventy years, that alliterative name has swung in 4/4 time, marking the center of the known jazz universe to an international circle of musicians and music fans."[14] While Kahn could refer to the club as "the center of the known jazz universe" in 2005, when Max Gordon first opened his doors in 1935, the place was anything but. In the 1930s, it was not much of a jazz club at all but rather a space for a wide variety of yet-to-be-established performers. At first, liberal young poets at home in the bohemian atmosphere of Greenwich Village, led by master of ceremonies Eli Siegel, provided the bulk of the entertainment at the fledgling establishment. According to Gordon, "In addition to poetry, there was music and dance."[15] These musical performances were indeed additions, not central acts by major stars but brief and often humorous numbers by members of the audience or service staff. As New York City nightlife developed in the early decades of the twentieth century, Greenwich Village had become known as a locale full of the possibility of adventurous escape from conventional daytime responsibilities and respectability. As Lewis Erenberg describes, "The Village, an authentic bohemian and Italian ethnic community in the 1910s, had increasingly become a tourist area and nightlife zone for uptown whites since 1917. The cafés offered secrecy to young and old of college and noncollege background. The area had other potent associations. As a bohemian section the Village became a playground where uptowners could indulge in wilder forms of sensuality. The Village's overtones of free sexuality attracted uptowners and out-of-towners, for in the Village they could see people apparently uninterested in success, caring little about money, desiring only to live the good life without responsibilities."[16] It was not until 1939 that Gordon, seeking to discourage some of the more raucous patrons who had found their way to the Vanguard, began to book more organized nightclub acts, and even these were not typically jazz-oriented. The first was a comedy troupe called the Revuers that performed satirical musical numbers and skits featuring a young Judy Holliday in her first forays onto the stage. In the Revuers's place came blues singers Huddie "Leadbelly" Ledbetter and Josh White, followed by Richard Dyer-Bennet, a lutenist and performer of English ballads from the seventeenth and eighteenth centuries, comedians Carol Channing and Lenny Bruce, singer Harry Belafonte, and many others.

This array of performers does share common ground, although jazz has little to do with their work at the Vanguard. First of all, they held appeal for the bohemian audiences of the left-leaning club that explored anything and everything with an air of counterculture. Whether they were hearing Leadbelly, a blues singer recently released from prison, or Lenny Bruce, a comic who would soon end up there on obscenity charges for the nature of his performance material, Vanguard audiences came out to see artists who pushed against the establishment. In addition, none of the performers booked in the club's early decades were well-known mainstream artists when they came to the Vanguard. They were generally closer to the beginning of their careers than the end, and their Vanguard appearances would eventually pale in significance when compared to their other achievements as performers, which included Academy Awards and Carnegie Hall performances. The Village Vanguard of the 1930s and '40s was not a point of arrival for performers but a point of departure.

In 1943, the Vanguard seemed a step on the way to bigger, better things even to Gordon. The steadily growing success of his small club in the Village had reached the point that he was able to open a newer, larger, more upscale club in midtown with business partner Herb Jacobi. To Gordon, the Blue Angel was, "indeed, quite a joint while it lasted," catering to a much wealthier and more glamorous clientele with its décor set to match "what New Yorkers thought a smart French nightclub looked like." Gordon's wife Lorraine described it as the primary focus of his business operations for the next two decades. For some of the aspiring artists at the Vanguard, the Blue Angel served as a second step. For example, Lorraine Gordon remembered, "Eartha Kitt got her start at La Vie en Rose and actually bombed there, but Max liked what he heard and, especially, I guess, what he saw of Ms. Kitt, enough to bring her to the Village Vanguard, where she really took off. Her next stop, of course, was the Blue Angel, which fit Eartha Kitt like a custom-cut gown." Nineteen-year-old Barbra Streisand followed the same path, performing first at the Vanguard and then at the Blue Angel before going on to theater and film.[17]

The Blue Angel flourished for twenty years, until the heyday of successful nightclubs in its style ended. Max Gordon cited as the reasons for his own club's ultimate demise the increasing difficulty in competing with television for acts and audiences, the aging of his core audience, and the change in the Blue Angel's neighborhood from primarily residential to primarily commercial as more people moved from the city to the suburbs. By 1963, he decided it was time to "let the curtain fall" and accordingly "closed up and went back to the Village Vanguard, where [he] came from."[18] In the meantime, however, the Village Vanguard had become a jazz club, and it has remained one ever since.

Although jazz did not constitute the primary entertainment on the Vanguard's stage until sometime in the 1950s, its history with the club reaches back further than that. Lorraine Gordon described the way that jazz began to make its way into the club's repertoire in the 1940s, when she was in her late teens and not yet acquainted with Max. "The biggest reason my pals and I went to the Vanguard, though, was because there were jazz jam sessions in the afternoons on Sundays. You could go hear Lester Young, Ben Webster, all the greatest jazz musicians for fifty cents at the door, or something like that. Those afternoon jazz shows were not run by Max. Not really. I don't believe he even knew all the musicians. He may have heard of them, but he did not know Lester Young in those days. A record company executive named Harry Lim, along with some other jazz insiders, organized things." In addition to these Sunday matinees, jazz musicians eventually also appeared in evening shows, although perhaps not always with Max Gordon's complete approval. In 1948, Lorraine, then working with her first husband Alfred Lion at Blue Note Records, convinced Gordon to give Thelonious Monk his first week at the Vanguard. Although today Monk's status as a major contributor to jazz history is secure, his music at the time was not widely known outside his immediate circle. Lorraine Gordon colorfully described her earliest attempts at marketing Monk to the public, "Did Monk's records sell at first? No, they didn't sell. I went to Harlem, and those record stores didn't want Monk or me. I'll never forget one particular owner. I can still see him and his store on Seventh Avenue and 125th Street. 'He can't play, lady. What are you doing up here? The guy has two left hands.'" Monk's unconventional approaches to both music and presentation, though destined to be emulated by countless later jazz players, composers, and hiply attired, goatee-sporting fans, were at first difficult for many people to take. According to Lorraine Gordon, his debut at the Vanguard was no exception:

> Opening night was September 14, 1948. And nobody came. None of the so-called jazz critics. None of the so-called cognoscenti. Zilch. Alfred and I sat there in a banquette at the Vanguard, and Thelonious got up at one point, did this little dance and announced, "Now, human beings, I'm going to play..." whatever the song was. Max came running over to me in acute distress, "What kind of an announcement is that?"
> "That's how he talks," I said.
> There was almost no audience. And Max kept crying, "What did you talk me into? You trying to ruin my business? We're dying with this guy."

While Monk would ultimately establish an important relationship with the club, his initial booking there provided no indication of his "making it" in the jazz world, the major rite of passage that appearing at the Vanguard represents for musicians today. Like the other artists who appeared at the club in its first decades of existence, the earliest jazz musicians to play there were not necessarily widely appreciated performers when they initially took the stage. The Vanguard was home to a wealth of artistic experiments, some more successful than others.[19]

Only musicians appear at the Vanguard now, and the majority of them are among the most prominent performers of what could be categorized as acoustic mainstream jazz. In Gordon's earlier decades as a nightclub owner, jazz had been one of many forms of popular entertainment that could appeal to his target audience. In the 1950 and '60s, however, the place of jazz in American culture was shifting at the same time that mainstream nightclub acts were moving to television. In redefining the booking practices of the Vanguard as a jazz club in 1957, the Gordons and the musicians who performed on their stage were beginning to lean away from the popular entertainment business and toward the art world, and the Vanguard's location in Greenwich Village and historical relationship with left-leaning bohemian culture made it an ideal venue in which to present the newest and most controversial of art musics. Lorraine Gordon described the transition as follows:

> In 1957...Max was finding it increasingly difficult to book the comics and the nightclub performers who had carried the Vanguard. Television was consuming them all....Max steered the Vanguard more and more toward jazz. Only in retrospect does this seem brilliant. But it was....You think I understood what Coltrane was doing when I heard him in the Vanguard in the sixties? I should say not. I didn't know what the hell I was listening to....The litany of jazz names Max brought in during this period established the Vanguard's peerless jazz identity for all time: Carmen McCrae; Charles Mingus; Thelonious Monk; Stan Getz; Ben Webster; Mose Allison; Anita O'Day; Teddy Wilson; Miles Davis; Horace Silver; Chris Connor; Dizzy Gillespie; George Shearing; Jonny Griffin; Lambert, Hendricks & Ross; Zoot Sims; Max Roach; Red Garland; Ahmad Jamal; Dinah Washington.[20]

This impressive list of performers that characterized the Vanguard of the late 1950s and '60s included both established jazz artists and the avant-garde characterized by Coltrane's increasing turn to free jazz during that period, music Lorraine Gordon described as so foreign to her at the time. While controversial during its emergence, Paul Lopes points out that free jazz was fairly quickly incorporated "within the general modernist paradigm of innovation and exploration" that characterized the shift to an artistic rather than entertainment-based understanding of jazz in which critics and historians ultimately "canonized John Coltrane as a jazz visionary."[21] Looking back, Lorraine wrote that, "Max booked a lot of acts I couldn't or wouldn't today."[22] As jazz heritage accumulated around the Village Vanguard and the live jazz scene surrounding it both locally and globally continued to change over the next six decades, the nature of booking practices at the venue gradually shifted as well, trending generally toward mainstream jazz performed by established artists as the most frequently performed music of the space today.

Though their work continues to play a role in expanding the borders of their musical genre, developing and embracing new techniques and ideas, the contemporary artists who play there have typically earned the right to do so by proving themselves to be extremely capable performers within a recognizable mainstream idiom. Despite a slipperiness of terminology and constantly shifting goalposts, there has long been discussion of jazz as understandable in terms of a core set of sounds, practices, and cultural meanings that—in their given place and time—are deemed central, and a related but external jazz-adjacent periphery. John Howland writes, "the boundaries of the jazz tradition actually include a wealth of sounds and approaches that musicians, critics, and aficionados have resisted calling jazz, despite the fact that much of this music overlaps with core jazz practice in performance, style, arranging conventions, and even in the participation of musicians from the accepted core tradition."[23] Coined by critic Stanley Dance around the same time the Vanguard cemented its role as a jazz club, the term *mainstream jazz* originally referred to the persistence of swing music after the advent of bebop—Monk, a key bebop pioneer, would have been the antithesis of mainstream by Dance's measure in the 1950s. Over time, however, the meaning of the word shifted in reference to the ever-expanding outer reaches of jazz, and Monk is now one of the jazz composers whose music is most frequently performed by contemporary artists, including those of today's mainstream. A later definition as penned by James Lincoln Collier suggests that the mainstream encompasses "any jazz improvised on chord sequences in the essentially solo style," typically excluding "free or aleatory jazz of the avant garde, rock-based jazz, and dixieland and other traditional forms."[24] Another way of describing the mainstream is to place performances in relationship to bebop as a central style—music that typically features a small ensemble of acoustic instruments, including a rhythm section, and features intricate solo improvisation. As Scott DeVeaux puts it, "Bebop is a music that has been kept alive by having been absorbed into the present; in a sense, it *constitutes* the present. It is part of the experience of all aspiring jazz musicians, each of whom learns bebop as the embodiment of the techniques, the aesthetic sensibilities, and ultimately the professional attitudes that define the discipline."[25] I use the term *mainstream* not to pigeonhole music at the Vanguard as bland or passé in comparison to some more real or vibrant current style but to take advantage of some of the tension native to its historical and contemporary definitions that mirrors the musical process currently playing out at the Vanguard: the mainstream is neither too traditional nor too experimental, and borders are constantly in flux along with the rest of the musics under the broad jazz umbrella. It is recognizable as relevant jazz, indeed as the current core of the genre to many jazz players and listeners, because it partakes of the music's past without taking on the role of direct recreation or revival of older music. Much of what is performed at the Vanguard has clear links to the bebop-related small ensemble jazz described as central by DeVeaux, and the regular Monday night big band offers a large ensemble version that is similarly viewed as central. In *Making the Scene: Contemporary New York City Big Band Jazz*, Alex Stewart describes various bands and elements of the scene as "inside," "the edge," and "totally outside," and it is the Vanguard Orchestra that constitutes the middle. He writes, "From the mid-1960s to the present the Thad Jones/Mel Lewis Orchestra and its later incarnations as the Mel Lewis and Vanguard Jazz Orchestras have been at the heart of the New York jazz scene. Whether as full-fledged members or regular substitutes, affiliation with these bands has marked for many musicians an important rite of passage, signaling the entry into the highest professional ranks."[26] The Vanguard holds onto a central place in jazz through live performances and recordings that embody both heritage and new modes of creativity and spontaneity widely considered to be essential ingredients in this genre, and it has a reputation for hosting the performers who can play mainstream jazz at its very highest level.

REDEFINITION AND REPETITION

Recording played a key part in the Vanguard's transition from the margins of New York City nightlife to a center for a significant contingent of jazz culture. By the end of the 1950s, the Vanguard's role as a major jazz venue was taking shape, in large part due to the influence and jazz connections of Lorraine Gordon, the venue's owner from Max's death in 1989 until she passed away at the age of 95 in 2018. The year 1957, when Max Gordon "began reinventing the Village Vanguard as a jazz club exclusively," was also the year that the first in a very long line of "live at the Village Vanguard" records was made, this one by saxophonist Sonny Rollins.[27] Blue Note Records, the company for which Lorraine had worked with Alfred Lion, released Rollins's *A Night at the Village Vanguard* in 1958. Since then, over a hundred recordings made at the club have been released as commercial records or compact discs. A myriad of artists, including John Coltrane, Betty Carter, and Wynton Marsalis, and a variety of labels, including Impulse!, Columbia, and Winter & Winter, have joined forces with the club to create recordings that carry the Vanguard name and sound. In effect, the Vanguard simultaneously became a place to hear jazz and a point of origin from which it was disseminated to a widespread audience via records.

One of the earliest recording sessions at the Vanguard has proven to be one of the most enduring and well respected. The material recorded Sunday, June 25, 1961 by pianist Bill Evans, bassist Scott LaFaro, and drummer Paul Motian is often cited as monumental in the history of the jazz piano trio, an ensemble type that has served as a Vanguard staple for decades. The material was initially released by Riverside Records as two albums that met with favorable reviews early on and have only grown in their significance to the jazz canon over time: *Sunday at the Village Vanguard* and *Waltz for Debby*. Yet the live aspect of *Waltz for Debby* held little charm for *DownBeat* reviewer Leonard Feather in 1962, "The set was recorded, like one of Evans' best previous albums, at the Village Vanguard. I don't know what that meant to Evans—possibly he is one of those artists who needs the stimulation of a club crowd—but to me it only means that somebody who had an irritating cough that day should have stayed home."[28] C. Michael Bailey's review of the rerelease of the same material in 2005 as *The Complete Village Vanguard Recordings, 1961* reflects a very different perspective on the audible liveness of the now-canonized Evans recordings from the now-canonized Village Vanguard. In the twenty-first century, with both Evans and the Vanguard holding honored places in the jazz pantheon, "tinkling glasses and audience patter" reveal the capital T, "true *Truth* of the recordings."[29] While Feather's view of background noise was not universally shared in the 1960s, indeed, the growth and persistence of live recording in jazz prove otherwise, the idea of a reviewer criticizing an artist's choice to record at the Vanguard today seems almost unimaginable—after all, those are Village Vanguard glasses heard on the recording, not just any background noise but audible traces of the specific physical space in which the record originated. The sound of a clinking bar glass is treasured by listeners like Bailey because it is a "real," "live," Village Vanguard bar glass, and anything "live at the Village Vanguard" has developed a certain cultural currency.

Much of the Village Vanguard's present fame stems from the recordings that have been made there. That both Max and Lorraine Gordon's autobiographies are titled with plays on the phrase "live at the Village Vanguard" hints at how often "liveness" is coupled with the idea of this space. Yet, specifying that a performance is live is of course only necessary if it in fact no longer is: performers that appear in person before audiences at the club do not need to be advertised as live, only the recordings they produce there do. As Philip Auslander points out in his study of live performance since the advent of mass media, "historically, the live is actually an effect of mediatization, not the other way around."[30] Live Village Vanguard recordings are not simply a means of preserving events that occurred at the club, they are unique new products that themselves play a major role in how the venue is understood. Indeed, as musicologist Travis Jackson observed in his study of the New

York City jazz scene, the production of live albums at the Vanguard can involve not just the inconspicuous recording of sounds that would occur anyway, but careful and conscious preparation and manipulation to transform a typical set of live music into a viable recording project:

> When artists like Joshua Redman and Joe Lovano made their live recordings at the Village Vanguard in the 1990s, it was likely as apparent to other audience members as it was to me that these were *not* typical performances. Intricate networks of wires and cables ran from the stage to other areas of the club and up the stairs to large mobile recording units parked in front of the club on both occasions. If that weren't evidence enough, the musicians took care to inform us in each case that the evening's performance was being recorded for commercial release. Moreover, as is standard with studio recordings, some recorded material, such as the intervals between songs or "extraneous" audience noise, didn't appear on the final releases. Finally audience applause was recorded on separate microphones to be mixed in later, and the individual tunes chosen for inclusion on the final recordings were sequenced in a manner that didn't replicate their order on the evening(s) of performance.[31]

Pointing out the liveness of recorded material from the Village Vanguard on the surface appears to tie it to the ordinary day-to-day business of the venue's pre-1957 existence, but it in fact marks a significant shift in the history, geography, and sonic possibilities of the space. From the very beginning, the origin of these recordings has been regarded as a significant part of their identity. Of the one hundred plus recordings made at the Vanguard in the past sixty years, the vast majority offer some suggestion of their creation in ephemeral, live experiences, public events now recalled as history in the making. From Rollins's *A Night at the Village Vanguard* and Evans's *Sunday at the Village Vanguard* to a plethora of fill-in-the-blank name plus "Live at the Village Vanguard" combinations by McCoy Tyner, Earl Hines, Dizzy Gillespie, and at least a few dozen others, the authority of records is based in the memory of the music's spontaneous performance in front of the Vanguard audience. As they are repeated, these albums function not only as musical sound but as objects defining both a heritage and a place.

It is no coincidence that the Vanguard's rebirth as a jazz club and its debut as a recording space occurred at the same time. Max Gordon was losing many of his most successful nightclub acts from the Blue Angel to television as the funds available through door receipts from a small live audience could no longer compete within the developing mass media economy. The new Village Vanguard that emerged in the late 1950s and early '60s proved well designed to appeal to a niche market with which television would not so directly compete, and the club's transformation during this period also engaged with the increasing presence of mass media that was changing the entertainment landscape. While Gordon continued to maintain a live performance space, he, Lorraine, and the network of musicians and recording companies with whom they collaborated also turned that very "liveness" into something that could be distributed on a larger scale. Making records at the Village Vanguard allowed the club to become a recognizable institution to jazz audiences regardless of location. Suddenly, John Coltrane fans from the Midwest and Bill Evans listeners in Europe had reason to know about the Vanguard. The club was no longer selling itself to just a neighborhood or a city but to an international audience, and it was no longer just a small basement room where a small group of listeners sat at crowded tables but also an imagined space with growing prestige in the minds of record audiences. The "liveness" of the Vanguard began to be experienced by only a small proportion of the music's total audience, a change that served to make that liveness more highly desirable. While live performance at the Vanguard might have struggled on its own during the decline of nightclub culture, the sale of its mediatized replacement reinstated its value by selling its absence and the events of its past, transforming the space into one that could play in a wide geographical and temporal landscape.

HOLDING ON AND MOVING ON

In his seventieth anniversary piece on the club, Kahn writes that "a 'Live at the Vanguard' album has become a rite of passage for modern jazz players" at this hallowed place where, "the best living jazz talent aspire to record."[32] This emphasis on recording rather than live appearance is significant in that it points to the strong relationship between the Vanguard as a performance space and as a recording space, but an essential aspect of what the recordings valorize is the idea of actual presence. The Vanguard has become a major landmark for audiences seeking that presence in live performances of jazz, and there are a number of factors beyond the distribution of recordings that have contributed to the venue's current cultural capital. What changed as the Village Vanguard moved away from its early status as a stepping-stone to a performing career toward its current role as a jazz destination in and of itself? As far as the inside of the Vanguard is concerned, remarkably little. But outside its red doors, the broader jazz scene in which the club is embedded has been drastically transformed by the gradual disappearance of other spaces like it and their replacement by institutions like universities and large-scale nonprofits modeled on classical music venues. By selling the idea of liveness at a historically significant club through recordings marketed to distant audiences unable to witness it for themselves, the Vanguard became one of the few small jazz clubs left capable of actually providing that liveness.

The 1950s and early 1960s brought the high-water mark in the success of the small jazz club scene. The dates of operation for another famous New York club named for Charlie Parker mark the borders of this era fairly well. Birdland first opened at its original 52nd Street location in 1949 to a show featuring Parker himself, and numerous jazz greats followed in the next decade and a half. The club shut down just two years after Gordon's Blue Angel, however, in 1965, due to what the owners describe as declining success in the face of Americans' new love affair with rock 'n' roll. The club would be revived with its old name at a new location, but not until 1986.[33]

Numerous other jazz clubs have come and gone, but the general pattern has been one of decline. Of all the purported deaths jazz has suffered, the first one noted as early as the 1930s and the final one surely not yet declared, no era was considered quite as dire for the music as the 1970s. Gordon and the Vanguard managed to weather the storm, however. Nat Hentoff describes one evening in the late 1970s that he arrived in the Village to take in a performance of the allegedly passé form only to find a line stretching around the block.[34] Gordon remembers his increasing difficulty in booking top tier artists like Miles Davis who found they could make more money with fewer hassles from concert-style performances at universities and similar venues, but the musicians continued to return, year after year.

Despite the club's growing prestige in jazz circles, the Vanguard has never achieved the kind of financial success that the Blue Angel did at the height of its popularity. Although an iconic one, it is still a small business that has only 123 tickets to sell to each show in order to cover costs and pay musicians. When Lorraine Gordon took over the club in 1989, she immediately found that "business was not great."[35] Through such tactics as taking the linens to the laundromat across the street rather than hiring a laundry service, she kept the place open and eventually found greater stability. Her efforts did not go unnoticed, and though many contemporary players have lauded her for holding on to the Vanguard, as usual, no one has put it quite as emphatically as Wynton Marsalis.

"She's maintained the integrity of the room. It's a great feat, especially in our time, when *integrity* is a curse word and selling out a religion."[36] By praising Gordon in these words, Marsalis presents an opposition between "integrity" and commercial success, suggesting that maintaining the Vanguard is a service to the jazz community that aligns with other nonprofits despite its history as a traditional business.

Lorraine Gordon's unique achievements in maintaining the Vanguard contributed to her recognition as a National Endowment for the Arts Jazz Master in 2013. At the age of 90, however, she had by that time passed much of the day-to-day operations of the club to her daughter Deborah Gordon and longtime employee Jed Eisenman, who have continued to operate the Vanguard since her death. This passing of the torch has so far unfolded as another of the Vanguard's subtle shifts, blending past and present values as the new leadership works with a deep respect for past practices. On one side is a continued need for musical change, and Eisenman echoes Lorraine Gordon's notion that "everything changes," saying, "The music changes.... If you want to look for what is valid and exciting and real in jazz, you can't just keep hashing out the same stuff."[37] Simultaneously, he and Deborah Gordon both stress the importance of continuity. In the following passage in *The National*, Deborah highlights both sides of the tension, "'I certainly value the history,' said Gordon, who works with her 92-year-old mother Lorraine to keep the Vanguard alive in its ageless state. 'Part of what I do is to guard that in a city that changes constantly. But we're not a museum, and we don't want to be. It's a real living place that responds and tries to keep up the name 'Vanguard.'"[38] Deborah Gordon's comments highlight a significant tension in the contemporary Vanguard's relation to its world: the constantly changing city. Eisenman is more specific in defining the change Deborah alludes to as related to the drastic changes in property values around the club over the course of its long life, "The things that are great for the real estate industry in New York have hurt the art scene and the culture scene and the night scene and the jazz scene.... I think the fact that New York is more homogeneous now is a little bit of a letdown to those of us who remember the city when it was a little bit more rough and tumble."[39] The homogenization that Eisenman refers to here can be interpreted as a late stage of gentrification, a process that came to Greenwich Village earlier than many other Manhattan neighborhoods; sociologist Sharon Zukin describes "an early form of gentrification" in the neighborhood inspiring some artistic residents to relocate to Brooklyn as early as the 1920s.[40] The poets that the

Vanguard catered to in the 1930s were a part of the bohemian culture that continued to thrive in the neighborhood through the majority of the twentieth century, however, as the neighborhood famously played home to folk singers, beat poets, and other countercultural artists. It was around the same time that the Vanguard became a dedicated jazz space that the more marked gentrification of the area picked up steam, beginning in the 1950s and '60s.[41]

At this point, the Village Vanguard's immediate neighborhood is number thirty-one on the *Forbes* list of America's fifty most expensive zip codes with a median home price of $3.6 million.[42] Maintaining a small business there is surely no easy feat, and, indeed, many family-owned businesses have long since been replaced by upscale chain retailers. In a 2005 lament on the loss of the neighborhood's "heart" written for *The Guardian*, Paul Harris wrote, "Many...once-famous cafes, bars and theatres have closed their doors. Tiny family-run stores are on the retreat before a wave of big name brands. On the main thoroughfare of Bleecker Street there are no fewer than three Marc Jacobs stores. Another Village block has three Ralph Lauren outlets."[43]

Although New York City in general, and Greenwich Village in particular, has continued to serve as a major jazz hub with numerous venues in close proximity, other individual venues have not had the staying power of the Vanguard. For example, during the mid-1990s, although interest in jazz was described as on the rise by critics Larry Blumenfeld and Peter Watrous, Travis Jackson observed frequent turnover in spaces that catered to jazz listeners, pointing out that although the two authors cited six new clubs opening around that time, only two were still in business and regularly presenting live jazz after a year's time.[44]

Simply staying open at all for the length of time that the Vanguard has is more than any other New York jazz club has done, yet the Gordons and their collaborators have maintained not just the business itself but also its atmosphere of jazz authenticity. From the musicians' perspective, the Vanguard is one of the only establishments that continues to consistently book players for a full week at a time, creating the opportunity for a kind of on-the-job ensemble development that once characterized jazz playing but has become relatively rare. For audience members, there is nothing garishly touristy about the club—no glossy posters or glowing screens advertising upcoming shows, no historical placards, no merchandise displays. Although T-shirts can be purchased at the bar, the overall vibe is simple and understated, all the way down to the establishment's cash-only policy that remained in effect through the first decade of the twenty-first century. In contrast to other contemporary venues, the Vanguard's connections to and consistency with the atmosphere of a mid-twentieth-century jazz club are palpable: as listeners walk down the stairs, they are not in a historical recreation of a jazz club funded by a corporate sponsor, or a new place with stylish retro furniture, or even the reborn Birdland that has rechristened itself The Jazz Corner of the World—they are simply in a jazz club, the sort of space that other newer spaces can only contrive to evoke.

Being one of the only places of its kind to stay by and large as it was half a century ago has, ironically, also forced certain changes at the Vanguard. Continuing to succeed as a business in a shrinking field and changing urban environment created a need for different hiring practices than those that made sense in its days as the more experimental of Max Gordon's two (and at one point even three) clubs. Lorraine Gordon described having to turn down relatively unknown players seeking employment as one of the most difficult parts of her job. Faced with a constant onslaught of aspiring musicians, Gordon reported, "Sometimes I just say, 'Look, I only book people who've played here before.' Which is almost, but not entirely true, of course. 'How do I get a start?' they ask me. Good question. Go to a smaller club. Start there. But you can't start here. This isn't a jumping-off place anymore. Maybe it was years ago, but not now. I have to fill this room every night to survive." Gordon singled out Ethan Iverson as an exception to the rule, "someone who actually [got] their big break at the Vanguard" in recent memory. Gordon describes how she heard him as a sideman and "fell in love with his playing." As Iverson remembers, "I was playing with Mark Turner, the saxophonist, a little bit on the side, and he…was playing [at the Village Vanguard.]…He said, 'We'll set up the piano—why don't you play a couple tunes with us?' And Lorraine heard it.…And then she actually encouraged Kurt Rosenwinkel to get me on piano.…I'm sure that Kurt, if he didn't want to get me, he wouldn't have had to. It was just more like a suggestion, you know, 'What about Ethan?' And he said yes, and that was the first time I played the Vanguard." As Gordon put it, at a certain point, she asked him to play with his own group, and "Boom. Done deal. Moreover, the band that he brought in for the occasion, the Bad Plus, has had a lot of success since."[45]

Yet, even Iverson was not another teenage Judy Holliday or Barbra Streisand getting started at the Vanguard. Over a decade passed between the night he came to the Vanguard on the eve of starting college and his first appearance with the Bad Plus there in 2002. As "big breaks" go, what Gordon referred to as Iverson's came much later in his career than those of early Vanguard performers, and he had considerably more professional experience than Holliday or Streisand did at their Vanguard debuts, even as he appeared young and untested to Gordon among the established jazz heavyweights gracing the stage at the turn of the twenty-first century. While Holliday came to the Vanguard straight from working as a switchboard operator with no real experience as a performer, Iverson had been working as the musical director for the Mark Morris Dance Group for the past four years, a position that, while noteworthy in and of itself, also allowed him to perform with major stars like Mikhail Baryshnikov and Yo-Yo Ma. He had also recorded several albums, including one with the Bad Plus, a complete album of his own original compositions, and one with well-known tenor saxophonist Dewey Redman. His appearances at the Vanguard certainly brought Iverson to the attention of a larger pool of jazz listeners, and the Bad Plus rocketed to national and international jazz prominence in the years that followed. If Iverson represents the twenty-first-century version of the young unknown artist getting his "big break" at the Vanguard, however, times have certainly changed.

Today's Village Vanguard is not the place to go to catch an act by an unknown young performer whose experimental work may or may not prove to break interesting artistic ground. This certainly does not mean that the club has lost its significance; rather, it has come to be an important landmark and to take on a role in defining the sound of contemporary jazz. The musicians who appear at the Vanguard now are among the music's biggest stars, the same people whose faces appear on the cover of *DownBeat* magazine, people who also play in larger concert halls and make recordings that are well-received in a broad jazz community, not people who are just beginning careers in music. The venue has transformed itself into a space that promises prospective audience members that, on any given night, they can walk into the Village Vanguard expecting to hear world-class jazz. And as Fred Hersch, now one of the establishment's veteran performers, describes, many people do. "I think the Vanguard is one of those places where it's on everybody's consciousness. You know, if you come to New York and you love jazz, it's one of the first places you look—who's playing at the Vanguard. I think in the eighties when the Japanese economy was such that the Japanese were coming constantly and filling the club almost, it was kind of like Statue of Liberty, Museum of Modern Art, Village Vanguard. It was the thing—it was the authentic New York jazz experience. I think it still is."[46] During a Vanguard residence on a Saturday night in July of 2009, Hersch played to a full room. Undoubtedly, many people in the audience were there specifically to hear him because of a prior familiarity with his music. Yet, following the first set, a man who had slipped in late and sat down at the table next to me leaned over to ask me whom he had just been listening to. An Italian spending his vacation in New York City, he had stopped into the Vanguard because it was the Vanguard, not because he knew who was playing. He visited the club as one might visit a well-known art museum without prior knowledge of the specific exhibition on at that time, drawn by the prestige of the place housing the art rather than any particular relationship to individual artists or works.

FRED HERSCH AND TODAY'S VILLAGE VANGUARD

The artists who appear frequently at the Village Vanguard now are almost all highly accomplished and familiar figures in the jazz world, and pianist Fred Hersch certainly earned his place in the venue's roster of regulars through his decades of performing at the highest levels of the New York scene, first as a sideman for Vanguard-staple players of the 1980s and eventually as a leader of his own ensembles. Hersch, who celebrated his sixtieth birthday while playing a week at the Vanguard in October of 2015, is part of a generation of musicians who grew up in a world in which the Village Vanguard was already a noteworthy jazz destination. In fact, playing at the Vanguard with his own group was a long-standing goal for Hersch. A documentary about his life and music includes a photograph of Hersch smiling as he stands outside the door next to a sign that, for the first time, features his own name. Reflecting on the occasion while sitting in the club ten years later, Hersch said, "I'd been wanting this for fifteen years. That was certainly a big night.... It's a privilege to play here."[47] His attitude toward the Vanguard is representative of many of the players who perform there today: they came of age as musicians as playing the Village Vanguard increasingly meant reaching a status of respectability in the New York jazz scene, a scene that in turn is often regarded as representing jazz performance at its highest level. A close listen to how Hersch plays there through the analysis of recordings made both inside and outside the club demonstrates the ways in which this venue influences the music that is made there. Just as memories of past artists are palpable in the way the Vanguard is now perceived, the venue itself leaves audible marks on the music of the present.

Hersch began playing jazz in the 1970s and witnessed vast changes in the live performance scene as his career was taking shape. When he moved to New York, he first began working in an environment in which "everything took place in clubs." This type of scene extended outside his home city, "There used to be a circuit around the country where you could go....There were certain bands...who worked forty-some weeks a year. And so, if you got a gig with them, that was your job.... You could...make a living. Now that doesn't happen anymore. I mean, with very rare exceptions, you know, nobody works that much." Hersch points out that today, not only are there fewer clubs for musicians to play in but those that do exist are of a different nature. "Especially in the smaller clubs that I used to play in New York, there was more of a connection between performer and audience." More recently, in addition to the fact that "clubs have become more expensive," he says, "there are not that many clubs around the country that are like the old clubs...they're slick, they're too big." The experience of playing and listening in an intimate space has become increasingly rare, thus heightening its value for today's performers and audiences. By continuing to present music in much the same way it has since the late 1950s, the Vanguard now serves as both the club it has always been and a monument to all the others that were once like it but have since disappeared.[48]

In the contemporary club scene, Hersch feels that "the Vanguard is still the most soulful one." To him, "what's going to be exciting to people about jazz, and what's going to keep them supporting it and coming back to hear it is...more than likely at a place like the Vanguard" and less likely in larger settings like concert halls and festivals. Hersch now plays at the Vanguard regularly, the result of a relationship with the club that he cultivated for a number of years. It took until the late 1990s for him to convince Lorraine Gordon to allow him an opportunity to perform as the leader of his own group. "There was a gap between the end of my sideman time and the time that [Lorraine Gordon]...was convinced to give me a chance as a leader. It was about a six-, seven-year gap. When she was finally persuaded to give me a week, it was, frankly, kind of quite an event—sell-out, everybody showed up—and I think she was kind of surprised. Then, of course I made a live album there, a few times later, and...kind of solidified my relationship as somebody who's always in the mix over there." Hersch has since distinguished himself as the first pianist ever to play a full week of solo performances at the club. He was also one of the artists featured during the club's 80th anniversary celebration and has been added to the gallery of portraits on the Vanguard's walls, "I was very honored...Lorraine Gordon put my picture on the wall....That's a big thing. It was great...just that my relationship with the club has been acknowledged." On Hersch's end, that relationship involves a sense of loyalty to the Vanguard, and he is conscious of how playing at other venues can reflect conflicting interests. For example, he said, "I know it would be very painful for Lorraine if I were to work at, say, Dizzy's Club Coca-Cola," the smaller club venue that is a part of Jazz at Lincoln Center. "Because they're quote 'nonprofit'...they get all kinds of free advertising and a board of directors and very deep pockets," factors that can make it difficult for the Vanguard to remain competitive as a business. Hersch's respect for Gordon and the space she maintained directs his own choices about where to appear as a performer.[49]

VANGUARDS AND STANDARDS

Despite Hersch's close relationship to the Vanguard, however, he acknowledges that, as a venue, it is better suited to some of his musical projects than it is to others. In particular, though he has appeared there as both a soloist and part of a quintet, he recognizes that Gordon was happiest to book his trio, the group that, of the ones he leads, tends to stick to the most easily recognizable jazz style and repertoire. Hersch remembers a Vanguard performance by his quintet at which Gordon told him that she was "really looking forward to the trio." As a result of Gordon's preferences, he often chooses alternative spaces when pursuing more experimental interests, like other clubs, art museums, and concert halls. While his loyalty to the Vanguard discourages him from playing some venues, he says, "I do play at the Jazz Standard [another New York club], but the kinds of things I'll do at the Jazz Standard are not things that would interest Lorraine." In 2009, Hersch saw it as unlikely that his quartet called the Pocket Orchestra would end up playing at the Vanguard because of their more experimental sound. Indeed, Hersch has continued to present his less bebop-oriented new music at a variety of other venues while maintaining a consistent presence at the Vanguard with solo and trio jazz.

Like some of Hersch's other projects, the Pocket Orchestra falls somewhat outside the jazz mainstream. While, as can be seen through his Vanguard performances, Hersch is highly accomplished in a contemporary version of bebop, his broad interests in a wide variety of musical styles as well as visual arts, literature, and dance have led to compositions that are not necessarily grounded primarily in established jazz styles like bop, swing, or the blues. For instance, he has composed such diverse pieces as a set of variations on a Bach chorale, a tune inspired by ballerina Suzanne Farrell, a setting of selections from Walt Whitman's *Leaves of Grass*, and a musical theater piece called *My Coma Dreams*, based on his experience of a two-month-long AIDS-related coma in 2008. The Pocket Orchestra is another of Hersch's artistic pursuits that has more to do with his individual experiences, interests, and dedication to exploration than it does with the traditional jazz canon. An atypical combination of piano, voice, trumpet, and percussion with no bass player and a repertoire made up almost entirely of Hersch's original compositions, this project definitely strikes out in a more experimental direction than the trio, which sticks to standard jazz instrumentation and performs a very normative and equally divided repertoire of original tunes, jazz compositions by other artists, and standards from the American songbook.

The Pocket Orchestra's performance of Hersch's piece "Light Years" wanders further from the typical jazz path than any of the group's other tracks recorded at the Jazz Standard with its use of recited poetry and percussion that is more coloristic than metric. With trumpeter Ralphi Alessi sitting out this tune, Hersch is left with an enormous amount of melodic and harmonic freedom as the only provider of pitched material through substantial stretches of music. The flexible approach to tempo throughout creates a very open-ended atmosphere in which all members of the ensemble interact freely. The piece's beginning provides an example of the kind of malleable musical backdrops to spoken poetry that recur throughout the work. Drummer Richie Barshay's use of small chimes and rattles creates the initial texture into which other musical layers will be added, an approach to percussion that draws listeners outside of a typical jazz sound world both in its use of nonstandard instruments and its lack of a consistent groove. Hersch joins with freely improvised, light, pointillistic playing, creating melodic material that is neither abrasively striking nor easily grasped. Into this context comes Jo Lawry's spoken rather than sung entrance. One minute into the piece, Lawry moves from speech to song, and Hersch moves to a harmonized piano part and a temporarily perceptible, though still flexible, pulse. This gradual, collectively improvised movement from sound to song is repeated in a variety of forms throughout the piece, providing ample opportunity for the kind of spontaneous creation and interactive risk-taking that Hersch values. As he puts it, "I like frameworks...that are specific but not specific. It has an intent, but if it goes somewhere else, I'm not going to control it." While "Light Years" may not have the kinds of sonic or cultural characteristics that some audiences deem essential to jazz, it offers the kinds of creative challenges that Hersch finds engaging.

In contrast to "Light Years," one of the tunes in the Pocket Orchestra's repertoire that is most closely aligned with mainstream jazz is also played by Hersch's trio at the Village Vanguard, offering an excellent opportunity to compare his work at the Jazz Standard to what he performs at the more heritage-driven Vanguard.[50] In the trio rendition, "Stuttering" comes across as a more or less straight-ahead jazz tune with a few fun and memorable twists, whereas the Pocket Orchestra plays up the tune's oddities to a greater extent. "Stuttering" has a much more normative rhythmic feel than Hersch's most adventurous Pocket Orchestra repertoire, with its constant tempo and swing groove, and it also features a standard thirty-two bar formal structure.[51] As the title implies, however, the piece is still quirky: the "Stuttering" bass line lilts along in a steady triple meter that is at odds with the standard four-four jazz ride cymbal pattern painted over the top, making it, metrically speaking, one of the most unusual tunes in a typical trio set. Its meandering, stop-start melody does not commit fully to either of the work's two metrical camps, and a lack of repeating phrases makes it difficult for listeners to pinpoint any landmarks in the form.

In the trio's performance at the Vanguard, Hersch, bassist Drew Gress, and drummer Nasheet Waits play within historically established instrumental roles to create a collaborative three-part musical texture in which the drums keep time, the bass plays a walking line that defines the harmonic structure, and the piano presents the melodic material. Hersch continues this established approach into the first portion of his improvised solo. He chooses to use the piano as a melodic rather than harmonic voice, even in his solo, generally avoiding chords in favor of a single treble line. This choice creates continuity between the opening and closing presentations of the composed melody and the improvised material that falls in between, and Hersch's note choices lead to an equal continuity in terms of pitch by largely avoiding notes from outside the key. The metric complexity caused by simultaneous use of groupings of three and four beats continues to add novelty and interest to the performance, especially after Waits displaces his drum pattern by one beat, but, in general, the conflict between the various voices is downplayed by the normative and continuous texture of single-line piano melody with walking bass and drum groove accompaniment. In the end, the performance comes across as one in which the musicians casually and effortlessly play in different meters at the same time without ever really highlighting challenges to expected jazz norms.

The Pocket Orchestra version of this tune from the Jazz Standard emphasizes the strangeness and incompatibility of the "Stuttering" layers to a greater extent. Beginning with the choice of instruments performing the melody, the sense of uncertainty created by the lack of symmetrical musical phrases in the composition is played up in this setting by the addition of untexted voice to selected moments in the melody. The piano and muted trumpet play the majority of the melody together in a casual manner reminiscent of the trio performance, but they are joined by voice on irregularly spaced longer notes that punctuate the otherwise quick and steady feel of the tune. The long notes now stand out more strongly because of their doubling by the vocalist, bringing their odd temporal distribution into focus. Hersch's piano solo with the Pocket Orchestra is also more disorienting than its Village Vanguard counterpart. While the trio's bassist, Drew Gress, maintained the waltzing bass line that accompanied the composed melody throughout the first chorus of the Vanguard piano solo, allowing the strange metric mix of fours in the drums and threes in the bass to gradually become more predictable through repetition, Hersch, in providing his own accompaniment with the bassless Pocket Orchestra, very quickly departs from the steady triple bass pattern. His bass line quickly slips out of a clear triple feel without moving to a clear four-beat pattern, leaving listeners without any metric underpinning to grab on to. Hersch also departs from the tune's initial spare texture of a single melodic line with walking bass, creating a wide variety of constantly changing ones instead, including passages with multiple melodies played in counterpoint and portions of clear melody with chordal accompaniment. Additionally, Hersch's melodic and harmonic choices in this solo stray much further from the tonal simplicity of the composed melody, resulting in a more jagged and unpredictable version of this piece than was performed at the Village Vanguard and drawing greater attention to Hersch's departures from mainstream jazz norms with this composition.

Comparing Hersch's variations in approach to his own material between performances with the trio at the Vanguard and the Pocket Orchestra at the Jazz Standard already points to the differences between how these two venues situate themselves with regard to mainstream and experimental music. When one considers the full range of repertoire covered by the trio, these differences become even more apparent, suggesting that the specific choices made by the ensembles in the two renderings of "Stuttering" do indeed relate to variations in the contexts of their performance. While the Pocket Orchestra plays all original material, the trio divides its sets among what Hersch refers to as his three "food groups": standards from the American Songbook, jazz compositions by other artists, and original material. Three sets from the group's July 2009 Vanguard residence show that this division between standards, jazz compositions, and originals is reasonably even and consistent.[52] In making roughly two-thirds of each set from material already familiar to jazz-educated audiences, the trio provides a much more easily recognizable mainstream jazz product than the Pocket Orchestra, giving listeners aware of the jazz canon but not acquainted with Hersch's work an easy way to relate to a set, even if it stretches somewhat outside of boundaries with which they are familiar. This aesthetic is well suited to the Vanguard of today, as it offers easily recognizable surface features of the mainstream, maintaining aspects of the type of acoustic, postbop playing that has now characterized the space for decades, while also enacting the venue's avant-garde heritage with unusual and experimental details at a more microanalytic level.

Conceptualizing the Vanguard as a stronghold of the mainstream does not equate to thinking of it as antithetical to creativity. It may seem that playing in a context like the Vanguard that defines jazz more conservatively than some other settings would not appeal to a player who values ingenuity and risk. Yet, for Hersch, these characteristics do not need to be removed from his essential approach to playing when performing standard repertoire—they are rather relocated. In performing standards, navigating the divide between respecting historically engrained norms and expressing individuality creates a whole different set of challenges than playing originals. Accommodating the Vanguard's reverence for heritage actually creates opportunities for novelty and personal expression by encouraging artists to refer to history without repeating its material, an intellectually and artistically demanding task. Playing standards and jazz compositions is an important facet of what Hersch does as a musician, and he develops performances of precomposed material similar to that of his original music, "Well, I think any tune you have to learn well and spend time with it. Standards, you know, for me, it's partially knowing the words. Then deciding...the key, where it wants to live tempo-wise, then being familiar with it enough that I can just be free with it. With my own tunes, even though I wrote them, I still have to go through the same process." A performance of

Harry Warren's "I Wish I Knew" (1945), a standard Hersch used to open several of his sets during his week at the Vanguard in July 2009, offers a glimpse at what it means to "be free with" a tune.[53] Compositionally, "I Wish I Knew" falls squarely in the middle of the mainstream jazz repertoire. It is a thirty-two–measure popular song in four-four time that he performs at a medium swing tempo—just about as standard as standards come. The trio's performance playfully engages with the normative aspects of this work, maintaining the predictable tempo and form that make it easily recognizable as a jazz tune, while adding new elements that make it more challenging for both players and listeners. Specifically, this performance with bassist John Hébert and drummer Eric McPherson employed two tactics that expand "I Wish I Knew" beyond its usual boundaries. The first of these is beginning the performance without clearly stating the melody, a technique Hersch has discussed with regard to another composition. "Sometimes this week we were playing 'Played Twice,' a Monk tune, and we would just start improvising and then play the melody at the end. And that's fun, because, you know, everybody's...very attentive at first....Then gradually it [the melody] kind of reveals itself. And I like doing that kind of stuff too. It puts me in a different spot." The motivation for this formal modification, as Hersch describes, is both to engage the audience more fully and to lead the performers to different choices by interrupting usual habits. In the Vanguard performance of "I Wish I Knew," Hersch begins an improvised solo right away. He only briefly hints at a few of the primary pitches of the tune's opening phrase at the beginning of the performance, waiting until the very end to provide a clear statement of the tune's composed melody. A second alteration technique applied to this rendition of "I Wish I Knew" is a gradual change of key—the performance begins in G major and ends in A flat. As with the casual approach to rhythmic oddities in the Vanguard performance of "Stuttering," what could be a rather jarring move to a very distant key—G and A-flat major share only two notes in common—is smoothed over, allowing listeners expecting a typical jazz performance to remain undisturbed while still playfully engaging those that hope to hear something personalized and imaginative in the presentation of a familiar tune. A jazz specialist listener could note a series of playful harmonic substitutions that, over the course of four choruses, leads to the new key.[54]

Like beginning with improvisation, changing keys is a method Hersch uses at times to add interest to pieces well known to him or to his audience. "Sometimes," he confessed, "just playing a standard, say, in two different keys...a chorus in one key, a chorus in another key, doing that—just something simple, is fun. It just kind of makes it sound intentional." As with his description of the first alteration technique, Hersch again points out the value of reworking standards for both players and listeners. He expresses his concern that performances sound "intentional"—that the musician's efforts to engage personally with a particular tune come across in performance. "Often I'll have a student come in here, and I'll feel like they're obligatorily playing 'Stella by Starlight' or 'In Your Own Sweet Way' or 'Alone Together,' but it's like, do you know anything about this tune? Why are you playing this tune? What does it mean to you? Why did you pick it? I hate going to a show and just feeling like there's no intent behind the piece. And I also really dislike feeling like people are not really, really improvising....To me that's anti-jazz." For Hersch, simply playing a tune that is drawn from the traditional repertoire of jazz standards does not necessarily mean performing traditional jazz. From this perspective, a standard without evidence of concepts that, for Hersch, are essential to jazz like creativity and improvisation is no more "real jazz" than a less traditional work like "Light Years." The challenge in playing a standard becomes making it just as personal as an original tune, and just as relevant to the present historical moment.

RESPECT, REMEMBRANCE, AND TILTING TOWARD TRADITION

Hersch is not the only performer who tips his choice of ensemble and repertoire toward historically recognizable jazz styles in his work at this particular venue. Returning to Ethan Iverson and his former band The Bad Plus, which achieved prominent notice from jazz publications and audiences in the first decade and a half of the new century, we find another example of a musician who regularly pushes the boundaries of jazz as a genre yet wishes to maintain the identity, and even the sanctity, of the Vanguard as a jazz club. If anything, Iverson seems to see the task of carrying on historical models of jazz as a process that is only becoming more difficult over time. He expresses a sense of the increasing weight of history that separates even his generation from that of Hersch, his former teacher, "[Hersch] played with jazz masters, and you can hear that in his playing. He played with Sam Jones, he played a week here [at the Village Vanguard] with Joe Henderson, Ron Carter, and Al Foster....That's the sort of experience I could only ever dream of having."[55] Holding on to a deep appreciation for jazz of the past, in spite of a sense of distance from its most original or authentic cultural and musical origins, represents a recurring theme in Iverson's discussions about his own place in the jazz world.

Iverson and bandmates bassist Reid Anderson and drummer David King caught jazz audiences and critics a bit off-guard with their rapid ascent to popularity in the early 2000s, performing and recording a sizable body of music in the nearly two decades they worked together. One journalist described them as "a lightning rod for opinion and controversy" because of their tendency to perform tunes from outside usual jazz realms.[56] Their 2009 album *For All I Care*, a collaboration with vocalist Wendy Lewis, demonstrates their eclectic approach to repertoire. On this album, a version of "Lithium" by '90s grunge icon Kurt Cobain challenges jazz norms in the direction of the popular, and the inclusion of the high modern serialism of Milton Babbitt's *Semi-Simple Variations* crosses boundaries along an entirely different front. Along with these two works are songs by Pink Floyd, Wilco, György Ligeti, Yes, the Bee Gees, Heart, Roger Miller, Igor Stravinsky, and the Flaming Lips. Despite the rather startling breadth of source material here, it is worth noting that none of Hersch's jazz "food groups" are represented. While The Bad Plus has performed all three of these types of pieces at one time or another on prior albums, there is not a single standard, jazz composition, or original tune on *For All I Care*. Though musicians from jazz's earliest history onward have regularly drawn on popular songs and classical music as source material for improvisation, the boundaries of what is often conceptualized as mainstream jazz hardened somewhat between its move toward high art in the 1950s and '60s and the dawn of the twenty-first century. Efforts in the 1970s and '80s to stave off the forces of jazz-rock fusion made interpretations of more recent pop targets for criticism by jazz purists, and assertions of jazz as a unique non-European art music left contemporary classical music equally off limits. Making an album exclusively from these two sources certainly speaks to a willingness to break with mainstream jazz conventions on a considerable scale.

In addition to their choice of music, the band is known for their rock-influenced stage presence and antics during performance. According to jazz writer David Adler, their "non-purist ethos carries over to the group's live show" in which Iverson "has been known to recite song lyrics in a grave monotone; sling off his tie during the group's rendition of 'I Will Survive'; stare blankly at the audience during King's 'Freelance

Robotics'; even crouch behind the piano and render the bridge to 'My Funny Valentine' in a crazed, stuttering wail."[57] Despite being an acoustic piano trio that plays improvisatory music, The Bad Plus, originally in its incarnation with Iverson and later with his successor Orrin Evans, is just as likely to appear in rock venues as jazz ones, and their manner of performing reflects the spaces in which they play.

Even with his forays into rock and modernist art music, Iverson is clearly an artist with an extensive knowledge of and profound love for canonized, historical jazz styles. Hersch explains this aspect of his friend and former student by describing him as "wildly interested in everything in a very deep way." Iverson himself talks of an emotional attachment to the music of the past that even occasionally makes it difficult to maintain his composure while interacting with younger musicians and students he feels have not taken advantage of the opportunity to learn from the recordings of past jazz masters. As he puts it, "I think I can actually be a bit of a hardass, unintentionally, because I don't think that's necessarily the best way to teach. I think a lot of the best teachers are sort of more...open and encouraging. But I care about it a lot, and if you're coming to me, and you're playing Monk tunes out of the *Real Book*, it's very hard for me to keep my cool entirely." If students have only looked shallowly at lead sheets of standard tunes rather than learning them from historically significant recordings, Iverson finds himself frustrated. He described a master class gone awry in which he found the students' level of historical and musical knowledge troubling, "I played James P. Johnson's most famous piece, the 'Carolina Shout,' and none of them recognized it. And I felt like none of them had even heard of James P. Johnson. And I just sort of—I actually started to cry a little bit. Like, I just couldn't understand why you wouldn't know a bit more about some important heritage—again, the coin that was paid. James P. Johnson paid heavy. He paid dues no one I've ever met has had to pay, given his time and place and what he was up against." Not surprisingly, Iverson's enthusiasm for the music and musicians of the past spills into enthusiasm for the Vanguard. Iverson talks about himself as an outsider to some of the more central aspects of jazz, especially as compared to players who grew up in communities where jazz was commonly performed and heard. To him, some players better represent "the real... jazz tradition than [he does] for sure." In Iverson's view,

> Someone who does represent it, for example, is the Marsalises. They're from New Orleans, the dad is a great jazz pianist....Wynton and Branford met all the heaviest jazz musicians on the planet when they were just idiots in high

school that cared more about basketball. You can actually hear it in their music, even if you don't like it. That's fine, but you can hear that they know something about what the real jazz is, and they've known it for a long time. And that if you talk to Wynton or Branford about jazz, the way they phrase their sentences is actually like some real jazz type of thing. It's not me from the Midwest. My scene is like a different universe.

Iverson describes himself as someone who has had only a "couple of the bites...of the real jazz tradition," and, significantly, "they've actually been connected to this club [the Village Vanguard], for sure." When playing the Village Vanguard, Iverson balances his identity as a musician who works both inside and outside the jazz world with his respect for the heritage of the club.

> Well, the band I'm mostly in is The Bad Plus, which is not representative... particularly, of the world of jazz clubs. We do happen to play the Vanguard, and it's a great honor for us to play here, and we love doing it....When The Bad Plus does play the Vanguard, we do think about it a little bit....Whatever is in our repertoire that is a little more like jazz, we program it when we play the Vanguard, as compared to if we're playing a rock club or the festival Bonaroo or something. It's not like we rewrite the whole book or something, it's just how you tilt it.

Iverson did not set out to transform the Vanguard into a rock club with The Bad Plus. While he also did not attempt to turn The Bad Plus into a traditional jazz trio, he showed a willingness to meet the club and its audience halfway by tailoring sets for the Vanguard out of jazz-related material to the extent that it was possible within the band's performing repertoire. When he does play as part of a more typical jazz trio rather than in his former band, his work conforms more neatly to the work of other Vanguard regulars. A performance at the club in July of 2009 by Iverson, with drummer Paul Motian, Vanguard staple since the 1960s, and The Bad Plus bassist, Anderson, contained repertoire choices practically indistinguishable from those made by the Hersch trio the week prior: four original compositions by the performing musicians, two jazz compositions, and three standards.[58]

Despite the ways in which they fit their work to the jazz-specific environment at the Vanguard, neither Hersch nor Iverson seems to feel that the establishment has become overly restrictive. Both make a point of noting that Lorraine Gordon was open to the inclusion of a variety of musical styles as she booked musicians for the Vanguard. In Iverson's view, "Lorraine has been interested in getting different kinds of music in here...and it's not music that sounds like traditional jazz." Similarly, Hersch said, "I give Lorraine a lot of credit for keeping it as it has been, and also expanding to include new artists, which she has." Yet in examining Gordon's own statements on the matter, continuities with the past are easy to spot. In fact, the very expansions that Iverson and Hersch describe were, for Gordon, continuations. She was quite frank in descriptions of her own hiring practices, "How do I choose whom I hire? Basically, I just start with what I know. I like what I like, so that's what I hire....I also read everything about jazz that's available; I try to keep up with the jazz world." The fact that Gordon had an interest in "keeping up" in the present jazz world should come as no surprise when her earlier career is considered. Collaborating on projects for Blue Note records over seventy years ago, Gordon remembered being "entirely into older jazz" but still "going to clubs like the Royal Roost and Birdland, on Broadway near 52nd Street, because that's where all the new young guys were playing this new music called bebop." Gordon's extensive career took place in a jazz world characterized by constant stylistic changes, and continuing her own typical practices meant "always [having her] ears open for the new man, the next phase of jazz history."[59] As she described her perspective in a 2013 interview with Will Friedweld,

> Everything changes. Look at me, look at you. Of course it changes—it's a growing art form. Anything that's artistic and pure will change. Otherwise it's a static thing that you don't care about. What's new is the name of the game; if it comes out of the musical ability of artists who play and compose, then it's a valid art form." But Ms. Gordon does insist on some traditional values. "I encourage everyone who plays here to include at least one standard or ballad in every set—I say, no one's going out the door humming that original you wrote 10 minutes ago."[60]

Striking a balance between heritage and change is at the core of what the Vanguard has come to represent.

While the cast of musicians appearing at the Village Vanguard has changed over time, the basic premise behind what they are there to do has instead gradually solidified. In a contemporary market in which jazz clubs in a mid-twentieth-century model have become scarce—now competing with concert halls, repertory movements, and festivals—holding on to this particular manner of doing jazz business has become a hallmark of the Vanguard's twenty-first-century identity. For Iverson, the Vanguard and a handful of other small clubs maintain spaces in which musicians can continue "practicing a certain way of thinking about the music" that is not possible in all areas of today's live jazz scenes. He expresses some concern over recent trends in jazz toward overvalorizing the past, citing, in particular, things like Ken Burns's 2000 documentary, *Jazz*, that strive to present historical jazz players in the most glowing possible manner, and, in the process, discourage contemporary players from exploring new interests.

> I think that there's…too much reverence, but not enough respect.…You get into this zone where you're talking about Louis Armstrong [being] as great as Shakespeare.…I think if you're a writer, you can't just sit around praising Shakespeare all day. You have to be irritated with Shakespeare sometimes. Shakespeare isn't funny. And what about some of those historical plays? A couple of them are great, but some of them aren't so good. You know, you have to sort of interface with it in a non-reverential way.…Know it, and then eat it up and spit it out however you're going to do it. I'll be playing some Monk tonight. I won't be playing it how Monk played it.…But I really know Monk's original piano parts. I'm very careful to do that. I don't play any of them that I don't know Monk's piano parts. Then I can discard them.

Not many years have passed since jazz first came to be considered the sort of art form that could have a figure analogous to Shakespeare. The institutions that have taken shape since the last quarter of the twentieth century have highlighted the significance and uniqueness of the Vanguard in the context of today's scene, but they have also brought questions of influence starkly into focus. The concern Iverson expresses about both knowing and carefully avoiding replication of Monk's performances of his own music speak to a level of canonization relatively recent in the jazz world, a musical idiom that originally carved out a space for itself as countercultural and transgressive.

In many ways, the culture surrounding the Village Vanguard positions itself in opposition to the forces of institutionalization—it is a place in which creativity, improvisation, and artistic change are held in high regard and a place that openly celebrates the countercultural credentials of its origins and early history. Yet there is no denying that it has become an institution in its own right. Maintaining the identity of the Vanguard has become a careful balancing act. It is no longer just a nightclub that can present the moment's most novel and promising entertainment. Sixty years' worth of records have piled up as a very tangible reminder of the direction the space has gone, records that simultaneously serve as reminders of the past and guidelines for the present and the future, as they copy and repeat history verbatim in their mediatized form and demand consciously inexact reference through carefully constructed live performances that are both the same as and different from what has come before. Performances like those by Hersch and Iverson, creatively quirky standards and standard-adjacent interpretations of originals, serve to keep the Vanguard in its tenuous space between past and present as well as its neighborhood and broader marketplaces. Now that the Vanguard has become an iconic jazz landmark, its recognizable identity is linked to its ability to hold on to what it already is and what it was. These remain two different things, however. The Vanguard of the past, preserved in so many photographs, stories, collective memories, and, above all, treasured records, is an essential part of the Vanguard of the present, a part that forces a more complicated, careful way of carrying on now. Bassist Christian McBride describes the experience of making a twenty-first-century recording at the Vanguard like this: "All of a sudden, when those microphones went up, I had this sense of, 'We'd better bring it harder than we've brought it anywhere else before.... This is going down as a document at the world's most legendary jazz club.'"[61] With the esteem brought by a stage so many have used before, the respectability now prearranged for new acts at the Vanguard, comes a certain trust that the past will be built upon rather than shattered or cast aside, a gesture that presents this place as one in which jazz heritage, though always contested and in flux, is audible.

CHAPTER 2

Phantom Partners

Large-Scale Venues on a National Scene

After climbing up the dark, narrow stairs of the Village Vanguard onto the crowded sidewalks of Greenwich Village, away from the tight basement that has become so iconic as a physical representation of jazz culture, a contemporary jazz listener can travel to a nearly opposite building in search of this same genre of music. A couple hundred miles to the south, along the bank of the Potomac River and adjacent to the National Mall's two miles of generously spaced monuments and museums, stands Washington, D.C.'s John F. Kennedy Center for the Performing Arts, one of a handful of arts presenters in major American cities that now routinely offers live jazz on an enormous scale. There is a malleability to jazz due to its loose and contested genre boundaries that allows it to symbolize a wide range of geographically and culturally defined values. Various constructions of its history can symbolize America, diversity, risk, African American experience, creativity, freedom, sophistication, populism, New Orleans, New York, or San Francisco, among plenty of other ideas, places, and identities. Nationally visible large-scale venues define themselves in part through their relationships with each other and the differing versions of jazz history they relate, and their monumental physical spaces help lend weight to the stories they tell about jazz, themselves as institutions, and each other.

Like the nearby Washington Monument, much of the visual impact of the Kennedy Center comes from its sheer size. At 100 feet tall and 630 feet long, the massive rectangular building can be seen from a substantial distance by an approaching pedestrian. Its specific placement along the wide river, while visually striking, emphasizes the building's role as a major national cultural site rather than an element of an interconnected urban neighborhood; the Center is almost completely cut off from the surrounding city by a tangle of highways, making the Watergate Complex and the Saudi Arabian Embassy its only easily walkable neighbors. Cars and shuttle buses deliver audience members to the building's impressive entrance leading into the dramatic, high-ceilinged Hall of Nations and Hall of States that separate the three large theaters on the first floor, the Concert Hall, Opera House, and Eisenhower Theater. The two hallways end in the Grand Foyer, an overwhelmingly enormous space spanning the full length of the building that is described on the Center's website as "one of the largest rooms in the world." To again put the Kennedy Center in perspective with other D.C. landmarks, the 555-foot tall, 55-foot wide Washington Monument, if laid on its side, could fit neatly into the Grand Foyer with plenty of room to spare on all sides.[1] Upstairs on the Terrace Level, however, a room that once housed a library has been converted into the Terrace Gallery, a multiuse space at times set up as the KC Jazz Club, a 160-seat room with cabaret tables and a modest raised stage, a Vanguardesque room tucked inside a vast monument of American art as both a memorial to and a continuation of jazz club culture.

The KC Jazz Club, which opened in the early years of the new century, was originally a project of Billy Taylor, the first artistic director for jazz at the Kennedy Center, beginning in 1994. While the Kennedy Center had programmed jazz intermittently since its opening in the 1970s, Taylor's concerts in the 1990s provided annual seasons of what he called "America's classical music," a development at the venue that followed the rise of Jazz at Lincoln Center in New York a few years earlier. Taylor remained at the helm of the Center's jazz programming up until his death in 2010. In 2011, The Kennedy Center appointed Jason Moran as Taylor's successor. Immediately, Moran was expected to make noteworthy changes. Born fifty-four years after Taylor, who was known for fairly traditional programming, Moran was viewed as an iconoclast who would shake things up. Yet when he took the position, Moran sought advice from the leader of the biggest and most widely discussed large-scale jazz presenter, Wynton Marsalis of Jazz at Lincoln Center. One area in which Moran has decidedly not followed in Marsalis's or Taylor's footsteps is in the diverse and experimental nature of his programming for the Center. Not following Marsalis's model does not equate to ignoring his advice, however: "'I told him we don't all have to have the same vision,' Marsalis recalled.... 'Your tastes govern your program. It's important to be independent in your taste and your decisions, and to stand by your program. Do what you believe in.'"[2] Moran's work at the Kennedy Center has indeed been independent from Marsalis's hotly debated canonical approach, reaching outward to other art forms and musical genres he can connect to jazz rather than shoring up barriers around a clearly defined genre.

Moran took on the Kennedy Center role as an opportunity and a challenge, a chance to reshape jazz at large-scale arts institutions. In an interview with reporter Fred Kaplan, Moran reflected on the generational divide separating him and his peers from earlier institutional leaders. "All the yelling we did about institutions when we were in our 20s—now we're in our 40s, and we're in charge of these institutions.... What are we going to do with them?"[3] According to Kaplan, Moran has already done a great deal at the Center and is poised to do more with his contract extension carrying into 2021, a full decade from the date of his initial appointment. "Not so long ago, Moran's eclectic, adventurous approach to jazz would have placed him well outside the aesthetic boundaries of Washington's John F. Kennedy Center for the Performing Arts. But in the past few years, the big white box on the Potomac has opened its venues to jazz in tandem with skateboarders, stand-up comics, dancers, painters and rappers. This redefining of what it means to be the 'national cultural center' is, to a large extent, the doing of Jason Moran."[4] Rather than focusing on jazz exclusively, Moran has encouraged the Kennedy Center to bring in more diverse forms of American music, including advocating for the first artistic director for hip hop culture, rapper and producer Q-Tip. Meanwhile, Marsalis has maintained his commitment to swinging, blues-based jazz in New York alongside encouragement for Moran's different path. "Marsalis said he likes a lot of what Moran is doing in Washington. 'I like the skateboarding, I like the live painting, the diversity of art. I applaud the things he does, which are so unlike what anybody else could do,' he told [Kaplan]. 'I don't like hip hop, but it doesn't matter. It means one person doesn't like it. I support Jason, and I'm glad they brought him in.'"[5] In the second decade of the twenty-first century, large-scale American performing arts institutions look large enough to contain multiple visions for jazz, its history, and its future.

Thirty years ago, discourse on jazz reflected much more concern and uncertainty about the potential of large-scale, nonprofit arts organizations to homogenize and control the future of jazz. Nervous commentary speculated on a musical future fixed as firmly in place as the heavy edifices in which it was performed. Leading up to the first full concert season of Jazz at Lincoln Center (JALC) in 1991, musicians, journalists, and listeners were already criticizing the organization for the ideological ramifications of its plans for an unprecedented million-dollar budget for jazz programming. In an article for the *New York Times* in August of 1991 titled "Good News in Jazz, with a Big Caveat," critic Peter Watrous wrote, "Even nationally, the brute force of a million-dollar first-year budget and a string of 18 concerts, all emanating from an American institution dedicated to the preservation of classical music, has to act as a legitimizing influence."[6] Watrous's use of the word "preservation" is key here; at the root of outcries against JALC's grand scale was a fear that preserving jazz would mean a retreat into the past and a loss of development and innovation. He warned that JALC was set to become "a partisan in an ideological argument, and it should not be when its program is the only one of its kind in the country."[7] Because of its sheer size, high level of financial support, associations with high culture, and commitment to educational outreach, JALC has played—and will likely continue to play—a defining role in how the general public sees jazz and the historical canon of performers and composers, many of them long dead, that are central to its programming. It is no longer the only program or space of its kind in the country, however, and the jazz story told by JALC has not led to one homogenous jazz narrative but a multivoice national conversation with diverse and at times conflicting visions of jazz, its past, and its future.

Since the early 1990s, JALC itself has amassed even more support and influence, but it is has also amassed company on a national scene. Taylor and Moran's work at the Kennedy Center offers a corollary in Washington, D.C.; SFJazz opened its own major San Francisco venue in 2013; and, though considerably smaller, the New Orleans Jazz Market, which opened in 2015, drew inspiration from JALC's model. The massive shadow of JALC has indeed shaped all of these venues, and connections exist in the scale, structure, and mission of each one. An aspect of JALC's influence, however, has come in the form of opposition: comparison is one element of what has caused each space to develop individual identities and definitions of jazz in their programming. Each nonprofit presents jazz as a service to their city rooted in a long-standing tradition, and each shapes the stories told about that tradition to the places and institutions that surround them. The ways these large-scale jazz venues have crafted partnerships between living and dead musicians have allowed them to leverage jazz history to validate the presence of their institutions, controlling the interpretation of past masters while presenting the work of today's artists. While many observers voiced concerns that the enormity of Jazz at Lincoln Center would cause its particularly narrow version of jazz history to dominate widespread understandings of the music, what it means, and who makes it, the subsequent addition of parallel jazz programming efforts at large venues in other American cities has led to a form of national scene in which these presenters partner not only with dead icons of the jazz canon but also indirectly with each other. JALC's strict definition of jazz allowed it to take hold at Lincoln Center, and it also created a demand for contrasting definitions that have emerged in other venues. What follows will first explore the rise of JALC and the way it used contemporary constructions of historical jazz figures to validate the permanent and consistent presence of jazz in large nonprofit performing arts spaces. In a discussion of Hall of Fame concerts featuring the music and biographies of Fats Waller, Mary Lou Williams, and Bill Evans, I argue that JALC shapes its presentations of historical jazz to shore up an aesthetically and philosophically unified blues- and swing-based canon grounded in a particular vision of African American masculinity. Next, I will describe the recent growth and success of SFJazz as both a parallel and a response to JALC's model, analyzing a Miles Davis festival that follows JALC in celebrating a canonic jazz master but departs from their model by foregrounding living artists and stylistic diversity in a physical space that mimics classical music presenters while also asserting its independence from them.

MAKING A CASE FOR JAZZ INSTITUTIONS

Jazz at Lincoln Center originated as a summer program called Classical Jazz that offered its first three-concert series in 1987. As the title of the series implies, the act of drawing this repertoire into the same performing arts complex that houses the Metropolitan Opera, the New York Philharmonic, and the New York City Ballet presented jazz as an art more closely allied to high culture than to popular entertainment. Four years later, JALC had become a year-round endeavor, and in its second season, its first collaborative program with the New York City Ballet further cemented the presence of jazz as one of Lincoln Center's fine arts. By 1995 support for JALC had grown to the point that the venue granted the organization at least three landmark criteria for recognition:

(1) JALC was given equal status with Lincoln Center's other arts programs; (2) JALC was the first significant addition to Lincoln Center in nearly forty years; and (3) before the end of the program's first decade of existence, its organizers had plans already underway to build a substantial new space dedicated entirely to hosting jazz events. Programs for public television and radio, including Ken Burns's popular documentary *Jazz* (2000) for PBS, brought attention to this growing jazz institution from places far beyond New York City.

In addition to presenting jazz in a high-art setting at Lincoln Center, JALC's leadership took on the role of jazz missionaries from very early on in the program's history. Administrative director Rob Gibson told the *New York Times* in 1992, "We want to be the model for the nation in terms of jazz and presenting this music."[8] In a similar vein, JALC's director of education, Laura Johnson, described her work as "sort of a crusade" in which the organization made a point of bringing jazz to the world.[9] While jazz communities might be expected to support such a project, the process has not been straightforward or lacking in contention. The basic concerns repeatedly voiced by JALC's critics relate primarily to what they see as the organization's overly conservative programming.[10] Summing up arguments against JALC near the end of its first decade, Peter Applebome noted that much opposition to the programming was based in a perception of its being "cautious, static and dated."[11] Although the range of styles included in the organization's musical offerings has expanded over time, in his reflections on the program's thirtieth anniversary, Giovanni Russonello wrote, "At a time when canon-busting is nearly the national consensus, Jazz at Lincoln Center's founding artistic director, Wynton Marsalis, maintains that jazz is a classical music with a fixed roster of heroes, and a nonnegotiable rhythmic foundation."[12]

Despite controversy over limited programming, JALC racked up an impressive number of popular and financial successes in very short order, and it has continued to increase its amount of programming each season from its very beginnings. The organization's second season grew considerably from the first, presenting nearly one hundred events, four times the previous year's number. Education programs quickly multiplied, and the Lincoln Center Jazz Orchestra embarked on a twenty-eight-city tour that took JALC's influence outside New York. Ben Ratliff reported in the *New York Times* that by 1997, each concert JALC put on at Lincoln Center had to be presented twice rather than once to "accommodate an increased demand for tickets," and Applebome echoed this in 1998, commenting that "most concerts play[ed] to sold-out houses."[13] The following year's centennial celebrations of the birth of Duke Ellington throughout the 1999–2000 season brought on another growth spurt with a twenty percent budget increase. The Lincoln Center Jazz Orchestra's tour that year included one hundred cities on four continents, and the Essentially Ellington educational program expanded to all fifty U.S. states. By 2017, it had distributed free transcriptions of Ellington's music to approximately five thousand participating schools. In 2003, JALC's annual operating budget had hit $12 million, and in 2004 its $128 million facility opened at Columbus Circle. Less than a decade later, the new space had been fully paid off, and the organization was operating with a budget surplus.[14] Writing in 2017, Russonello commented, "Jazz at Lincoln Center typically sells out more than 90 percent of its seats for these major shows, so there is clearly a New York audience still interested in standard-issue jazz."[15]

The audience Russonello describes is one that has been carefully cultivated through JALC's programming and educational mission, a topic best understood against the backdrop of the life and career of Marsalis as the organization's highly visible artistic director. His status as a Grammy-winning, Juilliard-trained, virtuoso classical musician has given him a unique level of influence in his efforts to promote jazz as refined and artistically important to classical institutions and audiences, and his roots in an established New Orleans jazz family lend credibility to his perspectives on jazz. Winning a Pulitzer Prize in 1997 for his jazz oratorio, *Blood on the Fields*, was a notable mark of his progress in the direction of successfully pulling jazz into the classical world, as the Pulitzer board had to alter its requirements in order for his work to be eligible.[16] Outspoken and charismatic, Marsalis made *Time* magazine's list of "America's 25 Most Influential People" in an era when even the most popular jazz musicians were far from household names. While irksome to his adversaries, the fact that Marsalis has been called "the most celebrated jazz musician of his time" is essentially accurate in terms of his worldwide fame.[17]

Also famous are Marsalis's opinions on what constitutes jazz, especially as he voiced them as a young man in the 1980s. In a 1985 interview with Herbie Hancock for *Musician* magazine, the two musicians clashed over the issue of jazz's relationship to popular music. While one might expect the younger man, Marsalis, to be the one to come out in favor of his generation's popular music, he instead criticized Hancock's success in the realm of jazz-rock fusion. In fact, Marsalis's critique of popular music was founded not only on musical terms but on moral ones as well. According to Marsalis, pop music was "really geared to a whole base type of sexual thing." To the young Marsalis, pop music was a manifestation of low physicality, while the goal of more legitimate music was to "elevate the people to a certain level rather than go down."[18] Earlier in its history, jazz itself received the brunt of criticism linking music to a lack of morality in articles like "Does Jazz Put the Sin in Syncopation?" for the *Ladies' Home Journal* in 1921.[19] By the 1980s, however, when more and more people had come to associate jazz with sophistication and high art, Marsalis was able to pass the stigma of loose morals onto a new generation's popular music as a way of further elevating his own musical idiom, redefining jazz's relationship to the body along the way. In fact, one of the frequent criticisms of JALC, voiced here by longtime jazz producer and manager Marty Khan, is that it has built a monopoly based on a new, sanitized jazz removed from any troubled past of hypersexualized or countercultural deviancy. To Khan and other proponents of the smaller jazz organizations and venues that predate JALC, this enormous player in the global jazz scene has "been able to manipulate the minds of an ignorant public by portraying itself as the only 'safe' access to a world populated by junkies, deviants and other various forms of social misfits or generally distasteful characters."[20] By contextualizing jazz within one of the most respected high-art institutions in the country, Khan argues, JALC is able to present its musical offerings as the most wholesome and respectable jazz on the market.

As the artistic director of JALC, Marsalis has been an important part of presenting jazz to an audience that is clearly tied more to the world of art music than to that of popular culture. As Khan puts it, JALC's "concerts are geared to draw audiences like those who attend the symphony, or those who watch public television," in large part by framing jazz as socially responsible.[21] While Marsalis's rhetoric has grown more moderate in recent years, many of his core ideas about jazz's superior moral qualities remain intact. In his 2008 book, *Moving to Higher Ground: How Jazz Can Change Your Life*, Marsalis develops his ideas about the social function of jazz into a full-fledged manifesto. He expresses his basic viewpoint in the introduction to the book, telling readers, "In this book I hope to deliver the positive message of America's greatest music: how great musicians demonstrate a mutual respect and trust on the bandstand that can alter your outlook on the world and enrich every aspect of your life—from individual creativity and personal relationships to the way you conduct business and understand what it means to be a global citizen in the most modern sense." The beliefs Marsalis outlines here about how jazz creates a type of musical discourse that ought to be a model for other forms of human interaction are central to the overall project of JALC. In addition to his focus on providing jazz high-art status, it is significant that Marsalis refers to it as "America's greatest music." Jazz and its essential but indefinable cooperatively improvised "swing" is held up by JALC as America's unique musical and cultural heritage, something capable of helping form a harmonious national identity and secure a brighter future for the country. According to Marsalis, "Our current lack of respect for the swing can be likened to the current state of our democracy. Balance is required to maintain something as delicate as democracy, a subtle understanding of how your power can be magnified through joining with and sharing the power of another person."[22] Through this type of rhetoric, Marsalis, and JALC under his leadership, frames learning about and listening to jazz as a democratic responsibility that will lead to a better social and political situation.

Even as Marsalis makes the case for democracy and shared power in music and life, he did so from what was for many years a position of unparalleled power and influence in his field, a position many jazz commentators have accused him of abusing. While this does not necessarily invalidate Marsalis's efforts to analogize jazz and American political ideals, it does expose less palatable versions of both elements. As Dale Chapman writes, "It is not difficult…to problematize the easy collapsing of jazz values with those of the American nation-state: after all, African-American jazz artists have often defined themselves in opposition to the more self-congratulatory accounts of American democracy, and have themselves often been subjected to its least democratic impulses. Moreover, numerous observers have argued that the very same nation-state that is celebrated for its 'jazz-shaped' dynamism and inclusivity has engaged in practices (racist, patriarchal, neo-imperialist) that belie its claims to democratic virtue. Nevertheless, the efficacy of this jazz-centered narrative of American exceptionalism has been remarkably difficult to dislodge."[23] More specifically, Chapman makes the argument that Marsalis's neoclassical approach to jazz pairs with concurrent trends in neoliberal politics, writing, "A key irony here is that, even as the conservatism of neoclassicism has rendered jazz palatable for the consumption of large institutional actors by putting a brake on innovation, what these actors see reflected in jazz neoclassicism is precisely a quality of nimble, dynamic, and democratic innovation that they would like to see in themselves."[24] Marsalis's institutionally viable version of jazz and its history represents a set of innovative, experimental, inclusive values to its new audience even as it draws criticism from some jazz musicians and audiences that feel their version of the music is excluded by JALC's rigid conservatism.

Nonetheless, JALC's projects of upholding strict borders around jazz as a clearly defined art music and claiming value for that music based on its American identity have been central to its musical programming and the rhetoric that promotes it. Early on, JALC made no apologies for its quest to designate a canon of jazz masterpieces. The following statement by Stanley Crouch, an important mentor to Marsalis, introduces a collection of live recordings from the early 1990s, one of the first to be released by JALC:

> To some extent, this recording of performances gathered from concerts presented by Jazz At Lincoln Center is a history of art. It is arrived at through aspects of a developing canon rich with vitality. The performances selected for this document are part of our mission at Lincoln Center, which is to present first-class performances, regardless of style; to create a viable jazz canon; to provide education for young musicians and listeners; and to build a jazz archives worthy of the music and the premier arts complex in America...sustaining and extending our most democratic art, bringing the dreams of our most enlightened social propositions into the arena of aesthetic vibrance.[25]

Jazz at Lincoln Center has thus presented itself as a steward of not just aesthetically viable music but socially uplifting music. By extension, the musicians who are embraced by the JALC canon are positioned not only as artistic leaders but also as moral ones. The ability to create great jazz that draws on the music's multicultural history and takes advantage of its improvisational freedom is offered as a model of responsible and productive American citizenship, and the grandeur of the venue in which this story is told adds significance and polish to the telling.

PERFORMING CONTROLLED DIVERSITY

The establishment of a canon requires the selection of musical and cultural leaders, a task that has taken on its most concrete form in JALC's establishment of the Nesuhi Ertegun Jazz Hall of Fame. Now comprised of over sixty musicians, the Hall of Fame formerly consisted of a multimedia display in the lobby of JALC's Rose Concert Hall that allowed visitors to explore written, photographic, and musical material documenting each musician's contributions to jazz, an online version of the same exhibit available to viewers and listeners anywhere in the world, and a live concert series of programs devoted to recent inductees. Hall of Fame concerts were specially designed to guarantee listeners, especially those who were new to jazz, a high-culture experience based in the work of respected and celebrated artists. While the Hall of Fame concert series no longer exists under the same name, concerts in a similar spirit continue to be presented by JALC under new headings, such as the Visionary Voices series, which features music associated with famous icons, including historical figures like Billy Strayhorn, Frank Sinatra, Billie Holiday, Tito Puente, and Art Blakey, among others.[26] The Hall of Fame creates the sense of a common ground for jazz audiences, a body of artists and their music that is officially recognized as important and worthy of attention. In a jazz landscape as diverse as the present one, a concert built around a historical figure provides a safe choice for listeners uncertain about where they would draw the boundaries of the genre or whom the most significant, interesting, or entertaining contemporary players might be. As Tracy McMullen argues, JALC rose to prominence amidst a late-twentieth-century "culture of fear." She writes, "Faced with perpetual discourses of insecurity and fear, it is unsurprising that audiences were increasingly drawn to reenactments that offered performances of the *known*: performances that provide a sense of stability and mastery, a respite from the open-endedness, insecurity, and 'loss of a sense of grounding' characteristic of postmodernity generally and fueled by political discourse."[27] Rather than choose from a broad, unfamiliar, unpredictable array of current musicians, audiences can escape into jazz history in much the same way that classical music audiences can take comfort in repeated listening to Bach and Beethoven. Although one can no longer go see Duke Ellington, Charlie Parker, or Ella Fitzgerald, these concerts make it possible to attend live performances where historical characters are the stars of the show.

The catch, however, in a contemporary live concert is that the music of these dead but widely recorded artists must be played by someone else. The jazz repertory movement's re-creations of earlier performances are certainly not a new phenomenon—Alex Stewart traces the history of jazz bands performing preexisting music from records back to the 1930s.[28] They certainly intensified, however, as celebrated giants of mid-century jazz like Duke Ellington and Count Basie disappeared from the scene, yet demand for live performances of their music continued. Many commentators, however, have questioned the relevance of these posthumous performances in light of recordings by jazz masters of the past. For example, jazz critic Konrad Heidkamp asks, "Who would in this day and age rack their brains about new interpretations of Bach, Mozart or Beethoven...if we had recordings of their performances, if their sound were documented in audible form and repeatable?"[29] Because Miles Davis's *Kind of Blue* (1959) is readily available on record as played by its original creators, one might argue that there is no need for contemporary performers to rehash the album's old material in concerts that will never be perceived as equal to or greater than the revered recording. Yet, the very lack of famous deceased artists creates a desire to connect with them and their music, which allows JALC to successfully market and present these concerts, year after year.

According to Jason Stanyek and Benjamin Piekut, "Music has been a particularly fertile growth market for dead talent."[30] In their work on what they call posthumous duets, such as the 1991 collaboration between the living Natalie Cole and her deceased father Nat, they argue, "In late capitalism, the dead are highly productive. Of course, all capital is dead labor, but the dead also *generate* capital in collaboration with the living. What is 'late' about late capitalism could be the new arrangements of interpenetration between worlds of living and dead, arrangements that might best be termed *intermundane*."[31] Dead artists hold a special attraction for audiences, and the ability of the living to recast the work of lost performers in new guises has proven quite fruitful, simultaneously offering listeners old favorite recordings and something new they have never heard before. The unique role these intermundane projects can fill lies in their use of both living and dead creativity, the collaboration between past and present.

Of course, thinking of deceased performers as sharing responsibility for posthumous projects raises questions about both the musical and ethical impacts of working with the dead. Stanyek and Piekut are frequently asked, "How are these 'collaborations' when the dead cannot respond, cannot change or adapt to their living counterparts?"[32] Their response points to the idea that denying the agency of the dead in these projects may exempt them from responsibility for the less savory aspects of living-dead partnerships, but it also denies their continued ability to affect the present through their preserved artistic legacy. "For us, agency is not merely an individual's capacity to respond to changing conditions....We might even say that this is the only guarantee that sound recording offers: being recorded means being enrolled in futures (and pasts) that one cannot wholly predict nor control. Crucially, having a future means having an effect."³³ In presenting music of dead artists after their passing, the power relationships between present and absent artists must be read as more complex than the simple statement that the living take advantage of the dead once the latter can provide no resistance to such cooption. Financially, certainly, living people benefit from their presentation of the dead, but, artistically, the collaborative relationship proves much richer and much riskier. These concerts can use the cachet of deceased artists to create opportunities and audiences for the living, but much of the credit and prestige flows back into the past as today's performers are framed as vehicles through which audiences access yesterday's great masters.

JALC's concerts based around historical artists demonstrate the ways in which the organization's canon-forming mission translates into live performances, performances that became emblematic of the power of large-scale jazz presenters for many jazz musicians and critics during JALC's ascent to prominence in the 1990s and early twenty-first century. This power seemed to carry both promises and threats: defining a jazz canon on a large stage opened new doors to larger audiences, greater influence, and increased resources, but it also had the potential to foreclose some of the music's messy, complex past and possible futures. Before exploring how subsequent large-scale jazz presenters responded to JALC's canon-building concerts, the following analysis of a season of Hall of Fame concerts explores how they created a sense of the presence of historical jazz performers, both to engage live audiences and to craft a version of jazz history in line with the organization's goals. While the concerts presented by the organization are the product of numerous individuals working in collaboration, I described JALC as a singular figure in these stories as both a convenient shorthand and a reminder of the overall trend toward offering a unified image and message. While the three concerts in the 2009–2010 Hall of Fame series featuring the music of Fats Waller, Mary Lou Williams, and Bill Evans celebrated a diverse range of artists who had been dead for decades, the presentational techniques JALC employed were calculated to leave audiences feeling as though they had connected personally with three historical greats representing a single clear musical style. The versions of these artists audiences saw and heard were new constructions that resulted from intermundane collaborations between dead icons and live performers and presenters. Through careful curation of the Hall of Fame artists' legacies, JALC was able to grow its canon without eroding the firm boundaries the organization had constructed around jazz as a genre.

With posthumous artists, JALC has considerable leeway in crafting ideas about the bodily traits of these absent musicians, and it uses that power to bring people who in life had a variety of different traits into a unified version of jazz history. Nichole Rustin-Paschal's concept of racialized "jazzmasculinity" is helpful in understanding how this process unfolds in a JALC concert celebrating an absent artist, as it offers a sort of physical corollary to Marsalis's version of jazz history and values. As Rustin-Paschal argues, culture surrounding jazz tends to value qualities or ideas associated with black masculinity, including "aggression, competition, arrogance, discipline, and creativity associated with men," regardless of the specific race and gender of any particular artist—indeed, she uses the concept to help explain the music and careers of figures like Hazel Scott and Mary Lou Williams, showing "how much women were invested in the principles of jazzmasculinity, even as they reveled in their femininity."[34] JALC's canon and version of jazz history is certainly characteristic of jazzmasculinity, and the intermundane nature of Hall of Fame concerts is ideally suited for placing historical figures within its bounds. The following three vignettes demonstrate how JALC's massive scale can be leveraged to infuse historical figures with oversized doses of jazzmasculinity to form a larger-than-life canon. By focusing on the constellation of values tied up in jazzmasculinity, JALC creates a sort of controlled diversity within its jazz historical narrative, bringing in musicians of a variety of backgrounds while aligning them with a unified set of musical sounds and associations. Intermundane negotiations between the live bodies on stage and the missing bodies of featured performers pull all artists involved in line with the JALC story.

FATS THREE WAYS

Few bodies in jazz carry more mythological weight than the one belonging to Thomas "Fats" Waller, a man who stood nearly six feet tall, weighed 285 pounds, and composed around four hundred tunes in his less than forty-year life, all while purportedly consuming what his biographer Alyn Shipton calls "vast meals" and "a daily alcoholic intake that would have killed most normal people in a few days."[35] To celebrate the enormous legacy of this jazz giant, one concert by one pianist must not have seemed enough. Instead, on April 16 and 17, 2010, Jazz at Lincoln Center put on its Fats Waller Festival, an event that featured two separate programs, one in Rose Hall and the other in a more intimate performance space called the Allen Room. The program in the large concert hall entitled "The Music of Fats Waller" featured celebrity host Ben Vereen, a Tony Award–winning Broadway actor, as the singing, joke-telling embodiment of Waller, sharing stories of the pianist-composer's life between performances by a small ensemble led by the concert's music director, saxophonist Andy Farber. In addition to his many jokes that evoked the idea of Fats Waller as a personality, like taking the announcement of the tune "Everybody Loves My Baby" as an opportunity to proclaim, "Everybody loves my body," Vereen took a more serious tone to sum up Waller's important contributions to jazz into three basic categories, "Fats Waller's known for three things. One, he's a great pianist, greatest pianist of his generation. Second, he's a brilliant composer, wrote more standards than anyone of his particular time.... Third, as I said, he was one of the greatest performers."[36] Meanwhile, another concert across the hall devoted to the solo piano music of Fats Waller presented these three aspects of Waller's career: impeccable pianistic technique, compositional and improvisatory creativity, and entertaining audience engagement. In honor of Waller's gargantuan reputation, it took a separate pianist to represent each one of these traits. Also, Waller's epic size, both physically and metaphorically, was pointed to by the fact that all his contemporary interpreters eventually joined forces to play at the same time. "Fats Waller: A Handful of Keys" featured Judy Carmichael, Dick Hyman, and Marcus Roberts as modern-day representations of the many sides of the iconic Fats Waller: the entertainer, the virtuoso, and the innovator. As Carmichael describes, the three pianists involved all "have very different personalities," both musically and in terms of their interactions with the audience.[37] These diverse players, all highly accomplished on their own, were combined to elevate the status of Fats Waller and make him the star of a show he did not live to see, presenting him as a single artist who had once done the work of three. While Waller was not physically present, his oversized personality and body and identity as an African American man were palpable themes of the concert.

The role of entertainer was taken up by Carmichael. Although the basic idiom in which she performs Waller's music is representative of a clearly recognizable, historically informed approach to the stride piano repertory, particulars of Carmichael's performance are not meant to reproduce Waller's specific vocabulary. According to Carmichael, she has "never tried to imitate Fats Waller." "Jazz should be about what you bring to it," she says, and she therefore strives to play older jazz piano styles in a way that is generally true to historical techniques and accessible to listeners but representative of her own improvisational vocabulary. In addition to playing in a clear, straightforward stride style, Carmichael took on the task of making the music understandable and accessible for the audience through her verbal performances. She says one of the central goals of her jazz career is "to spend [her] life making this music more accessible," and her interactions with the JALC audience demonstrate her welcoming attitude toward listeners who are unfamiliar with jazz. Before beginning to play her first piece, Carmichael took a moment to introduce the audience to what she was about to do: "I am thrilled to be starting us off tonight, and although I look at an audience that is simply riddled with sophistication, in case there is one person out there who doesn't know everything there is to know about stride, I was given the assignment of sort of giving you Stride 101. So, stride piano: it's called stride because the left hand is making a striding motion over the bass end of the keys."[38] In addition to her role as an educator, Carmichael saw herself as, of the three pianists, representing "the spirit of Fats" and his "joyfulness" through her stage demeanor, a sentiment that was repeated by her colleague Dick Hyman, who called her "the best entertainer." Like Waller, Carmichael sings as well as plays and connects with the audience through her sense of humor. Her explanation of stride included pointing out, "It's stride, s-t-r-i-d-e. I always spell it now, ever since a woman came up to me on the street here in New York and stopped me and said, 'Oh my gosh, you're Judy Carmichael, that famous snide pianist!'"[39] Carmichael stresses the importance for her of interacting with the audience, especially in a concert hall setting. "My goal at a concert is to make that place seem like a club," she says, and she hopes to create a sense of relaxed intimacy that makes listeners feel that they are "right there on the piano bench" with her. As Carmichael presented only one portion of the program, however, the event framed her as performing only a portion of Waller's full capabilities or worth.

Hyman's role in the three-part concert was to resurrect Waller's technical mastery of his instrument. For Hyman, a performance like this is an act of "recreating rather than innovating."[40] Although he is improvising while performing the music of Fats Waller, he says that he intentionally includes features reminiscent of Waller's playing, such as his stride bass and approach to right-hand figuration. Hyman is also careful to avoid anachronisms in his historically inspired performances. For example, when playing Waller, he chooses not to invoke the more complex harmonic language of players like Art Tatum and Bill Evans, even though he has studied their work in detail, because pianists did not adopt their approach to harmony until after Waller's death. Carmichael described Hyman as having a more "intellectual approach" to his contributions to the concert, and he agreed, noting that most of his speeches to the audience were intended to "explain what [he was] about to do." While Carmichael introduced the basic style of stride piano, Hyman focused more intently on the specific musical structure of the selections he performed. He offered musical details to help orient the listener and clear up the boundaries that distinguished Waller the composer from Hyman the performer. "Minor Drag," for example, was described as a loose framework for improvisation, "just messing around, as Fats would have called it," while "My Fate Is in Your Hands" featured a more structured composition Hyman thought of as "almost Gershwin-esque in the kind of melody and harmonies and countermelodies he put to it." Hyman's verbal attention to details of individual pieces suited his musical role as a virtuoso interpreter of Waller's compositional and improvisational style.

In contrast, Marcus Roberts freely blends the old and the new in his interpretations of Waller. Roberts created a third distinct Waller persona by interacting with the audience only minimally, a move that compounded any disorientation the audience experienced in listening to what Hyman referred to as "daring" moves outside of Waller's style. When Roberts first came on stage, he did not speak at all, but instead simply played two solo selections, "Numb Fumbling" and "Viper's Drag," without introduction. These performances incorporated a variety of poststride elements including walking bass lines, bebop figuration, and postbop harmonic choices. After playing during the second set, Roberts attributed his own experimental attitude to Waller himself, saying, "Oh well. That was a 21st-century view of Fats Waller, but, don't get me wrong, if he was here right now, he could play what he played in 1933 and you'd be messed up." In a similar vein, Roberts had told the audience of the early set that Waller "just wrote a bunch of hip music, so, you know what I'm saying, you get a chance, check it out. It is all extremely hip." In both instances, Roberts's remarks allude to Waller's role as an innovator, the role that Roberts himself was playing in the context of the concert. By avoiding direct explanation of how he was approaching the music, Roberts created an image of Waller as a figure who once contributed to and now continues to inspire novelty and awe.

The combined work of the three performers created a performance that could connect with a wide variety of listeners, offering something for newcomers to stride piano through Carmichael's commitment to accessibility, echoes of Waller's own performance style that would resonate with established fans contributed by Hyman, and Roberts's evocation of a jazz tradition that looks back in order to move forward. Yet, the circumstances of the concert also served to remind audiences of the distance between their historical and physical location and Waller's, infusing collective memories of him with an exotic mystique. Although Hyman related an anecdote about a drunken Waller composing a tune during the cab ride to a recording session, the New York visible to the audience from the Allen Room was safe and distant. The venue's wall of windows five stories above the ground allowed glimpses of crowded sidewalks and constant traffic, but even a speeding ambulance, with lights flashing and presumably sirens blaring, was completely inaudible from the clean, modern vantage point of the concertgoers. An elegant little table on the stage, covered in a black cloth and set with a pitcher of water and three glasses, offered another reminder that Fats Waller was not there, sipping from the bottle of gin that he famously kept on the piano, and that "there" was clearly not a crowded speakeasy or seedy old movie theater. In the Allen Room performance, there was a sense that Waller was being raised up above all the struggles of his earthly reality. There was also a sense that the era of jazz giants had passed, and that the representation of one pianist now necessitated the presence of three. To bring home that point, the performance ended with a three-piano version of "Handful of Keys," with all six modern hands at work to replace the two that were not there.

MARY LOU AND BILLIE JEAN

The absent body of Mary Lou Williams, a composer, arranger, and pianist who lived from 1910 to 1981, also played a significant role in how her music was framed in the concert celebrating her induction to the JALC Hall of Fame. While Waller's body presented a straightforward opportunity to showcase magnified jazzmasculinity at the core of a swinging jazz tradition, Williams's inclusion in that same canon allowed JALC to demonstrate that women can also harness the qualities of jazzmasculinity to pursue successful jazz careers. In the case of the Mary Lou Williams concert, the specific choice of the evening's host was symbolic of what JALC wanted Williams to represent to the concert audience: proof that jazz is a democratic art springing from a diverse community that includes women. In order to convey the significance of

Williams in the context of JALC's canon, audiences needed to perceive her as not just composer and performer but one with a female body that was capable of matching the efforts of her male colleagues.

In Williams's absence, a stand-in female body was provided by host and former professional tennis player Billie Jean King. While not particularly connected to the jazz world, King is a well-known public figure for both her athletic ability and her feminist activism. Born in 1943, King's tennis career coincided with the high-water mark of Second Wave Feminism in the 1960s and '70s. In addition to her accomplishments as a master of her sport—she won thirty-nine Grand Slam tournaments in the course of her career—King was a significant pioneer for women's professional tennis. She was one of the first ever professional female tennis players and agitated for more equitable pay for women in a heavily male-dominated system.[41] In addition to her activism within her sport, King has been an outspoken advocate of other social issues that make her a clear symbol of struggles for greater support for diversity and equality in American culture. For example, King spoke publicly about an abortion she had in 1971 and became the first openly lesbian professional athlete in the 1980s. The event that best established King as a cultural icon, however, was her 1973 defeat of Bobby Riggs in the so-called Battle of the Sexes. Riggs, who, as King describes, "claimed *any* man could beat *any* woman, that the women's game was dull compared to the men's, and that there was no reason for [women] to get equal prize money," challenged her to the match.[42] They played in front of over thirty thousand live audience members, the largest crowd ever to watch a tennis match, and a reported forty million television viewers.[43] When King defeated Riggs by winning the first three sets in a best-of-five competition, she became an instant symbol of progress in the women's movement. According to sports and literature scholar James Pipkin, she came to be "viewed as the sports equivalent of Betty Friedan, Gloria Steinem, Bella Abzug, and Jane Fonda."[44]

JALC's choice to have King host the Mary Lou Williams concert invited listeners to view Mary Lou as the Billie Jean of the piano, and therefore the Betty Friedan, Gloria Steinem, Bella Abzug, and Jane Fonda of jazz. King's verbal introduction to the performance made this suggestion explicit.

> The story of Mary Lou Williams and her success in a male-dominated field has been an inspiration to us all. This is a case where the triumph of one woman helped uplift everyone, both men and women, musicians or athletes, and everybody else. She is truly a pioneer.[45]

King continued by describing Williams's career as follows:

> Mary Lou Williams was a giant of jazz and a colossus of the piano. She was virtually the only major figure to have participated in every stage of the development of jazz, from ragtime to stride piano to hot jazz to big bands to swing to bebop to symphonic jazz to soul jazz to the avant-garde. She was certainly the only pianist in jazz who in 1925 showed Jelly Roll Morton how she would play one of his classic tunes, and then, more than fifty years later, she would share the stage with the iconoclastic free jazz master Cecil Taylor.

The program that followed this introduction essentially gave a chronological tour of Williams's six decades in jazz that included both her first arrangement for the Andy Kirk band from 1929, "Messa Stomp," and her last arrangement before her death, "Shafi," from the late 1970s. A transcription of her first recorded piano solo, a stride tune called "Nite Life," was performed by Geoffrey Keezer, and Geri Allen played one of her late compositions, "Blues for Peter," in a more modern solo piano style. Many of the other works featured on the program came from the body of work Williams composed and arranged for some of her better-known male contemporaries and their bands. The Jazz at Lincoln Center Orchestra performed two arrangements Williams had done for the Duke Ellington Orchestra ("Lonely Moments" and "Blue Skies"), a boogie woogie hit she wrote for Benny Goodman called "Roll 'Em," and a bebop-style big-band vocal number popularized by Dizzy Gillespie, "In the Land of Oo Bla Dee."

In addition to the fact that promotional materials and King's speeches referenced Williams's nickname, "The First Lady of Jazz," programming that highlighted her work with Ellington, Goodman, and Gillespie presented her as the closest female equivalent of the Duke, Count, or King of Swing. King introduced a bebop tune of Williams's from the late 1940s called "New Musical Express" as proving to audiences that "Mary Lou's music was so modern...that she was just as innovative as Bird, Dizzy, and Monk," again presenting Williams in terms of her more famous male colleagues. Meanwhile, the program featured three different pianists in the playing role of Mary Lou, two white men, the resident orchestra's regular member Dan Nimmer and guest Geoffrey Keezer, and African-American woman Geri Allen. This constant shift from one pianist to the next made the consistent presence and voice of Billie Jean King the one most likely to be associated with the absent Williams in the minds of audience members. The spectacle of King as announcer and the narrative of female struggle that she both voiced and symbolizes served to present the athletic power of King's physical body as a metaphor for Williams's musical and creative power. The concert also suggested that Williams, like King in the tennis world, had been an important force for women's rights, able to play and compete with men just as King proved her ability to best Bobby Riggs.

On closer inspection, however, the views that Williams expressed during her lifetime on women, gender equality in jazz, and feminism prove not to be mirror images of King's activism in the athletic world. While Williams enjoyed a major comeback in the later years of her life that corresponded historically with the height of King's tennis career, the two women did not share equal levels of participation in the women's movement. To begin with, Williams did not acknowledge any particular challenge in navigating the jazz world as a female instrumentalist, an attitude that starkly contrasts with King's outspoken critiques of inequality. In 1980, she told an interviewer, "I've never had problems with being a woman musician," echoing similar statements she had made in the past when asked about how gender issues had shaped her career.[46] She also routinely described proficiency in women jazz instrumentalists, herself included, by saying they "played like men."[47] According to Williams biographer Tammy Kernodle, "At times, Mary was pushed into the center of discussion regarding women's place in jazz and criticized heavily for her claims that she had not experienced prejudice or discrimination because of her gender."[48] Kernodle also asserts that, "Mary had no intention of being an activist or spokesperson for what could safely be termed feminist causes."[49]

This is not to say that Williams remained uninvolved in all arenas of social activism. For example, her hiatus from performance during the 1950s resulted in part from a belief that her obligation to serve others outweighed the importance of her music. Williams converted to Catholicism and devoted her time to prayer and to caring for impoverished or drug-addicted people, particularly musicians. Much of Williams's music making after her return to performing and recording demonstrated her continued devotion to the cause of cleaning up jazz and its public image. Essentially, Williams worked to bring her religious feelings to her jazz colleagues—a project that went as far as dragging a drunken Thelonious Monk to six a.m. mass—and to establish jazz as a viable form of sacred music.[50] After years of campaigning and composing, having her work performed as a Catholic liturgy at St. Patrick's Cathedral in New York City in 1975 marked a major achievement for Williams in gaining respect for both jazz and the place of African Americans within the Catholic Church.

While Williams's religious work was mentioned in the JALC performance, it was not featured in the musical programming. King's verbal description of Williams's life included her hiatus from music and conversion to Catholicism, but, unlike the other musical styles described including stride, boogie woogie, swing, and bebop, none of Williams's sacred music was actually performed. King said, "Mary Lou brought her two passions together, jazz and church, in *Black Christ of the Andes*, an album glorifying the sixteenth-century South American saint Juan Martin de Porres. "Chunka Lunka" is a rousing number that appears on the album, and the title is actually no mystery when you listen to what the rhythm section is doing behind the piano and then the horns." King referred to the boogie-style bass and shuffle drum feel that make "Chunka Lunka's" title onomatopoeic, so the tune's title is indeed no mystery. The more mysterious question is why this particular piece would be offered as the only representation of Williams's sacred work when it has no directly religious content and was not released on the original *Black Christ of the Andes* LP. The CD reissue from thirty years after the initial release (and over a decade after Williams's death) included "Chunka Lunka" as one of four bonus tracks, all of which are secular. Of the ten tracks Williams released during her lifetime, four feature explicitly sacred texts while a fifth, "Dirge Blues," is a spiritually tinted memorial for Martin Luther King, Jr.

Turning our attention to the music from *Black Christ of the Andes* not featured on the program reveals a unique side of Williams that was not readily apparent at the JALC event. For example, the first track of the album, "Saint Martin de Porres," seems to have been very important to the overall project because, in addition to its placement as an opening statement, it is both the longest performance and also the track from which the title is drawn. The piece held great significance for Williams for a variety of reasons both personal and musical. The project was a collaboration with her close friend and spiritual advisor, Anthony Woods, who encouraged her to compose religious music and provided the text. It is one of Williams's most innovative and original works, written primarily for *a cappella* chorus with brief passages of piano solo and accompaniment, and it recognizes the social themes most important to the composer by celebrating the canonization of the first ever black Catholic saint, a man who was known for taking in the poor, through the complex harmonic language of jazz. In addition to tying together jazz, the black Catholic community, and Williams's own commitment to serving the poor, "Saint Martin" was the piece that marked Williams's return to work as a composer and began her comeback to the musical world in earnest. In creating a program that sums up significant moments in her life and sounds in her music, this piece seems an obvious choice, yet it went unplayed in the JALC tribute, as did the entire body of sacred pieces Williams composed, performed, and promoted during the second half of her life.

While a performance of "Saint Martin de Porres" would have required the addition of guest performers for the choral parts or a new arrangement of the piece for big band, neither of these adjustments would have been unprecedented in a Jazz at Lincoln Center Hall of Fame concert.[51] Indeed, while "Chunka Lunka" as played on *Black Christ of the Andes* was performed by a piano trio, the version presented in the concert was arranged for a full jazz orchestra. Also, its original incarnation on the album was incredibly spare and simple in terms of its precomposed elements, just a repetitive boogie woogie bass line outlining a basic blues progression, a steady shuffle rhythm from the drums, and three brief melodic gestures outnumbered by the long rests that surround them. Williams's improvised solo constitutes the main substance of the track, not the short head that precedes and follows it. Transferred to the big-band context by JALC, this piece essentially featured soloists from the band, not Williams as composer, and certainly not Williams as proponent of sacred music. Given these circumstances, it is reasonable to interpret the choice to omit Williams's sacred music as aesthetic and philosophical rather than simply practical. Choosing "Chunka Lunka" instead of *Saint Martin* allowed a straightforward blues tune with a traditional, swinging shuffle feel to stand in for Williams's music that fell outside the musical and ideological mainstream of the jazz tradition as defined by JALC.[52]

Along with the parallels the program drew between Williams and King, the decision to feature arrangements Williams wrote for her more famous male contemporaries and her own works that shared stylistic elements with those well-known men presented Williams as a mainstream jazz musician and a feminist, equivalent to the male musicians already familiar to most jazz audiences in all ways but her gender. Until Williams's induction, the JALC Hall of Fame had only three women among its thirty-five members, and none were instrumentalists; indeed, Williams remains the only female instrumentalist on the list a decade later. Having a strong feminist figure as a member of JALC's jazz canon supports the image of jazz as the quintessential American democratic art, so that is how Mary Lou Williams came to be defined in the JALC version of jazz history. It is worth remembering, however, that Williams, given her own voice in a democratic system, fought for an entirely different cause through both her life and music. By channeling Williams through King's feminist body, JALC lost important aspects of her artistic and social vision as her individual voice was sacrificed to the broader project of showing jazz to be socially progressive without broadening the musical definition of jazz put forward by the institution. JALC called Williams a pioneer, but prioritizing her "swinging" music over her experiments and anchoring her work to a material, gendered body became more important than unique elements of her musicianship, values, and ideas.

BILL EVANS AT THE HOUSE OF SWING

The physical body of the third pianist inducted to Hall of Fame that season, Bill Evans, was in his own way as distinct from Waller's as Williams's was, but, by the mid-1960s, his reputation in the jazz world had reached Waller-like proportions. His work with Miles Davis in the late 1950s, particularly on the album *Kind of Blue*, and his trio recordings with bassist Scott LaFaro and drummer Paul Motian had brought him a great deal of attention and laid the groundwork for his present place as a player just as influential to the generation that followed him as Waller had been years before. Pictures of the thin, white, pianist, his face hidden behind glasses and bent low toward his instrument, cropped up regularly during the 1960s in the jazz press and on the covers of many of his albums like *Sunday at the Village Vanguard*, *Time Remembered*, and *Conversations with Myself*. In one of four feature articles written on Evans in the early 1960s for *DownBeat* magazine, John Tynan described a commonly mentioned parallel between the pianist's body and his music, "Evans, at 35, is grave of mien and sober of dress. Introverted at the keyboard, he plays with head bent to his inventions, seemingly oblivious to all but the secret messages running among piano, bass, and drums that emerge in musical translation as some of the most memorable jazz in our time."[53] Visuals of Evans body line up neatly with a particular perspective on his music, leading interpreters of his work to focus on him as an intellectual, sensitive introvert, the keeper of musical secrets that require great delicacy and attention to discover. While this stereotype has been presented both positively and negatively, suggesting that the hidden intricacies of Evans's work are either fully worth discovering or too obscure to merit the energy, descriptions of his playing are permeated by language describing a man who was brilliant but withdrawn and inaccessible to the average listener. As jazz scholar David Ake put it, "Had he possessed a more robust physical stature, such as that of Fats Waller, say, or Count Basie, Art Tatum, or Oscar Peterson, Evans would almost certainly have been perceived differently."[54] In the absence of his conspicuously unjazzy body, however, the JALC Hall of Fame concert featuring Evans reframed him and his music in terms of the institution's accessible, swinging canon.

While a lack of present, living Hall of Fame artists can allow JALC the leeway to create, magnify, or exaggerate body-based stereotypes with relative impunity, it also gives them the opportunity to combat prejudices and assumptions about historical figures if they so choose. Unlike the cases of presenting a feminist Mary Lou Williams via Billie Jean King or an irreplaceably giant Fats Waller requiring three stand-in pianists, the missing body of Bill Evans was left in the past rather than revived or idolized, a choice that gave JALC a chance to present him as a part of the same tradition of expressive, passionate, swing-based jazz that underpins their take on jazz history. Painting Evans this way may be convenient for the organization in the sense that it draws him closer to the blues-steeped, spiritualized, African American jazz that dominates Marsalis's vision of jazz history and away from the staid world of western art music with which he was often associated. In the process, it also restores a part of Evans's musicality to today's audience that often went unappreciated by those of his contemporaries who could not see past his body.

The particular era in which he came to prominence determined the extent to which the physical Evans defined the musical Evans during his lifetime. As Ingrid Monson argues in her rich study of jazz and the civil rights movement, "From the early 1950s to the mid-1960s a general shift took place from a colorblind ideology on race within the jazz community to the assertion of a black-identified consciousness on the part of many African American musicians and their supporters."[55] Evans came of age in a jazz climate where many saw the most authentic jazz voices as stemming from uniquely African American culture. In contrast, white players tended to be viewed as imitating their black peers or even stealing popular recognition from them. One reaction to this situation that Monson describes was the decision by many African Americans to pointedly present what they played as an aspect of their black identity rather than a musical language potentially accessible to and playable by anyone. "In response to the commercial and popular success of white jazz musicians, which was viewed by many as depriving African American musicians of a fair economic return on their creativity, many African American jazz musicians of the 1950s and 1960s seemed determined to emphasize and develop black difference rather than witness a repeat of the 1930s, when Benny Goodman was crowned the King of Swing."[56] As black difference came to be increasingly valued in jazz circles, white players were more frequently deemed to be lacking some essential jazz quality, often the indefinable but essential "swing" that many, Wynton Marsalis and JALC included, still insist permeates the best music. For example, Lennie Tristano, who Monson calls, "perhaps the strongest white contender for the status of innovator in a field of competitors resoundingly dominated by African American musicians," was, in the 1950s, denounced by some as a cold, unswinging intellectual.[57] Jazz writer Bill Cross referred to Tristano's work as being "as tangible as an algebra problem," criticizing him for musical complexity and a lack of clearly communicative emotion, in much the same way that others would treat Bill Evans a few years later.[58] It would be overly simplistic to regard this treatment of these two white pianists and their penchant for musical complexity as reverse racism, however, as the judgment actually relies on deeply imbedded tendencies to paint African American artists as more simple and natural, reserving the role of the misunderstood intellectual for descendants of Europeans.

Evans might have avoided the brunt of musical critique based in racial tension if it had not been for his brief stint with the Miles Davis sextet in 1958 and 1959. Although Davis famously defended his white pianist, Evans's biographer Peter Pettinger asserts that "Evans was uncomfortable in the band for a number of reasons, not the least of which being his status as a racial minority of one."[59] According to Davis,

> Some of the things that caused Bill to leave the band hurt me, like that shit some black people put on him about being a white boy in our band. Many blacks felt that since I had the top small group in jazz and was paying the most money that I should have a black piano player. Now, I don't go for that kind of shit; I have always just wanted the best players in my group and I don't care about whether they're black, white, blue, red or yellow. As long as they can play what I want that's it.[60]

Despite Davis's assertions in support of Evans's musical ability, Pettinger states that, "From the black patrons in the clubs, Evans received a lot of flak for not swinging as hard as [Red] Garland," the band's former pianist, a criticism that may well have been commentary on Evans's race masquerading as a critique of rhythm.[61]

Certainly, however, more than race was involved in Evans's developing reputation for introversion. A surge of interest in Evans came on the heels of the death of his friend and bandmate Scott LaFaro in a car accident in 1961. The loss left Evans severely shaken both musically and personally and spiraling into depression and drug addiction. Evans's longtime friend Gene Lees remembers having "found Bill's life and career in hideous disarray" even a year after the accident.[62] Meanwhile, several records featuring live recordings made by LaFaro, Evans, and Motian just before the bassist's death were garnering a great deal of critical and popular attention. Just as Evans's celebrity was intensifying, his personal and professional lives were crumbling, drawing him into the spotlight as a melancholy, sensitive figure.

Critics doubted the ability of the withdrawn, tragic Evans—despite his technical brilliance—to play jazz to its full expressive potential, establishing a lasting discourse framing Evans in terms of introversion that JALC would have to one day counteract in order to embrace him in their story of jazz history. In a review of *Sunday at the Village Vanguard*, one of the final LaFaro recordings, Martin Williams wrote, "I think Evans has a problem with audiences and with the emotional communication of his music; I think he has, with so fine yet so fragilely introverted a talent, a problem in reaching people."[63] In a similar spirit, though he blames inattentive listeners rather than Evans for the disconnect, John Tynan said in his article on the pianist, "Visually, Bill Evans is a hunched mass of back and shoulders to the audience, his face barely a foot above the keys, his concentration mentally and almost physically bearing down on his listeners. Sometimes they don't understand. A sweet young thing, visibly bemused by it all but eager to please her date was heard to remark after a particularly trying set: 'Y'know, it makes you want to rub his back.'"[64] Evans was perceived not as an exciting, swinging performer but as a focused intellectual who demanded an equally intent and informed audience. His body and posture did not look like the model jazz musician of his time, and his playing was perceived as lacking the emotional immediacy that other players could more easily inspire. Furthermore, Tynan's anecdote here (in addition to reflecting misogynistic views so prevalent in jazz literature of the era) notes a failure of Evans's masculinity: rather than inspiring awe with his talent, he is an object of pity to a young woman unable to grasp the significance of his performance. Even the positive reception of Evans in the 1960s tended to focus on delicacy and inwardness rather than exuberance or swing. Paul Allen Anderson writes about the critical description of the "poignant" in Evans's playing as a more positive and masculine framing of the pejorative and feminine-coded "sentimental." While Evans's slow, soft performances of ballads were often celebrated for their poignancy, Anderson writes that, "This kind of 'ruminative and withdrawn' ballad performance (to borrow a slightly later description from the critic Whitney Balliett) made up a small portion of Evans's live repertoire but had an outsized impact on his reputation."[65] In order to successfully place Evans in their Hall of Fame, JALC reshaped his image away from the distant, delicate intellectual described in the press at the height of his career.

As it turns out, an earlier discourse on Evans's playing exists that helped tie him more neatly to the JALC story. It would be easy to accept the idea of Evans the fragile musical introvert as a consensus genuinely based on the sound of his playing if it was not for the very different reactions his work generated before his association with Davis and trio work with LaFaro and Motian brought him into the spotlight. In 1957, reviewer Nat Hentoff described Evans's work on a feature piece for him by George Russell by saying, "*Billy the Kid* packs a mad wallop, especially when Bill Evans spurts out a series of solo breaks as smoothly as a Texas gusher," and, the next year, Dom Cerulli referred to Evans's playing as, "pulsing with life, and driving with stated and implied rhythms and accents."[66] Hentoff's review of Evans's first album as a bandleader, *New Jazz Conceptions*, refers to his favorite track on the album as "blues-virile" and notes that Evans "swings deeply."[67] *Portrait in Jazz*, another Evans trio album from two years later, still communicated to critics the idea of a manly, forceful pianist. Don DeMichael wrote, "Above any of the details of Evans' work, I admire the firmness with which he plays. There's never any doubt of his control of the instrument. The music he produces makes clear that here is a *man*."[68] Evans's first impression on the jazz world was not that of a sensitive, withdrawn intellectual but an assertive extrovert, and a notably masculine one whose authoritative voice was not questioned even in the African American idioms of blues and swing.

Following his rise to fame, observations on these qualities in Evans's playing did not altogether disappear, but they were recontextualized in reference to emerging critical tropes about his fragile body and fragile sound. Even a reviewer that had noted Evans's firmness and masculinity in the late 1950s seemed surprised by his extroversion and capacity to swing by 1963. DeMichael said the following of *Interplay*, "This blowing session—I'm tempted to say swing session—is certainly a departure for Evans as leader, since all his other as-leader albums have been trio efforts and usually marked by that exquisite introversion so much a part of Evans' piano playing.... There is possibly more extrovertism [sic] displayed by Evans on this release than on any other LP on which he plays. It is a healthy departure for the pianist."[69] This description conveys that the music seemed to swing, but that such an assessment of Evans would now require some kind of excuse or explanation. DeMichael was not the only one to recast Evans's moments of forcefulness as out of character. Pete Welding described an up-tempo track from *Undercurrent*, a duo record with guitarist Jim Hall, as "something of a dark horse" because of its "powerful rush of extemporization, producing a seamless whole of force, intensity, and impassioned fervor."[70] The language used here hints again at the strong, masculine Evans that was heard early in his career, but this style of playing is presented as a surprising exception to the norm rather than one commonly used aspect of Evans's multifaceted musicality.

Without a thin, white, glasses-wearing body bent low over the piano keys, it was much easier for JALC to reclaim the muscular, percussive, masculine Evans and present him as a musician who balanced intellect, emotion, and swing, qualities that made him a perfect candidate for a Hall of Fame based in an African American–identified version of jazz history that now embraces twenty-first-century multiculturalism. From the remarks by guest musical director, host, and pianist Bill Charlap to the musical selections and their arrangement, everything about the concert was directed toward presenting Bill Evans as, first and foremost, a versatile, multifaceted musician capable of demonstrating the same affinity for black jazzmasculinity that characterized the rest of the JALC canon.

The concert began immediately with music rather than words, the Lincoln Center Jazz Orchestra launching right into an arrangement of Evans's well known, classically tinged "Waltz for Debby," but Charlap's spoken introduction after the first piece made clear that the Bill Evans who studied classical piano and loved Debussy would not be the only one celebrated in this concert. "Lyrical, passionate, graceful, swinging: the music of Bill Evans is all of these things and many more. He was one of the most influential musicians in jazz, combining the impressionism of Debussy and Ravel with the swing of Nat Cole and Bud Powell, and, while he developed his musical foundation with the utmost care and discipline, all the listener experiences is the depth of his emotion."[71] Every word or phrase suggesting Evans the introvert is balanced by an evocation of extroversion: his lyricism is passionate, his grace swings, and his disciplined practice behind closed doors blossoms publicly as directly communicated deep emotion. Along similar lines, the second tune on the program balanced the delicacy of "Waltz for Debby" with its up-tempo exuberance. Charlap introduced "Five" as simply "Bill's take on George Gershwin's 'I've Got Rhythm'" before counting off a bright tempo for the rollicking performance. Focusing only on the fact that Evans's "Five" is a rhythm changes tune helps smoothly align him with mainstream bebop, positioning him as one in a very long and ongoing line of musicians to write a contrafact over jazz's most popular set of 32-bar chord changes. What Charlap left out of his verbal description is that Evans's version of the tune is intentionally obtuse, an excellent example of the composer's intellectual, complex side. "Five's" title relates to the various ways the number is used to create unusual rhythmic structures within the confines of the standard 128-beat cycle of Gershwin's original. Five measures in the A phrase contain quintuplets, and the B section is divided into two five-bar subphrases through a mixture of 3/4, 4/4, and 5/4 meters. The complexity of this structure is compounded by the use of polyrhythm, like a repeating 4-note figure divided into quintuplets that occurs in the last three bars of the A phrase over a mixture of half notes and triplets.

Although Charlap was prominently featured at the piano in both small and large group contexts, as in the Williams and Waller concerts, he was not the sole carrier of Evans's voice, ensuring that an imagined Evans rather than a concrete contemporary player dominated the narrative. Transcriptions of Evans's improvisations, both as a soloist and an accompanist, appear in multiple places during the concert, but not through the body of one man sitting at the piano. Instead, the combined forces of a full big band embodied Evans's characteristic voicings and phrases. For example, arranger Don Sebeski re-orchestrated improvised passages from a Bill Evans recording of the Jerome Kern standard "All the Things You Are" as ensemble passages in order to make an Evans-centric big-band version of the piece. Similarly, Ted Nash's arrangement of Evans's major contribution to the Miles Davis record *Kind of Blue* injected the piano improvisations from the original version into written parts for woodwind, brass, and rhythm sections. Every note Evans chose, whether as a supporting background behind another soloist or during his own featured moments, found its way into the arrangement, and the pianist's overall role in the piece became simultaneously magnified and diffused by its new omnipresent status. Even details like a rolled chord behind the opening trumpet melody became fixed in the score, appearing as slightly staggered entrances for a series of wind instruments.[72] Evans emanated not just from the piano bench, but from all sixteen men on stage, as strong, confident, present, and immortalized in this new treatment of one of his most famous recordings, his vitality and masculinity reasserted through the live presence of the band. Evans's problematically frail white body was transcended and replaced by the wealth of contemporary alternatives available in the JALC Orchestra, most of whom belonged to black men.

The concert did not leave listeners with the slow, subtle sounds of "Blue in Green" in their ears, however, despite their intensified form in a large rather than small ensemble arrangement. The last piece, in fact, was chosen for its ability to demonstrate the vivacious, swinging side of Evans, a rationale made clear in Charlap's final remarks, "Reflective, thoughtful, profound: all of these words come to mind when thinking of Bill Evans...but the truth is, Bill Evans wanted to reach as many people as possible. He's quoted as saying, 'The artist should be responsible to try to perpetuate the feelings which will contribute to a better world. Concentrate on truth and beauty. That's all that matters.' We're going to close with one of his most optimistic, happy, and swinging compositions, 'Peri's Scope.'" The links created here between Bill Evans and the philosophy of jazz as a path toward a more socially and politically harmonious world outlined by Wynton Marsalis in *Moving to Higher Ground* could hardly be more explicit. As described here, art should contribute to a better world, and jazz does its part through the optimism inherent in swing. Casting Evans in this light allows more immediate, accessible aspects of his playing to be restored to his legacy, and it also allows JALC to embrace someone known best as an introverted white intellectual into their canon dominated by a very different set of characteristics. Significantly, this portrayal of Evans, along with the Hall of Fame performances celebrating Waller and Williams, took place in a venue designed to give it the quality of an official, authoritative history. The very name of the organization, Jazz at Lincoln Center, points clearly to the role of Lincoln Center as a place with a reputation for important art, despite the organization's jazz arm having relocated to nearby Columbus Circle. The concert hall inside likewise wears its pedigree on its sleeve. While it is formally named for donor Frederick P. Rose, the nickname of the space commonly used in promotional material and live announcements in the venue roots it firmly in Marsalis's telling of jazz history as "The House of Swing."

CLOSED DOORS AND OPEN WINDOWS

The fact that JALC's canon-building concerts all point to a unified version of jazz history raises the question of how this aesthetic and rhetorical approach relates to the nature of the institution putting it forward. While JALC has endured considerable criticism for the conservatism and consistency of its programming, some commentators have also pointed out a relationship between the organization's specific, narrow framing of jazz as a genre and its success as a large-scale venue. Chapman argues, "What the stripped-down, reductionist historicism of neoclassicism achieves is to render itself *legible*, to bracket those components that might inhibit the intelligibility of its brand; it is to make the music market-worthy by, in Tracy McMullen's words, 'presenting jazz in easily digestible consumables.'"[73] Chapman goes on to quote Farah Jasmine Griffin on this issue, who in 2001 wrote, "Had Marsalis not struck such a conservative stance, whereby some of the most innovative practitioners are left out of the jazz canon, it is highly unlikely he would have been able to acquire the resources necessary to do the kind of work on behalf of the music that he has done."[74] Sociologist Herman Gray makes this case in detail in his 2005 book *Cultural Moves: African Americans and the Politics of Representation*. Gray states, "In my estimation, Marsalis and his supporters understood the political importance of establishing institutional recognition and legitimacy, if jazz were to be taken seriously as a cultural object with a permanent institutional status and resources."[75] He goes on to argue, "Marsalis's canonical project at Lincoln Center, while an expression of one form of resistant black culture, is also fundamentally conservative."[76] As a contrasting case, Gray analyzes what Don Byron describes as "the jazz left," and Gray positions the institutional home of JALC and the lack of a similar physical and cultural space for the jazz left as defining features of their different musical approaches:

> I want to consider critically the practices, spaces, networks, assumptions, and social relations of an approach to the music that emphasizes the expansive possibilities in jazz in terms of its *movement, innovation, and openness*. I contend that such projects often go unnoticed and are thus relegated to the margins of cultural discourses about jazz and black creative music, because the terms, spaces, and operations that structure them, define their practices, and position their practitioners very often exist beyond the logic of canonical recognition, institutional legitimacy, and conventional discourse.[77]

Gray explicitly ties aesthetic conservatism to the fixed space and institutional legitimacy of JALC, suggesting that musical innovation and openness go hand-in-hand with physical movement. Gray uses the metaphors of the road and the street to describe the music and workings of the jazz left, constructing them as fluid, dynamic, and portable in comparison to JALC. Chapman explains this line of thought from the jazz left as painting JALC as "a kind of philanthropic oil tanker, unable to respond to the innovations of the music as they unfold in the immediacy of cultural ferment."[78] This early twenty-first century assessment of the limitations of large-scale jazz institutions leaves little room for the possibility of institutional support for jazz outside of JALC's specifically swinging jazz history.

Perhaps in part because of analyses like McMullen's, Griffin's, and Gray's, additional large-scale jazz institutions that have emerged in the United States since JALC initiated its programming in the early 1990s have raised questions about the inevitability of pairing institutional support, large spaces, and conservative music. The heft of JALC and the discourse surrounding it have meant that SFJazz, Jazz at the Kennedy Center, and the New Orleans Jazz Market have borne considerable scrutiny in their fledgling years, with many explicitly asking the question of whether or not these new jazz giants will be satellites of JALC. While I believe that Marsalis's and JALC's conservatism fueled the success of the first large-scale American jazz venue, I argue that the controversy surrounding that conservatism has subsequently fostered the development of more adventurous, diverse, and locally specific programming in other places. JALC has indeed cast a large and powerful shadow over the development of other similar jazz presenters, but the impulse to define themselves in opposition to JALC has been just as strong as the impulse to recreate its model in other cities.

Press coverage of large-scale jazz institutions that have emerged in the wake of JALC's massive growth and success almost inevitably bring Marsalis and his programming into the story. A *Washington Post* story on Moran's work at the Kennedy Center offers an exemplar of this kind of comparison:

> This sense of art without boundaries has been a central theme in [Moran's] programming at the Kennedy Center—noticeably at variance with Billy Taylor's approach and with the approach of Wynton Marsalis, the trumpeter and artistic director of jazz at New York's Lincoln Center, the model for all the jazz institutions to come. When Marsalis emerged as a brash wunderkind in the 1980s, touting straight-ahead jazz and torching hybrids based on rock, funk or European avant-garde music, he triggered a schism within the jazz community: You were either with Wynton and his traditionalist approach, or against him. It was a cultural divide: uptown (Lincoln Center) vs. downtown

(the hybrids). The fight now seems silly—jazz has managed to accommodate many styles and genres—but it can still raise ruffles in the stuffier or more progressive quarters.[79]

The recurring question as more large-scale jazz venues take shape continues to be some version of, "Will this venue be with Marsalis, or against him?" While much of the concern about Marsalis's approach in the 1990s and 2000s was rooted in fears that such a massive and well-supported venue was bound to dominate jazz culture, the Kennedy Center, the New Orleans Jazz Market, and SFJazz have all chosen programming that contrasts with rather than replicates JALC's successful model. For example, *New York Times* coverage of the New Orleans Jazz Market emphasizes differences over similarities:

> The Market seems to be aiming at something beyond even the organization that inspired it: Though Jazz at Lincoln Center invests deeply in educational initiatives for underserved students, its concerts treat jazz as a high-priced commodity, and one with a fixed cultural identity rooted in its 20th-century heyday. But at the Jazz Market, both the free Wednesday jam sessions and the orchestra's own performances attract enthusiastic, majority-black crowds, seeming to articulate the argument that jazz ought to serve the community that gave birth to it.[80]

Writer Russonello goes on to discuss the Market's wellness and exercise programs, free rehearsal spaces, and connections to the public library, quoting former artistic director Irvin Mayfield as saying, "I thought jazz should be a public service, which is why we called it a 'market.' I wanted people to embrace it with the same open nature that they embraced food."[81] While a financial scandal involving Mayfield has forced the organization to scale back its staff and programs, the sense that this space is locally specific rather than a replication of JALC in New Orleans continues as new artistic director Adonis Rose and CEO Sarah Bell strive to build what Bell calls "a place of community access."[82] Musically, this sense of the local comes out in what Rose calls the "gumbo" of New Orleans music, an inclusion of other elements of locally popular styles that fall beyond strict definitions of jazz, leading to events like a Whitney Houston tribute concert with a second line parade through the concert hall aisles. The weekly jam session is not jazz-specific, inviting musicians but also comedians and poets to perform and local small businesses to participate. While Mayfield took inspiration from JALC, defining jazz does not hold a notable place on the Jazz Market agenda. To be appropriate for its own city and neighborhood, the Market must instead translate the definition of the large-scale jazz venue to its own specific geographic and cultural context.

FREE-STANDING JAZZ

The venue that has achieved a scope most similar to JALC has accordingly been subject to the most comparisons with it. Like so many others, SFJazz founder Randall Kline gives Marsalis and his narrow definition of jazz credit for the success of JALC, saying, "Wynton is criticized for his one-mindedness, but his one-mindedness is what makes it all happen."[83] Kline's organization, however, has not followed in Marsalis's footsteps, demonstrating that singlemindedness is not—or is no longer—necessary in the act of combining institutional support and jazz programming. Kline founded SFJazz in the 1980s, but the organization did not break ground on its own facility until 2011. When they did, they drew the interest of jazz commentators not just in San Francisco but all around the United States, and the question of how this new space would relate to JALC was frequently raised. *Chicago Tribune* writer Howard Reich explained the SFJazz project in terms of its similarities and differences to JALC as a point of reference, calling it JALC's "West Coast counterpart" and stating, "Though SFJazz clearly follows in the footsteps of Jazz at Lincoln Center, it also goes its own way."[84] In the discourse connecting JALC and SFJazz, two key differences are frequently noted: SFJazz's free-standing building and its diverse, genre-crossing approach to programming.

Emphasis on the SFJazz Center as a free-standing building fully devoted to jazz serves two important purposes with regard to the venue's assumed place in JALC's large shadow. The first relates to physical space. Though smaller in terms of square footage and cost than JALC's home, SFJazz can rank its space first in its class by pointing to its building's autonomy, "An approachable three-story structure in glass and concrete, the SFJazz Center is being billed as the nation's first free-standing building created for jazz. And if the careful wording of that claim suggests a hedge against comparisons with Frederick P. Rose Hall—the $128 million home of Jazz at Lincoln Center, ensconced within the Time Warner Center in Manhattan—it hardly diminishes the extraordinary scope and promise of SFJazz's achievement."[85] Just as significant as the organization's ability to claim a singular status with its independent building is the free-standing nature of SFJazz from an administrative perspective. It is not just the Time Warner Center that JALC fits inside; Lincoln Center remains the larger organization in which JALC sits, placing jazz as one of several performing arts and aligning it with long histories of high-art traditions. While a partnership with the San Francisco Symphony was an option SFJazz considered, the organization ultimately opted for the autonomy of their own space under their own control.[86] To emphasize that separateness, the building was designed to evoke a different aesthetic from the other arts institutions located nearby, "SFJAZZ Center will look nothing like the immense Davies Symphony Hall (where Michael Tilson Thomas leads the San Francisco Symphony) or the colossal War Memorial Opera House (home to the much-admired San Francisco Opera and San Francisco Ballet). Those buildings, and other historic structures in the Civic Center neighborhood, evoke an earlier kind of cultural palace: huge, towering and somewhat removed from the hustle of everyday existence. A jazz center, says Kline, needs to be different—more reflective of American life in the 21st Century than European culture of the 19th."[87] Instead of echoing classical concert halls, architect Mark Cavagnero sought an approach that evokes accessibility to the neighborhood and nonhierarchical seating. He cited Unitarian churches as models for the largest performance space, Miner Auditorium, noting, "they're places that are about people meeting, and there is no formal power relationship; it's about everyone being equal."[88] The exterior of the building pushes right up against the sidewalk, and critic Nate Chinen suggests its "glass exterior conveys a literal and conceptual transparency" that is immediately apparent from the street.[89]

Notions of independence and accessibility built into the physical venue are linked to the music programmed by SFJazz. The approach to programming since the venue opened in 2013 has defined SFJazz in opposition to JALC. Where JALC is headed by Marsalis as a single dominant figure, SFJazz uses a rotating program of four to five resident artistic directors per season. Moreover, these directors reflect considerable diversity, both musically and in terms of race, gender, and nationality. Directors have ranged from Afro-Cuban pianist Chucho Valdés to performance art icon Laurie Anderson to tabla virtuoso Zakir Hussain to singer-songwriter Rosanne Cash, reflecting SFJazz's strategy of featuring a wide variety of jazz-related musics that reach outward and its stark contrast to JALC's carefully defined genre boundaries. Chinen made the comparison explicit in a *New York Times* piece covering the inaugural SFJazz season in the new space:

The programming...that will feature multi-night appearances by the pianist Brad Mehldau, the fado singer Ana Moura, the tabla player Zakir Hussain and the banjoist Béla Fleck—speaks to an inherent curiosity in the SFJazz psyche....And to the extent that the SFJazz Center has enabled that breadth of style and approach, it disarms the very comparisons it invites. Jazz at Lincoln Center, taking its cue from Wynton Marsalis, its artistic director, has always used its programming to express a firm conviction about what jazz is (and by strong implication, what it isn't—or what isn't it). Mr. Kline and his team aren't naturally inclined toward that definitive sort of mission, and it's fortunate that they don't have to be.[90]

While Chinen does not directly explain why SFJazz need not stick to a clear definition of jazz, this statement within a comparison with JALC suggests that the two organizations are in some ways functioning as a pair. Part of what made the launch of the SFJazz Center possible was the precedent set by JALC's success, and part of what makes SFJazz's more open-ended style of programming appealing is the way in which it responds to the decades of criticism leveled at Marsalis and JALC's uncompromising canon. While that embrace of a diverse and expansive definition of jazz may not have succeeded in bringing jazz into the high-art world of Lincoln Center in the social and political climate of the 1990s, it creates a unique local and national identity for SFJazz that helps to foster its success in the present. Five years into its programming in its new building, SFJazz was able to invite a new set of comparisons to JALC. *SFGate* reporter Sam Whiting wrote in 2018 that, similar to JALC, "SFJazz is operating at an astonishing 95 percent capacity for 474 concerts a year," and "Membership has gone from 3,000 when ground was broken on the former site of two auto repair shops in Hayes Valley to 14,000, which is twice the membership for Jazz at Lincoln Center in New York, and more than any other jazz performance organization."[91] As the 2019–2020 program book declares in bold font, "SFJazz is the largest nonprofit jazz presenter in the world." With its organizational independence, free-standing building, and rapid membership growth SFJazz can claim a position of leadership in the world of large-scale jazz presenters, asserting an identity that makes it clear that it is not simply a second-place version of JALC.

EVERYTHING'S BEAUTIFUL

The independent programming identity of SFJazz is apparent not only in its offerings that reach far outside narrow definitions of swing- and blues-based jazz, like the avant-garde approach of Ken Vandermark or the country and Americana of Roseanne Cash. SFJazz's engagement with historical figures from the jazz canon also demonstrates noteworthy distinctions from similar concerts as presented by JALC. A May 2018 festival celebrating Miles Davis's ninety-second birthday constituted a significant departure from the type of canon-building concerts JALC used to celebrate Waller, Williams, and Evans. Although the Davis festival still crafted an intermundane collaboration, the scales were tipped toward the agency and prominence of living rather than dead artists, and Davis's status as a jazz icon was used in service of defining the music's outward reach rather than its internal characteristics. The four concerts all connected Davis and his legacy to jazz-adjacent musics, and his fusion-inflected late career formed a focal point rather than hiding behind his more mainstream and widely celebrated postbop of the 1950s and '60s. Spanish pianist Chano Domínguez evoked Davis's most popular album, *Kind of Blue*, from 1959, through flamenco, giving an international spin to a canonic favorite. With a similar concept and a different geographic connection, another concert titled "Miles from India" reworked Davis's music with a mix of Eastern and Western musicians and musics, blending Indian tabla and bamboo flute with trumpet and saxophone. The "Miles Electric Band" concert was subtitled "*Bitches Brew* to *Tutu*," drawing off Davis's fusion projects from the late 1960s through the '80s. Pianist Robert Glasper's contribution to the festival drew on his intermundane album *Everything's Beautiful* that combined recordings and outtakes of Davis with new material by Glasper and his band, and Glasper's translation of that album into live performance at the SFJazz Center leaned in a very different direction than a JALC posthumous tribute.

The choice of featuring Robert Glasper in a Miles Davis festival is unlikely to earn a Marsalis seal of approval. Though more moderate than his brother Branford, who said in a 2019 interview that "Glasper has a limited jazz vocabulary," Wynton told *Ebony* magazine, "Robert Glasper can play!" but went on to elaborate on his feelings about Glasper and others of his generation and stylistic bent as follows, "They make the choices that they make to deal with the environment the way they see fit—they're in a rough environment. We have personal relationships and we play. It doesn't mean that I'm going to embrace hip hop. I will never do that, ever! But does that actually make a difference? They're not going to stop playing that music because [I don't play it]. That's the beauty of democracy [laughs]. They're going to do their thing, regardless of what anybody else thinks about it—and they should."[92] While Marsalis is willing to leave room for Glasper's musical point of view in his jazz democracy, Glasper's connections to hip hop and other forms of popular music keep some of Glasper's projects firmly outside Marsalis's jazz boundaries, and Marsalis even frames hip hop as perhaps a necessary evil for Glasper, a tool for navigating a contemporary music world in which hip hop far eclipses jazz in popularity and commercial viability. Choosing Glasper to represent a jazz icon equates to choosing to blend jazz into an expansive, complex, and sometimes messy musical landscape, demonstrating that SFJazz is operating in a different musical arena than JALC, not just a different city. SFJazz noted Glasper's work as touring music director for Mos Def and appearances with Kanye West and Jay-Z in promotional materials for the concert, making his hip hop connections a selling point rather than a liability.

Glasper played two sold-out sets at the SFJazz Davis festival, the second of which drew a relatively young crowd with its 9:30 p.m. start time and open dance floor that replaced the four rows of seating nearest the stage in the Miner Auditorium. Although the historical Davis certainly possessed the kind of oversized public personality that would easily lend itself to the manner of resurrection that occurs in JALC's canon-building concerts through the use of celebrity hosts and biographical anecdotes, it was clear from the outset that Glasper, not Davis, was the star of the show. Glasper's name was the headline in the concert's promotional material, with "Miles Davis Reinterpreted" serving as a small-print subtitle that tied it to the festival while still emphasizing Glasper's artistic agency in presenting Davis's music in a new form. In addition, Glasper served as both the featured performer of the event and its de facto host, speaking between tunes throughout the set. His off-the-cuff rather than scripted remarks paid homage to Davis and his legacy, but they focused as much or more on topics of interest to Glasper and his fans in the present moment as to any connections to the celebrated trumpeter. For example, in a rambling speech lasting several minutes that he gave before playing the first notes of the concert, Glasper talked about food he had eaten while visiting San Francisco and the local NBA team, the Golden State Warriors, who were at the time in the midst of a postseason run that would lead to a national championship. He described the album that had inspired the performance he was about to begin, commenting that he had fought unsuccessfully with the record label not to have his name next to Davis's on the cover. Despite this nod to a sense of Davis's unmatchable greatness, Glasper talked at length about the album's relevance to the present and interest for audiences outside typical jazz circles. He expressed an interest in helping connect Davis and his music to new audiences rather than "preaching to the choir" of already devoted jazz fans, and he declared his success in this arena not by citing *Everything's Beautiful* as the number one album on the Billboard jazz charts at the time of its release, which it was, but by telling the audience that it had reached the top ten on both the R&B and hip hop charts at the same time as Beyoncé's *Lemonade*.

Of equal significance to Glasper's clear presence and personality was Davis's clear absence. While the Waller, Williams, and Evans concerts at JALC all prominently featured the piano, Glasper's Davis concert had no trumpet. Even the studio album that sampled Davis recordings did not make the trumpet a focal point, sometimes drawing instead on other members of Davis's ensembles or the sound of his voice. Glasper explained, "My idea for this whole thing wasn't for you to hear trumpet on every track so you'll know it's Miles Davis, you know. Cuz for me you don't need the trumpet to define Miles.... He was bigger than the instrument. Most times when you're talking about Miles Davis and somebody does a remix album, it's a trumpet record, you know. The reality is, everybody doesn't identify with the trumpet, nor do they want to hear the trumpet on every song."[93] While Glasper suggests Davis's greatness as one reason for limiting the use of the instrument, the framing of Davis as bigger than the trumpet, he also points to a desire to reach an audience that might not typically connect with the conventional aesthetics of acoustic jazz. In the live concert setting at the SFJazz Center, the role Davis's trumpet would have fit in the ensemble was filled by popular R&B vocalist Bilal, a guest on the program who joined Glasper and his rhythm section for several songs. Bilal sang his own lyrics on "Ghetto Walking," his contribution to the *Everything's Beautiful* album, but he also sang some wordless melodies to other tunes, processing his voice through an effects pedal in a manner reminiscent of Davis's trumpet techniques on some of his electric recordings. Bilal's presence was clearly a major draw for the concert's audience—his entrance to the stage elicited the most energetic crowd response of the night. The use of a well-known vocalist associated with a popular music genre in the space left by the absent Miles Davis served to connect jazz outward to different musics and listeners.

CREATING SPACE AND TAKING SPACE

Enjoying a fourteen-dollar cocktail on the SFJazz Center balcony during a beautiful and temperate northern California sunset before entering the carefully constructed Miner Auditorium where all seven hundred seats are within seventy-five feet of the stage is undoubtedly a luxury experience. The venue (and its cocktails) received a glowing write up in *Bespoke Concierge*, a lifestyle magazine with publishers that describe its audience as "affluent, educated and active travelers who have a taste for substance and have a passion for the finer things in life."[94] Yet, the walk from the bar to the sleek twenty-first-century concert hall takes audience members past a vivid reminder of the places where jazz sounded in the past in the form of two ceramic tile murals by artists Sandow Birk and Elyse Pignolet. Titled "Jazz and the City" and "Jazz and the Nation," the murals depict jazz history in San Francisco and in the United States largely through images of venues that no longer exist. The local-scene mural features renderings of Jimbo's Bop City, a club in the largely African American Fillmore District that operated in the 1950s and '60s and was forced out by urban redevelopment efforts, and Keystone Korner, a club that hosted major touring artists during the 1970s and '80s where a number of big names recorded live albums, including Bill Evans and Mary Lou Williams.[95] "Jazz and the Nation" shows many American jazz spots over the course of several decades, including a New Orleans parade, the Reno Club in Kansas City where Count Basie was once a regular, Harlem's Savoy Ballroom, and small clubs associated with mid-century bebop like the Famous Door and the Three Deuces. Interspersed with these venues are depictions of African American life in the era of Jim Crow, with weary travelers shown in a segregated waiting area of a train station and civil rights protesters marching with signs. Jazz and the places that present it are intertwined in these murals with struggles for social justice. They help to frame patronizing SFJazz as a continuation of the story on the wall in a new type of space, both a luxurious experience and a social good that celebrates the art of historically oppressed creators. One audience member described the experience of attending an SFJazz performance this way: "It has given jazz a much higher profile and a much posher audience.... It's a double-edged sword. In some ways it has taken jazz out of the clubs which used to exist here and made it respectable. But it has expanded the audience wonderfully, so I can't knock it."[96] SFJazz and JALC have both connected jazz to deeper pockets and more reliable funding by selling it in clean, beautiful spaces to affluent listeners. While SFJazz's success with wide-reaching programming demonstrates that large-scale jazz venues do not have to stamp out musical diversity and experiment to flourish, their size and resources do make them cast large shadows within their local scenes. As one San Francisco writer put it, half a century ago "jazz was dangerous, and everybody smoked in dives like Keystone Corner, El Matador and the Cellar, and later Kimball's, Pearl's, the list goes on. SFJazz is about all that's left, and maybe all that's needed."[97] While one major venue can serve just as many jazz patrons as a whole scene's-worth of clubs, they relate to their cities and neighborhood in very different ways than an array of small, locally owned businesses.

Despite the New Orleans Jazz Market's efforts to connect to and support local businesses and its neighborhood, it offers an example of the potential consequences these shiny new venues could have on cities that once sported very different jazz scenes. The building project benefitted from a number of subsidies and investments of both public and private sector funds, allowing a new home for the New Orleans Jazz Orchestra to take shape in the Central City neighborhood. While the project ostensibly provided a service to the generally low-income neighborhood in the form of a music and community space connected to the public library system, New Orleans musician Calvin Johnson still viewed the project as a clear example of gentrification, quipping, "It's not like they built them a grocery store."[98] The venue is on the former site of a discount store, and New Orleans *Uptown Messenger* opinion writer Owen Courrèges characterized its creation as an effort by city officials to force impoverished local residents out of the neighborhood. He wrote, "A discount store truly served Central City residents, but nobody was going to throw grants and low-interest loans at that kind of project....A discount store may not be as glamorous as a 'Jazz Market,' but it's more appropriate for Central City. The fact that a discount store folded and was replaced by a public-supported upscale jazz venue speaks volumes about the city's agenda."[99] SFJazz is much more glamorous than the two auto repair shops that once stood in its place, but that glamour is directed to audiences that can pay the ticket prices, not necessarily or specifically local residents. Large-scale jazz venues present jazz as a historically African American music representative of struggles for equality in an unjust society, but they also rely on funding from the affluent end of that society. All this is not to say that the service mission of organizations like JALC and SFJazz are not serious or substantial. In addition to JALC's Essentially Ellington program, discussed previously, they offer a tuition-free Middle School Jazz Academy for New York City students, and SFJazz also serves its local middle schoolers with programming in San Francisco and Oakland public schools. Both organizations also give away free concert tickets to families, schools, and community groups in their cities. Yet the primary recipient of the service provided by these massive, nonprofit, charitable organizations is jazz itself. With his carefully guarded canon and insistence on jazz as high art rather than popular music, Marsalis successfully made space for jazz in the philanthropy-supported art-music world, framing the music as both a luxury to enjoy and a resource to protect. By drawing fire as he did so, he has now essentially also created space for other programs like SFJazz and Jazz at the Kennedy Center that challenge his vision of jazz and its history. While these massive spaces cannot help but create powerful waves in their local scenes, their scope, visibility, and resources have pulled them into a form of national scene in which they pull, push, and shape each other, our understanding of the past, and the music of the present.

CHAPTER 3

Schools on the Scene

It is no longer remotely unusual for venues featuring professional jazz performers to overlap and intersect with educational programs and institutions. Even at privately owned clubs like Yoshi's in Oakland, school bands occasionally perform between big-name professional artists, and nonprofit performance venues like Jazz at Lincoln Center and SFJazz offer extensive educational programming that ranges from concerts for preschoolers to professional development opportunities for teachers. Additionally, professional jazz musicians have long treated college campuses as performance venues, with musicians like Dave Brubeck playing in university concert halls on a regular basis since the 1950s. Jazz has also been a subject of formal academic study since the middle of the twentieth century, yet, as Ken Prouty writes, "academic jazz programs often have been accused of being too far removed from the traditions of jazz as they developed through performance and informal learning situations."[1] Despite ever-stronger ties between jazz performance and education, a long history of skepticism surrounding formal jazz training has persisted into the twenty-first century.

Paul Berliner's ethnography *Thinking in Jazz*, written in the 1990s while jazz was widely taught on college campuses and had been for decades, describes informal apprenticeship as the primary or archetypal model for jazz teaching and learning. In his chapter "Hangin' Out and Jammin': The Jazz Community as an Educational System," Berliner introduces the idea of the jazz community by saying, "Record shops, music stores, musicians' union halls, social clubs for the promotion of jazz, musicians' homes, booking agencies, practice studios, recording studios, and nightclubs all provide places where musicians interrelate with one another."[2] Conspicuously absent from this otherwise detailed list is any mention of formal jazz study at universities. After describing in detail jam sessions, apprenticeships, and sitting in with groups as examples of learning opportunities in the jazz community, he adds, almost as an afterthought, "Besides the jazz community's own institutions for learning, improvisers have benefited in varying degrees from colleges, universities, and conservatories."[3] After interviews with over fifty jazz musicians, Berliner did not describe college jazz programs as one of "the jazz community's own institutions" but something somehow foreign to that community, a separate system provided by an outside source.

Since the mid-twentieth century, however, the presence of jazz in universities has been steadily expanding, as has the influence of universities on a broader jazz community. Even as Miles Davis was leaving Julliard in search of jazz, Clora Bryant turned her promise as a young jazz musician into a pathway to higher education, helping to pay her way through Prairie View College by performing with the school swing band.[4] By 1947, the University of North Texas offered the first jazz degree program—a major in dance band that eventually expanded into what is still one of the country's largest and most prominent jazz studies programs. College jazz remained fairly rare throughout the fifties and sixties, with only fifteen programs granting jazz degrees by 1972, but that number increased by nearly five times over the course of the next decade and reached approximately 120 by the mid-1990s.[5] In an essay suggesting that the time had come to reconsider the role of universities in today's jazz scene, David Ake listed around 150 professional jazz musicians born since 1950 who are included in *The New Grove Dictionary of Jazz* and formally studied jazz in schools.[6]

Criticism of jazz education is often based in notions of its uniformity and its separation from a more "real" jazz scene or community. Prouty notes that as jazz education has expanded, "the numbers of students who graduate with degrees in jazz has become a point of concern for some critics and musicians, who see the jazz world as being glutted with young musicians with no real professional experience, and who perform in very codified, standardized ways."[7] When jazz education is considered as a monolithic whole, the similarities between improvisation course sequences from one school to the next or the ubiquity of the big-band format stand out as some of the more obvious features of jazz curricula. From another angle, given that jazz is typically a relatively recent addition to a music program and university with a much longer history, formal jazz education faces marginalization from within higher education as well as from the jazz world outside. In looking at a small sample of individual schools within their geographic and cultural contexts, however, the variety of different possible jazz education experiences becomes more apparent, as do the efforts of jazz educators to help their students cultivate musical and personal relationships to professional artists both inside and outside academia. In the following study, I consider university jazz education programs as embedded in broader jazz scenes, both geographically and culturally, rather than as separate entities built to feed but not otherwise interact with those "real" professional scenes. From this vantage point, I argue that a significant part of the work done in contemporary jazz education programs involves building the variability and particularity that jazz education is often described as lacking and that the construction of universities as permeable and outwardly connected places rather than free-standing ivory towers is a central aspect of that work. In the following study, components of the jazz programs at the Eastman School of Music, the University of Nebraska Omaha, Oklahoma State University, and Loyola University New Orleans demonstrate several different strategies for weaving together professional jazz performers and student musicians that are shaped by their geographic locations and institutional identities.

UNIVERSITIES AS PLACES

As with other types of buildings, examining the physical structures of universities can offer insights into the uses and meanings of space and place. When viewed next to a romanticized vision of the freedom and countercultural cache of mid-twentieth-century jazz clubs, typical college buildings and classrooms can look like very unlikely places for jazz to thrive. Dick Hebdige writes,

> Most modern institutes of education, despite the apparent neutrality of the materials from which they are constructed (red brick, white tile, etc.) carry within themselves implicit ideological assumptions which are literally structured into the architecture itself. The categorization of knowledge into arts and sciences is reproduced in the faculty system which houses different disciplines in different buildings, and most colleges maintain the traditional divisions by devoting a separate floor to each subject. Moreover, the hierarchical relationship between teacher and taught is inscribed in the very lay-out of the lecture theatre where the seating arrangements—benches rising in tiers

before a raised lectern—dictate the flow of information and serve to "naturalize" professorial authority. Thus, a whole range of decisions about what is and what is not possible within education have been made, however unconsciously, before the content of individual courses is even decided.[8]

While the physical structures of universities and colleges can vary and inhabit a wide variety of geographic locations, jazz programs have been added into academic buildings and cultures that are shaped by their long histories, and those programs often find themselves forced to strike a balance between leveraging those institutional histories for resources and legitimacy while also pushing against them to reach toward histories of jazz performance spaces from the music's twentieth-century commercial landscape and its associations with experimentation, risk, professionalism, and improvisation.

In her 2017 book *Today's Medieval University*, M. J. Toswell outlines the many ways in which twenty-first-century universities remain deeply rooted in thirteenth-century traditions, from their governance to their rituals to their physical spaces. One perennial element of higher education she addresses that relates to the relationship between heritage and place in present-day universities is the valuing of autonomy, the separation of universities from other structures of power over daily life.[9] Philosopher and former university president Paul Gooch writes about this separation in terms of place in his work on contemporary universities, noting, "A bounded campus is, quite literally, a protected place proclaiming the autonomy of the university.... The defining characteristics of autonomy and academic freedom, essential to what it is to be a university, require this sense of *protected place*." As he describes, "a society's commitment to knowledge is expressed in the space and architecture of its libraries, archives, and universities."[10] While universities share this trait of functioning as physical spaces set aside to cultivate knowledge, Gooch also notes that two of the key elements that distinguish them from each other are the particularity of their geography and how that contributes to the sense of place on a specific campus and the history and heritage from which they have developed. He argues that, "It would be difficult to distinguish one [university] from the other by any substantive difference in their mottos and aspirational statements.... Two features are unique to institutions: their history and their location—their place in time and space."[11] In addition to the fact that, "a successful interrogative education will take advantage of whatever opportunities for conversation its locative place can generate," Gooch points to the central role of heritage in defining place at a university:

"Universities thrive when they grow from their roots, instead of trying to graft on shoots from different species. What works in one place to attract students might not grow as well in a different climate. The identity and reputation of an institution is wrapped up in its history, and the challenge of each new administration is to articulate and shape that historical identity in ways that honour the past while engaging the present."[12] Individual identities of universities are based in the intersection of heritage and place, so jazz programs within schools are substantially shaped by these forces.

Music programs at universities tend to reflect this heritage-driven quality of higher education in both their physical spaces and cultures. In his ethnography of an east coast music conservatory, Henry Kingsbury said the following about the institution's main concert hall as a physical and cultural center for the school:

> Over and above the visual impact made by the auditorium and by its unusually fine acoustical characteristics, this concert hall is a conscious symbol of the conservatory. In a dress rehearsal on the eve of a public performance, one conductor exhorted his ensemble by saying that "there's a great legacy to this hall, a lot of great musicians have played here. When you walk out on stage tomorrow night you have to reflect all the best qualities of this school." Indeed, I do not think I am pressing my anthropological bias unduly in suggesting that the entire building can be taken as a symbol of the conservatory's own past.[13]

In the majority of schools, jazz education has come as an addition to existing programs based in western classical music. As Bruno Nettl described in work on midwestern music schools,

> The center of the Music Building with its repertory of the central classical music, composed between 1730 and 1950, is surrounded by peripheral musics which have found their way into the institution—the experimental, computerized, electronic "new" music; jazz; non-Western music; folk and ethnic music; "early" music, from before 1700....These are not necessarily the musics of ethnic minorities, but in the society of musics that inhabit the Music Building, they are treated, by students and faculty but also, as it were by the central classical music in the way minorities have often been treated in American society....They are permitted into the Music Building only on the terms of the central classical repertory.[14]

Thus, the work of establishing and growing jazz programs in higher education has been characterized by efforts to bring peripheral music toward a classically defined center. Yet, victories in fitting jazz into established structures of classical music education in universities that have historically valued autonomy have come with increased tensions in how jazz education fits into a wider jazz world.

AN INCREASINGLY (UN)POPULAR APPROACH
TO LEARNING JAZZ

The more jazz is taught, learned, and written about in academic settings, the more outspoken the criticism of institutional jazz pedagogy has become. Even academic writing can be disparaging of jazz entering the academy. In the entry on "Jazz Education" in *Grove* available during the first decade of the twenty-first century, Gary Kennedy heartily condemned his own subject matter, writing, "Even fifty years after the movement began, 'jazz education' has yet to reach any of the serious artistic goals that the term would imply. Much of the reason for this failure, at least in the USA, is that most undergraduate-level jazz programs are concerned more with creating generic professional musicians and educators than jazz musicians."[15] Kennedy saw modern university training as not simply different from, but notably inferior to, earlier and less formal ways of learning jazz, producing technically proficient but uninspiring, stylistically similar players while the informal apprenticeship system produced the great individualistic performers of the historical jazz canon.

Indeed, this type of criticism is not unique to jazz but has often been applied to musicians in a variety of other situations. In the realm of western classical music, conservatories are sometimes described as mass-producing mechanical rather than musical players. A review typical of this rhetoric, for example, blamed the uninspired playing of an eighteen-year-old classical violin student on her conservatory training, saying that her "mechanical ability leaves no doubt she could go very far in her profession, but her curiously academic readings suggest it is high time for her to get out of the Juilliard practice rooms and sow some wild oats."[16] The implication is that Juilliard can teach her only technique; expression, on the other hand, must come from outside the formal educational environment. In northern India, a similar argument played out in a situation where formal schools largely replaced the older, individual-guru-based training system in practice but failed to measure up in terms of prestige. Andrew Alter's writing addresses the phenomenon of teachers working in formal institutions who "believe that the modern/Western institutional system has significant ills that must be redressed through the adoption of the *guru-shishya parampara*," the one-on-one instruction traditionally used to maintain a particular teacher-disciple lineage.[17] He describes trends away from set curricula, examinations, and degrees within musical institutions themselves due to a widespread belief among musicians, critics, and scholars that institutions based on western models graduate a wider audience of music appreciators but do not provide the necessary resources to "train competent performing musicians."[18]

In jazz, critiques of standardized conservatory training are particularly vehement due in large part to widely ingrained beliefs among its devotees about this particular music's highly individualistic and improvisatory nature when compared to other styles, especially western art music. Stuart Nicholson's chapter "Teachers Teaching Teachers" from his book *Is Jazz Dead?* suggests that the formal jazz education system does more to perpetuate itself than to produce meaningful art because of its heavy emphasis on classroom instruction in technique and theory. He discusses how widespread institutionalization has also meant widespread standardization of what it means to learn jazz, resulting in a university system that focuses primarily on teaching a single style. The most commonly taught type of jazz, according to Nicholson's analysis, is now the complex harmony of bebop, and teaching methods are aimed at maintaining that style as a static rather than developing language:

> This common language, its foundation based on the conventions of bebop style, is, as Mark Levine has pointed out in his excellent *Jazz Theory Book*, "explainable, analyzable, categorizable, and do-able." The problem was that by the end of the 1990s, rather a lot of jazz on CD and at clubs and festivals played by many younger musicians was *sounding* as if it was "explainable, analyzable, categorizable and do-able." Many critics ascribe this to the homogenization effect of jazz education, because most students follow broadly similar pedagogic routes to graduation while at the same time following broadly similar sources of stylistic inspiration.[19]

Like Kennedy, Nicholson makes a distinction between real jazz musicians and people who participate in formalized jazz education:

> In practice, large numbers of graduates are taught by educators who themselves have come through the jazz-education system, many of whom have little or no experience as professional jazz musicians and for whom the "jazz life" of paying dues in the hope that modest success might eventually come their way is more abstract notion than lifestyle choice. Others, from families who have made sacrifices to put them through college and university, feel they have to take advantage of the degrees and diplomas they have accrued and become teachers and lecturers and acquire status in the community, rather than turn their back on family sacrifices and scuffle for their living as a freelance jazz musician.[20]

Again the jazz education community is defined as separate from the actual jazz community: Nicholson describes students who are faced with a choice between being what he calls professional jazz musicians—freelance performers—or jazz educators who are not a part of the "real" jazz scene.

Voices from within jazz education have spoken out on behalf of their programs as meaningful components of contemporary jazz culture, however. John Murphy has defended the improvisation curriculum at the University of North Texas, suggesting, "Rather than argue that the university jazz program is a second-rate substitute for traditional ways of learning, scholars need to consider the university jazz program as a valid musical culture that blends academic and nonacademic approaches and is worthy of study in a holistic fashion."[21] Similarly, David Ake argues for the consideration of universities as sites of jazz culture, not production lines moving newly minted players out into a separate and somehow more real jazz world. He claims that even though jazz educators and students are not the best-known names in the jazz world, they are among the largest groups of people to make jazz a significant focus of their daily activities. "Why return to the topic of jazz education when most of the individuals involved in that field remain little known beyond their immediate regions? I do so because, by nearly any measure, college-based programs have not only replaced the proverbial street as the primary training grounds for young jazz musicians, but they've also replaced urban nightclubs as the primary professional homes for hundreds of jazz performers and composers."[22] Without denying claims made by writers including Kennedy and Nicholson that few graduates of institutional jazz programs become widely known artists, Ake suggests that there is more to be gained by thinking and talking about formal jazz education as an important element of contemporary jazz culture than continuing to rely on a discourse in which the "move from clubs to schools remains ignored, marginalized, or denigrated."[23] He writes, "It is true that college programs have yet to show an ability to turn every promising talent into an influential artist. Yet just because jazz programs cannot systematically produce musical geniuses, it does not follow that students in those programs fail to learn, improve, or otherwise benefit from their studies.... Some students become excellent, even important, musicians; some don't climb that high... just like those performers trained in the informal 'schools' of New Orleans, Kansas City, or Harlem in the last century."[24] Demystifying the informal educational system in which Louis Armstrong and Charlie Parker trained can help reduce the pressure placed on today's jazz educators to produce only students of their magnitude and encourage reasonable examinations of what contemporary jazz education can, does, or should do. In fact, accepting formal jazz education as a legitimate aspect of a broad jazz community rather than an independent entity makes it easier to see the ways in which college-level jazz is informed by a respect for the jazz apprenticeship model. While opportunities for young players to start their careers by touring with well-known bands are now few and far between, students still learn by listening to the masters and engaging with professionals in a variety of significant ways.

One aspect of the shrinking club scene and growing presence of jazz in universities that often goes overlooked in discussions lamenting the disappearance of the informal apprenticeship system is the fact that many of the most successful and prominent musicians in jazz now teach at universities or in other formal settings as one facet of their professional careers. For example, there is considerable overlap between the jazz musicians nominated for Grammy Awards in 2019 and the world of formal jazz education. The Best Jazz Instrumental Album category alone featured five current or former collegiate teachers: Tia Fuller, a faculty member at the Berklee School of Music; Fred Hersch, who taught at the New England Conservatory; Joshua Redman, who held a year-long appointment at Stanford; Ron Miles, director of the jazz studies program at Metropolitan State University in Denver; and Wayne Shorter, a professor at UCLA. For an increasing number of professional jazz musicians who have worked in the genre's most famous bands and venues, working in formal jazz education is also a commonplace aspect of jazz culture. For young players, the result is an option of attending colleges that, in Ake's words, "do offer all the benefits of the early twentieth-century nightclub-based mentoring system that Gary Kennedy extolled in his *Grove Jazz* essay, albeit in an admittedly less colorful (but also less toxic) environment than the popular after-hours-in-a-smoky-gin-joint image."[25] To be sure, not all jazz educators are in the national spotlight as the teachers at elite schools like Julliard, Manhattan, and the New England Conservatory tend to be, but Charlie Parker did not attend every jam session in the 1940s, either. Distances, both geographic and cultural, can separate jazz education institutions from the places, experiences, and scenes that are often perceived as central to jazz, but jazz educators can also leverage traits and resources of their intuitions in efforts to bridge these divides.

LOCAL AND GLOBAL

"I literally did not know jazz sounded like that in Omaha," enthused Ashlin Parker, a New Orleans–based trumpet player and educator, in response to a Jazz Education Network festival performance by the University of Nebraska Omaha Jazz Ensemble. While adjudicating a festival in New Orleans, the purported birthplace of jazz, that draws participants from throughout the United States, Parker could certainly use a version of the same line to address students from Bemidji, Minnesota, or Wichita, Kansas, who might feel equally separated from jazz capitals, but the joke landed well with his Omaha crowd. The suggestion that a person wouldn't expect to find great jazz in their city brought smiles and laughter from the student ensemble made up primarily of Nebraska residents, and they looked pleased when Parker concluded his clinic by telling them that their playing made him want to check out Omaha.

While the majority of the most prestigious college jazz programs are in large coastal cities like New York, Boston, Los Angeles, and Miami, the majority of college students in the United States enroll in schools near their homes, and schools with jazz studies programs can be found in a wide variety of settings throughout the country. Pete Madsen, coordinator of jazz studies at the University of Nebraska Omaha (UNO), says, "Most of our students come from the Omaha area. Outside of that, it's elsewhere in Nebraska, and outside of that maybe over in Iowa."[26] This represents the norm rather than the exception in American higher education; over seventy percent of students go to schools in their home state, fifty-seven percent stay within fifty miles of home, and only sixteen percent go beyond a state bordering their home state to attend college.[27] Working-class students, people of color, and people residing in rural areas are even more likely to remain close to home for school than their wealthier, white, urban counterparts.[28] While specialized schools, including dedicated music schools like the Berklee College of Music, tend to draw students from long distances at higher rates than standard universities, jazz studies programs in places like Omaha serve student populations that would be unlikely to receive formal jazz training if they had to relocate to New York or Los Angeles to do it.[29]

While Parker's quip offers a reminder that Omaha is not widely seen as a jazz Mecca, the jazz studies program at UNO offers an example of how geographic and institutional assets can be drawn on to enhance jazz education in terms of the connections between student musicians and a broader professional world. In describing his school's location, Madsen says, "Here in our little corner of the state, we've got about a million people, and then the entire rest of the state is maybe another million people all spread out all over the place. So, in terms of the state of Nebraska, we're very much the metropolitan hub, even though

Omaha compared to Chicago, New York, Kansas City—you know, we're not nearly as big as those cities. But we're definitely the hub in terms of the metro area for the state, and, so, I think because of that, there are a lot of opportunities here." As the largest city in its region, Omaha's jazz scene, though smaller in scope than those in larger cities, offers a gathering place for regional students and professionals and hosts nationally touring artists at places like its Holland Performing Arts Center and the recently opened Jewell jazz club. Through partnerships with the venues of this regional center, UNO jazz students have the opportunity to both hear and perform music outside of their college classrooms. Madsen describes working with local venues to bring in guest artists who perform at both the university and a concert hall or club on the same trip as one means of creating ties between the school and the local jazz scene, and he has also led student performances at local clubs, both with and without professional guest artists. In addition, the UNO Jazz Ensemble plays regularly for the Omaha Jitterbugs, a local swing dance organization that offers classes and weekly social dances.

While most of the students in the UNO jazz studies program don't travel far to get to college, another way in which their program pushes back against the stereotype of jazz education as insular and separated from the real world is through providing opportunities for students to travel while in college. For this, Madsen, himself a graduate of music programs at middle American state universities in Missouri and Illinois, draws on the strengths and connections available through UNO as an academic institution to expand his students' chances to engage a wider world. As he describes, "We have a very strong international studies program on our campus, so we have sister universities all over the place." By taking advantage of ties to sister cities and sister universities, the UNO Jazz Ensemble has traveled multiple times to Japan, China, Lithuania, and Latvia. These trips provide travel experiences to students who may not have had similar opportunities in the past. Madsen points out, "We've had some students, when we've taken them overseas, where it's not only their first time overseas but it's literally their first time on an airplane." This is possible because of UNO's institutional connections. As Madsen explains, "So with those relationships, then, we're able to make things very affordable because we'll do things like, we went to Latvia last summer, all we had to do was pay for the plane tickets to get there. And then, because they're on the ground there, they were able to figure out how to inexpensively house us and feed us, and then we did the same thing for them when they came to visit us." Through student and faculty exchanges, UNO Jazz Ensemble participants connect to other musicians outside their program. For Madsen, "It's really neat to see them making music together with other kids their age from another country. There's all the clichés, of course, about music being the international language and all that, but it's really neat to see those relationships being built, too.... I think it really just helps them get outside of themselves and their own American self-centeredness and see that there's just a whole other world out there." While Omaha may be relatively geographically isolated from the densest and most active jazz scenes in the United States, participation in jazz education at UNO allows students to experience jazz performance in a variety of contexts, build relationships, and travel to new places that can expand their understanding of jazz not only beyond the state lines that few college students cross but over international borders. While opportunities to join touring bands as a developing musician are now thin on the ground, taking advantage of the resources and connections of universities provides a different pathway for a young jazz player to become familiar with varying performance venues and broader horizons.

THE RECORDS' APPRENTICES

While some critique of formal jazz education has related to physical separation between educational and professional performance contexts, sometimes concerns relate more to theoretical or artistic separation. Much criticism of jazz education practices is directed specifically at methods that separate theories and techniques from the people who famously performed and recorded them. For example, Ake notes some of the drawbacks of the popular chord-scale system of improvisation study found in books by David Baker, Jamey Aebersold, and others that encourage students to memorize an abstract list of scales and how they fit over specific chords they might encounter in tunes from the standard jazz repertoire. As Ake argues, "While this pedagogical approach does succeed for the most part in reducing 'clams' (notes heard as mistakes) and building 'chops' (virtuosity), it presents a number of major and related drawbacks as beginners strive to play idiomatically within various jazz contexts. Most obviously, this approach ignores...sonic and rhythmic conceptions...but it also overlooks other important aspects such as musical interplay among players."[30] For jazz education critics who feel that over-privileging theoretical knowledge sends students down the wrong path, recordings of jazz masters are often prescribed as a corrective measure.

In April of 2009, the month that marked the 110th anniversary of the birth of Duke Ellington, students at the Eastman School of Music took the stage to perform his *New Orleans Suite* completely from memory. This concert, which students had prepared not by reading the score but by listening to and internalizing the Ellington band's 1970 recording, served as the culminating event in a year-long celebration of the composer's work. It also serves as an example of the essential role of recording in bridging two realms of jazz culture, the romanticized world of mid-century musical and cultural icons and the present reality of an ever-expanding system of institutionalized jazz education. Students and teachers I interviewed at the Eastman School of Music echoed the sentiment seen in critiques like Ake's that abstracting theoretical principles from jazz practice is not as effective a teaching strategy as encouraging students to look for those principles—and their exceptions and full musical context—in canonical recorded jazz. While a doctoral trumpet student, Mike Van Bebber differentiated between what he called "abstractions" and "actual music," saying, "People reduce jazz too far. They reduce it to a set of scales, and it's kind of ironic, because they reduce it, and then they exclude things that *are* totally necessary, like extracting principles from real music. It's weird. I've been a lot of different places, a lot of different workshops, and no one ever talks about *the music*, real music, jazz music. They talk about things that have been written about the music."[31] Van Bebber suggested that engaging with recordings of important players offers a superior alternative to written methods like the chord-scale system because it allows the student direct access to what he calls "real music." Ironically, records come to represent unmediated access to the real: "It's way better to just learn or memorize some classic recording or something that is jazz, a good representation of jazz, and then glean characteristics from that. And a lot of times it's a lot more valuable than the things that are written in books. It's always that way, because they [books] tend to overgeneralize." As an example, he describes a concept from a jazz textbook, "avoid notes," that he finds to be an overgeneralization that has a sanitizing effect on the music played by the book's adherents.

> In reality, in real jazz music, there's not notes to avoid or intervals to avoid, but that's just a perfect example of people teaching that you don't use a 4th and a 3rd in a voicing of a major triad, for example. But real musicians did do that, lots of times...It's like it's too much of a shortcut a lot of times.

Sure, it will sound okay, but you take away a little bit of what's interesting about the music in order to have more homogenous—harmonious and homogenous—sound. It's like you take a little bit of interest out of the music. I don't like that at all.

Van Bebber feels that by learning theory and performance practice through listening to and transcribing jazz icons himself, he is able to develop a more nuanced and musically satisfying approach to improvisation. Rather than rely on a set of fixed rules, he is able to use recordings as a point of reference for understanding why those rules exist and when breaking them might be musically interesting and successful.

Bill Dobbins, a professor in the Eastman department of Jazz Studies and Contemporary Media since 1973 and director of the Eastman Jazz Ensemble, describes a similar situation for his jazz composition and arranging students. He notices that the growth of institutionalized jazz since the 1970s has led to a greater number of incoming students who have learned from books rather than through directly studying the works of well-known composers. "It seems a lot of times jazz writing is approached in a very academic, abstract way. They just learn about a lot of techniques, but in most institutions they don't really do any score analysis or real—they don't really get into the nuts and bolts of how Neal Hefti and Sammy Nestico and some of the Basie writers work and what Ellington and Strayhorn did and how that's different from that."[32] Like Van Bebber's distinction between studying books and studying "real music," Dobbins prefers composition students "whose writing shows that they've really absorbed...actual music" to those who show only an abstract, academic understanding of standard jazz writing techniques. In terms of the playing ability of his incoming students, he often finds what he sees as a similar problem. Along similar lines to what writers like Nicholson have stated about jazz students, Dobbins takes issue with aspiring jazz players who learn from abstract theoretical methods and show a great deal of technical facility but are not familiar with how the scales and arpeggios they know were contextualized in performances and recordings by master players—in his words, "in a way that's a little scary, too—it's like the sorcerer's apprentice." From this perspective, the real jazz authorities are not teachers or books but the very same people that participated in the romanticized apprenticeship process of the twentieth century, the famous performers of the jazz canon. Dobbins says he hopes his students reach the point where they "realize that the way they really learn this stuff is to take advantage of the fact that jazz is probably the only sophisticated form of creative music whose entire history has been documented on records. And, fortunately for us, that's an invaluable resource." For both professor and student, one means of accessing "real" jazz in a university context is via recordings by master musicians.

Through the middle decades of the twentieth century, numerous young musicians had the opportunity to develop musical and professional skills by joining Ellington's band and serving as apprentices to one of the most celebrated jazz masters. Gabriel Solis points out in an article on the issue of canonic figures in jazz narratives that Ellington is often treated as the single clearest example of a jazz genius because he "is arguably the first, the most accomplished, and certainly the best-known jazz composer to create music that fits most of the conventional notions of a musical work."[33] Indeed, in discussing his rationale for putting on a school year's worth of Eastman Jazz Ensemble concerts devoted almost exclusively to the music of Duke Ellington, Dobbins used one of the most celebrated canonical figures in western art music, Bach, as an example to help explain how he understood the project's worth.[34] "I think that would be the same for a classical composer like Bach—I can see a real value in having classical musicians do nothing but Bach for a whole year, and maybe approach it in a similar way. If you did eight concerts through the year, try to concentrate in each of those concerts on a period of six or seven years in Bach's life, what repertoire he wrote then." In the western art music world, the music of J. S. Bach is essentially considered above critique—to many, the music of Bach and a handful of other greats *is* Western art music, and a person who appreciates this particular musical tradition necessarily also appreciates Bach. The student performers of the Eastman Jazz Ensemble participating in the Ellington programs tended to view him in the same way. An undergraduate trombonist, Tim Craig, compared the project to the resident faculty string quartet's two-season series of performances of the music of Beethoven, saying of both groups' efforts, "It's awesome stuff, so just do it, you know?"[35] Van Bebber agreed that the project was worthy because Ellington was a significant enough composer to merit the attention. "I didn't mind doing all of one composer, since it maybe was the best composer in jazz, you know? But if it was an obscure composer that wasn't really that good, then obviously I wouldn't—I don't think it's valuable." To students who accept as a given that the validity of the serious study of jazz is equal to the serious study of classical music, Ellington falls on the same plane as any of the greatest classical composers, and time spent on his music is considered well spent. In this case, the students performed four programs over the course of two semesters, learning over forty Ellington pieces or movements from longer suites.

Even with his reputation for being the most composerly of the historical jazz icons, though, his prolific career as a recording artist means that Ellington's work as performed during his lifetime is much more present in the ears and minds of students than is Bach's or Beethoven's. Ellington did not rise to fame through published scores that were widely performed by different ensembles but largely through recordings, radio broadcasts, and live performances of his works by the specific band with whom he collaborated, both in the act of performance and in the composition of works. Therefore, as the students learned to play his pieces, their written parts (when they had them) were not the most complete sources for what could be considered the definitive versions—the records were. On those records, Ellington was not the only author of the finished product under consideration. Each member of the Eastman ensemble had a specific individual to model his playing after, an individual that Ellington had in mind as he wrote the music.

For many listeners, a performance of Duke Ellington's music by any band other than his own would be unlikely to rank any higher than second best, a sentiment that makes the jazz repertory movement, an often controversial turn toward reviving historical works that emerged during the 1970s, most comfortably at home in educational contexts. Students, or professionals working in an educational context, can afford to perform versions of canonical recordings that are by default considered less valuable than the originals. In a jazz education system that is criticized for teaching through abstraction, giving students only technical information and leaving them to develop musicality on their own, encouraging students to emulate recordings provides an avenue for studying musicality by example. Instead of conceding that students simply "either have it or they don't," a popular notion of jazz that has historically contributed to its mystique and to both positive and negative assessments of the music's "naturalness," having students copy recordings opens the possibility that expression can also be learned, albeit in reverse as younger players seek to remove their own fingerprints from a performance in order to sound as much like someone else, someone who carefully cultivated a unique individual musical identity, as possible. For jazz education to be considered effective, students must learn more than theory and technique, but the qualities that go beyond the mechanical are subject to ownership. An alto player who learns, for example, to emulate the vibrato he or she hears on an Ellington record is more likely to be described as "playing with Johnny Hodges's vibrato" than "playing with musicality."

The Eastman Ellington project represents one attempt to navigate this difficult double bind faced by jazz educators, the challenge of teaching musicality and individual expression, qualities that audiences value as natural and untaught. By continually working on the music of just one composer-bandleader for a sustained period, Dobbins and his students sought an educational experience that would allow the young players to absorb as many musical details from Ellington's band as possible and also see as wide a perspective on his career as possible. According to Dobbins, "The obvious value of it is that when you concentrate on a particular repertoire like that, people do get into it to a depth that they just wouldn't if it was a couple of pieces on each program or one concert at a particular time of the year, and especially when it's a composer like Ellington, where there's so [many] different kinds of repertoire—where you can really hear things that he did later on that are a little different than what he did earlier on in his writing." The two advantages to an approach like this, as compared to a more theoretical approach like a chord-scale method alone, is that students are encouraged to notice specific details of an artist's style and also become familiar with a wide range of his or her work, not just the most celebrated highlights.

It is important to keep in mind that the all-Ellington project was only one element of the students' overall jazz education—they also continued to play in small jazz ensembles and take courses in academic subjects like theory and history as well as continue work in private lessons. Thinking about the music these students performed in their large ensemble, however, offers a chance to consider aspects of institutional jazz education that are often overlooked in other analyses of the system. Because much larger ensemble playing involves reading parts rather than improvising, it is often dismissed as less useful than other types of jazz learning, yet ensemble playing is one arena in which student musicians are encouraged to think about details of musicality like tone, articulation, and interaction. While theory or improvisation textbooks and transcription collections contain the kind of physical evidence that we often look to in thinking about what music students study—scores—listening to what students play and what they model themselves on reveals another aspect of jazz education and helps create a more complete picture of what a jazz degree entails by directing attention toward skills that are taught aurally and not documented in published educational materials.

Looking back on their experience playing Ellington, the Eastman students did find that they had come to notice details about performance practice that critics of jazz education often find lacking from programs that do not place "real music"—celebrated recordings—at the center of the curriculum. In his work on jazz curricula, Prouty writes, "Perhaps the most common feature in the institutionalized pedagogy of improvisation is the emphasis on *pitch*. Put another way, pitch structures, such as scales, chords, and the relationships between the two, are stressed above other factors."[36] Ake suggests that, in a pedagogical model dominated by coaching improvisers on appropriate note choices for particular harmonies, "musical elements less commonly considered in jazz pedagogy include sonority-based aspects such as timbre and intonation."[37] Van Bebber found that carefully studying Ellington's recordings over a long period of time helped him learn about issues of tone production that are not easily taught through written sources or abstract principles. "We've never worked on just one composer for a whole year. I've never done that before. It's much more in depth. You can work on much more subtle things than you normally can.... It got to be that we were working on just musical things, like the time feel, intonation, vibratos, articulation, stuff like that." Similarly, Craig felt like one of the major lessons of the project was "learning the importance of articulation and dynamics, learning the impact that that can have on the music, and really taking it from notes on a page to something that is music and is something that you want to listen to."

In addition to focusing on expressive details as a central aspect of the music, Dobbins worked to present Ellington to students as a complex and multifaceted artist rather than a composer who could be understood through familiarity with just one iconic aspect of his work, a type of pedagogical one-dimensionality for which institutional jazz programs have been critiqued. Ake criticizes, for example, the manner in which the music of John Coltrane is typically taught to college jazz students as too shallow and oversimplified because of the fact that educators tend to focus only on his best-known music and the aspects of his style most easily subjected to harmonic analysis.[38] For a more apprenticeship-like experience, students in the Ellington project used their rather limited time to learn as many skills as possible by listening to one ensemble rather than to learn one or two more basic traits of each of a wider range of composers or groups. Dobbins said, "I just really tried to pick things that, within the scope of a year's time, would introduce the students to as much musical variety as possible...so I tried to pick a number of more extended pieces...pieces that were different ways of approaching the blues, different ways of writing for individual soloists...ensemble virtuoso pieces...and different influences too, like the programmatic pieces...some pieces that had literary inspirations like *Such Sweet Thunder* or *Suite Thursday*, or pieces that were about locales or places that had a certain kind of cultural history like the *New Orleans Suite*." While the students I interviewed were all familiar with Ellington in some capacity before the school year began, they also all encountered music they had never heard or played before because of the wide range of pieces chosen for the various concerts. Reflecting on the year overall, Craig commented that the most memorable aspect of the experience was learning to see a more complete picture of Ellington:

> I think that really the thing that stood out to me the most was the variety of Ellington. I was very familiar with...very specific charts. But having my... Ellington spectrum widened as we played through different pieces of his... getting a broader understanding of what he was doing and also understanding the more I know of it, the more I see the different variety. As much as Ellington was writing for the same size ensemble, just the amount of color and just the variety he was getting out of that ensemble, from stylistic things to musical things to even individual parts. Like in the trombone section, I'd see how parts from one suite would be completely different and look different from other parts even though he's writing with the same harmonies, and it was just incredible to see, I guess, his awesomeness as a composer, for lack of a better word.

In addition to changing his understanding of Ellington's artistic and historical significance, Craig felt that the intense focus on a single composer created a different type of ensemble playing experience than he was accustomed to in terms of the way that he and his peers came to relate to each other as a band. In his words, "Any band, by the end of the year, the band's going to be much tighter, the sections are going to know each other...and things will just kind of continue to grow. But even, I feel, more so with the Ellington music because we all started to really embody what was happening. By the end of the year, I really just—it felt so much like the recording. It felt so much like being in the band." For Craig, the experience of focusing on Ellington felt closer to the kind of apprenticeship that his generation of young jazz players so rarely has access to than other aspects of his musical education. To him, feeling like he was accurately recreating a recording was like "being in the band."

Regardless of how accurately the students learn to recreate the sounds of the Ellington band, recreation as a finished product has little weight in a jazz culture that prizes improvisation and individuality as chief values. Young jazz players who learn to mimic canonic records have been criticized just as harshly as those whose playing is deemed abstractly mechanical rather than musical. Although addressing the 1990s, Nicholson's argument here against the practicality of emulating historical players, bolstered by trombonist, composer, and educator Bob Brookmeyer, continues to be echoed today:

> Original voices were becoming increasingly hard to find, exacerbated by the fact that learning solos of the greats was seen as a pathway to acquiring familiarity within the syntax of bebop. "I tell my students, I know what the real world is like," says Bob Brookmeyer. "I try to gently tell them that there are probably 35-45,000 Coltrane tenor players and you ain't going to make much money or even a living if that's how you want to play, even if you play fantastically well…I say it might be wise to broaden your spectrum, learn to become a musician rather than a focused imitator, which is what many of them become."[39]

According to this line of thought, while careful listening and imitation is one means of jazz study, it cannot be the end. For this reason, one of the themes that the Eastman students emphasized in their discussions of the Ellington performances were their efforts to "make the music their own." Van Bebber described the process as follows, "The first couple rehearsals, I would play exactly what they played and sounded exactly like them as much as I could possibly do, same vibratos and everything. And then Bill [Dobbins] would say, 'Okay, now let's start to play using that style, but with your own notes.' And so that's what we did from then on." Craig's memory of the same process on a solo of his own reveals the extent to which an improviser is seen to have ownership of the notes in a recorded solo, "I went to the recording, learned that solo, and then tried to grow my own solo out of that using similar material. I actually remember I stole his last two measures because they were really great, so I played those verbatim." In playing the same pitches and rhythms that an Ellington trombonist had improvised, Craig did not say he was mimicking, borrowing, or emulating—he said he was "stealing."

Overall, Van Bebber finds the basic skill of being able to observe and learn stylistic detail from a recording more valuable than the very specific skill of playing in the style of, for example, Cootie Williams. When asked if his work on the Ellington material affected his other playing, he said, "I don't transfer the playing in the style of Ellington band members, but I transfer the principle that you can learn a lot from copying people exactly, like every single element of the way they play, and there's a lot more information than I thought there was before." Van Bebber expresses a desire to be able to sound like various Ellington soloists, but only as an exercise. In his other playing, he would not intentionally choose to recreate another person's style. While the Eastman students expended a great deal of time and effort learning to recreate the sounds they heard on Ellington's records, there remained a sense that "real musicality" belongs only to players who sound fully distinct from their mentors. The Ellington performances seemed to be more valued by the students as mediated apprenticeships than artistic ends in themselves, but the opportunity to focus on musical skills not easily gleaned from books helped to supplement the theory and score-based elements of formal jazz training that have been so often called out as insufficiently representative of "real" jazz.

PROFESSIONALS ON CAMPUS AND STUDENTS ON THE SCENE

While the professional models for the Eastman students during the Ellington project were with them only in recorded form, jazz education programs can also function as sites of in-person interaction between students and professionals, even in programs that are geographically separated from large, active jazz scenes. Guest artists invited by colleges and universities to perform for and often with student musicians are commonplace in jazz education. Tommy Poole, director of jazz studies at Oklahoma State University (OSU), draws on guest artists to offer students opportunities to connect with professional musicians and experiences outside the classroom. In addition, universities themselves can help to create more robust performance scenes in areas that would not otherwise have them.

Stillwater, Oklahoma, a town with a population around fifty thousand, is home to OSU, but not to an extremely active jazz scene. Poole, who spent several years supporting himself as a gigging musician before pursing graduate degrees at the University of Miami and the University of Texas at Austin, described some of his students playing and listening to jazz in one or two local venues but also at times seeking live music experiences outside school by driving over an hour to get to the larger cities of Tulsa and Oklahoma City, where jazz clubs, jam sessions, and local professional musicians are more plentiful. While Poole notes challenges of working in a rural area as including a relative scarcity of local professional jazz musicians—a reality that makes it more difficult to have frequent, affordable guest artists from nearby—he also points out ways in which the resources of a large research university have allowed him to provide students with a rich variety of experiences and opportunities for professional training and mentorship. For example, Poole explains that there is not any particular advantage to locations in more populous areas when it comes to bringing prominent guest artists to a university setting, "The guest artist thing, I have as many at OSU as more widely known jazz programs have....If it's a big-name guest artist, they're probably living in New York or LA, anyway, so you're probably talking about a flight anyway....Any school can have to pay a ton of money to get Christian McBride out....The big marquee guest artist is not a problem."[40]

In addition to providing opportunities to hear prominent professionals live, Poole designs educational experiences that allow students to have interactive, memorable experiences with musicians who visit Stillwater.

> Every couple of years, I tend to release a CD. I do it usually with the top big band, though I've done it with a combo before, too. And so what I'll do is, say, a guest artist, like, a couple of years ago we had Michael Dease, who is one of the world's greatest jazz trombone players....We flew him down from Michigan, and he did our OSU jazz festival in early April, and then he flew down again in May, and we went to a studio in Oklahoma and recorded... and released a CD. And the CD has done extraordinarily well. And that's a guest artist experience that is exceedingly rare for students to get....I got three degrees, an undergrad, a master's, and a doctorate, and I never got to record a CD with someone like Michael Dease.

Part of the benefit of this recording project as Poole describes it comes in the form of connections to a jazz community outside Stillwater, as the presence of Dease as a prominent guest on their recording led to the album being reviewed in publications with a geographically broad readership like *JazzTimes, JazzEd* magazine, and the *International Trombone Association Journal* and played on the radio outside Oklahoma, including a thirty-minute spot on a Czech radio station. By bringing Dease to Stillwater, OSU also helped to bring its students' music to a wider audience.

In addition to bringing in musicians from off campus, OSU demonstrates another way in which university jazz programs can contribute to local music scenes and help students develop professional skills. Poole notes that only the most advanced of his students gig professionally in Oklahoma City or Tulsa, but OSU itself provides places for students in the jazz program's five combos to gain experience as performers. In 2018, OSU combos were hired for approximately fifteen paid performances, and Poole states, "Most of those were OSU, like if there's a regents' meeting over at the student union, and they want a group, or the provost had a gathering of Big 12 administrators, and he wanted a jazz combo for that...fundraisers, fundraising galas. So, the OSU community is becoming more and more aware of the jazz combo thing at OSU, so they're being utilized a lot." While there may not be a large number of local venues in Stillwater for students to work at as they learn to perform outside a school concert setting, the university itself provides contexts in which they can lean away from their identity as students in practice rooms and toward the status of paid professionals.

Conversely, due to its location in New Orleans, Loyola University students are able to gig regularly at off-campus venues, becoming active in the local professional scene before graduation. In addition to teaching vocal jazz, Kate Duncan is associate director of Loyola's School of Music Industry and coordinates student internships, including opportunities that pair students with local jazz venues. Duncan describes the relationship between Loyola students and New Orleans jazz clubs as follows:

> We have relationships with all of the jazz venues in the city,...and we often get asked for not only gigging musicians from our student pool, but the students will also work at the venues as well, so, getting that managerial experience, booking, stage management, all of that, in addition to the performance that they're studying in school. So let me talk about the relationships with venues. Tipitina's regularly, the Starlight Lounge regularly, Preservation Hall regularly....Either...they've got a hole in their Friday night and they need to book at Snug Harbor, or they've got a great band and they're like, "Hey, if any of your kids want to sit in"—that's also a great experience for them. Most of our students do form bands that are not their educational, academic combos, outside of school, and they do gig pretty frequently. It's...an embarrassment of opportunity riches for us as far as places for these kids to play. And...you're playing in historic, outrageously old places, and you're just doing your thing like any other student, for instance, in, like, Topeka, might be, but you're in Preservation Hall. So we facilitate those relationships with those clubs.[41]

As Duncan explains, the school's location within the active New Orleans jazz scene has a significant impact on the nature and quantity of opportunities students there have to connect with professional jazz musicians and performance contexts. While all the jazz educators interviewed in this study described guest artists as important contributors to student learning, Duncan stated, "Of course, it's like shooting fish in a barrel as far as getting guest artists that are just world-renowned heavy hitters who either come through regularly or are residents of the city.... At other universities that I've attended and worked [at], it was a special treat to get one or two people in per semester, but it's on a weekly basis that we have incredible, talented people walking through. So, for our college kids, that experience is super valuable." While schools in rural areas or those placed a significant distance from dense jazz scenes may function as anchors of local jazz activity, Loyola's jazz program is able to take advantage of New Orleans's ubiquitous jazz clubs and players to expand the professional world into the classroom and the classroom into the professional world.

In part because of its location, Loyola University New Orleans has considerably different demographics than larger state universities like UNO and OSU, which both have large majorities of in-state students, especially at the undergraduate level. Less than half of Loyola's smaller student population hails from Louisiana, and Duncan's observations suggest that location is one of the elements that draws jazz students from far away, "We do have a reputation for jazz education, we're in New Orleans, and we're also unique in that niche [of being a Jesuit liberal arts institution with a dedicated college of music], so all of those things create a confluence that, I would think, yes, that would be the reason probably that students are coming from farther than just a typical regional draw for most schools that aren't the big names." In terms of jazz education, Duncan says, "When you're the birthplace, kids kind of have that lofty goal of coming to school in New Orleans," a factor that allows Loyola to draw a share of the relatively small pool of students who travel far from home for college in its direction.

Duncan's experiences teaching vocal jazz in New Orleans also demonstrate other ways that geography interacts with jazz education, as local scenes each have their own strengths and norms. Duncan describes New Orleans as "a town full of horns" where "the tuba and the trombone are king." As she explains, "Because those horns and that brass sound is king, it seems like most of our vocalists are not formally trained like they are on their horn, but it's this secondary thing of everybody sings, everybody's been singing since they were doing nursery rhymes, so I'll just add this in—I'll take the trumpet [off] my mouth and I'll sing a little 'When the Saints Go Marching In.'" In addition to a stronger focus on brass instruments than specialization in vocal jazz, Duncan also found in moving from the Northeast to the South that different tunes made up the local standard repertoire, "I'm a Northerner, from the Pittsburgh area, and when I moved down, my book was very different than many of the players that I would sit in with. I would throw it out, and they would say, 'I don't know any of these tunes.' And I would look at theirs and be like, 'I don't know any of *these* tunes.'" In providing formal vocal jazz training and starting a vocal jazz ensemble at Loyola, Duncan found that some of the educational experiences that she had understood as norms in other parts of the country did not have much traction in her new home. Having gone to graduate school in Minnesota, Duncan observed that, "The Midwest is just show choir-, vocal jazz-laden, like it's silly if you don't have one of those in your high school, in your college programs. And I just thought that was everybody. I thought that was the way of the world....Coming down here, they didn't have a vocal jazz division at Loyola; they didn't even have an ensemble that was faculty run." Meanwhile, what New Orleans has in quantity is the opportunity to regularly hear live music by professional performers, a situation that Duncan sees as significantly shaping her students' time feel to match local conventions that are "in the water" in the city.

FINDING A PLACE

Prouty describes the relationship between jazz education and professional jazz scenes as a sort of balancing act in which students and teachers of jazz seek to satisfy expectations of both academic institutions and jazz musicians and enthusiasts. He writes, "In seeking to form their own community identity as practitioners of jazz within the academy, students and teachers of jazz are constantly finding their place within the communities of the institution and of the jazz tradition, both of which exert enormous historical and practical power. Negotiating the dynamics of such communities is difficult, but both teachers and students have made an effort to accommodate the respective traditions."[42] As Prouty also discusses at length, there is no monolithic "jazz community" with clearly defined traits and boundaries. While Prouty explores the concept of jazz community in part through outlining a practice-based definition of community rooted in the act of listening to jazz, a broader jazz world is also subdivided into countless smaller communities based in other shared traits and connections. While jazz education in general shares a need to connect educational and professional communities, or school and the "real world," each jazz school also has its own unique traits, geography, and community connections that shape how this process plays out. As the students and faculty at the four institutions considered here demonstrate, connections between educational and professional music making can take a wide variety of forms, a situation that means readings of jazz education as a single large entity tend to highlight more failures than successes in this particular aspect of jazz learning.

Yet, even the successes of jazz education institutions in forging connections to professional scenes may not earn uncomplicated praise. As university jazz programs continue to spread, grow, and amass institutional resources alongside the shrinking of commercially supported professional jazz, connections between universities and "real" scenes can also be read as threats to the sustainability of the real. As university programs approach professional jazz scenes, especially the romanticized image of these scenes as mid-twentieth-century, on-the-job apprenticeships in prominent touring bands and small clubs, they also replace them. Recreating past jazz learning environments and relationships in the more controlled atmosphere of the academic institution is in some ways the educational equivalent of reenacting past performances, a phenomenon that Tracy McMullen explores through her analysis of what she terms *replay*. McMullen describes jazz performances that resurrect the past as replacing improvisation's "repetition with a signal difference" with "a certain 'repetition without a difference' or 'repetition-in-control.'"[43] When the validity of a jazz practice is perceived as being rooted in traditions of the past, deviations from old ways, like the shift from informal apprenticeships to university degree programs, struggle to achieve respect, yet efforts to reconstitute traditional practices in new contexts can also be read as problematically artificial, as students can be taught to value a "real" professional scene over jazz programs supported by educational institutions even as these two settings increasingly overlap. In the following chapter, a fifth example of a connection between a university and a professional venue is explored in detail, and it demonstrates that schools and professional venues can both confer authority on each other and simultaneously draw that authority into question from other angles. The balancing act required to relocate John Zorn's experimental music space into The New School highlights both the challenges and the possibilities of further uniting educational and performance contexts in a twenty-first-century jazz landscape.

CHAPTER 4

Unearthing The Stone

From Underground to The New School

Two musical performances took place in two Manhattan neighborhoods on consecutive nights in June of 2017. The first, played by multi-instrumentalist Peter Apfelbaum, tubist Marcus Rojas, and percussionist Cyro Baptista, happened in a nearly unmarked space in New York City's East Village. Some small, peeling lowercase letters near the door handle listed the venue's name, becoming visible after the metal door covering rose shortly before the show. The audience lined up outside along the street, paying cash at the door once it opened—there were no tickets, reserved seats, or refreshments of any kind, and all proceeds went directly to the performers. Inside, folding chairs tightly packed together in a small rectangular room faced a performance area with no raised stage. A line formed there in the front—it was for the bathroom. Since one had to cross through the performance space to use it, it was off limits once the music started. The room's only decoration was a set of sixty black and white photographs, portraits of musicians associated in various ways with new music, that formed a grid on one of the exposed brick walls. The photos represented performers diverse in terms of age, instrument, race, gender, and level of fame and blended into a smooth, uniform, nonhierarchical display that emphasized their community and shared purpose. A staircase led down to a basement green room, and a small table at the back served as a station for the volunteer collecting the cover charge. The show began a half-hour after the listed 8:30 p.m. start time with a half-hour group improvisation. By the end of the set, the musicians had explored such diverse sounds as wild, elephant-like roars through a tuba and percussive uses of its metal surfaces; singing, muttering, and various nonverbal mouth sounds; shaking a DIY instrument that looked more or less like an octopus made of garbage, mostly bottle caps of various sizes; a throat-singing rendition of "Moon River"; and a nearly disastrous experiment in kicking over glass bottles and throwing a chair that led to knocking over some sound equipment. Fortunately, in this particular venue, which was intimate to the point of claustrophobic, the front row of the audience sat only inches away from the performers, so listeners were able to catch the toppling electronics.

The next night, trumpet player Dave Douglas led a group with Chet Doxas, Steve Swallow, and Jim Doxas in a performance of material by and inspired by the work of Carla Bley at a location about a mile and a half away from the former Chinese restaurant where Apfelbaum, Rojas, and Baptista had appeared. The music and musicians were interconnected—Apfelbaum is a former Bley collaborator for example, and the second performance still fit under the umbrella of the jazz avant garde—but this evening's show involved more composed material and no kicking trash around the room. The audience members were interconnected, too—I recognized a woman sitting in the middle of the front row from the prior evening's show. Perhaps the most obvious differences, however, stemmed from the performance space. Rather than entering through an easy-to-miss door on an unremarkable corner by a bodega, approaching audience members for the second evening could directly see the stage as they walked up the street. Large plate-glass windows adorned with performance-themed words and phrases visually open the venue out to the street, and similar windows, though clear, display the space to the lobby of the larger building that hosted it, Arnhold Hall of The New School, a university in the Greenwich Village neighborhood. The space contained the same number of seats as the venue across town, seventy-four, but with room to spread out; a few feet of empty space separated performers and audience, and one could take in the music without touching thighs with neighboring listeners. The space appeared clean and bright. The bathrooms were out in the lobby, reachable through the theater's two exits. Douglas created a feeling of intimacy in the performance as he chatted with the audience between tunes, at times pointing out fellow trumpet players. He also introduced a dean from The New School, Richard Kessler, who was at the show. At one point, Douglas, who is on The New School faculty, commented, "I feel like we're in school....Does anyone have any questions?"

These two performances both took place at John Zorn's music venue called The Stone. Zorn opened The Stone in 2005, and the bare-bones website that has long functioned as its only form of advertising labels it "a not-for-profit performance space dedicated to the EXPERIMENTAL and AVANT-GARDE" where "all expenses are paid for by the MUSIC itself" through benefit concerts, the sale of CDs, and donations.[1] June 2017 marked the start of a unique moment in The Stone's history, a nine-month transition during which Zorn presented shows in two different spaces, both the original The Stone location and The New School's Glass Box Theater. In March of 2018, the East Village location closed permanently, and The Stone began operating five nights per week, forty-nine weeks per year at The New School. In an interview for *The Village Voice*, Zorn explained the move by saying, "There's no negative or sinister backstory about gentrification. Last summer I walked into The Stone, which remains a magical space. And I thought it was time for a change. I thought we needed something better." Yet, in the same interview, Zorn stated, "Our aesthetic will not alter one bit."[2] Zorn's explanation contains tensions: he frames the move as simultaneously noteworthy and nonchalant, transformative and static. It was time for something better, yet the old space is magical and represents an aesthetic worth maintaining. Indeed, these contradictions in Zorn's artistic standpoint constitute the very aesthetic that defines The Stone. The old Stone established itself not just as a physical music space but as a set of practices and an artistic community defined in part by its location at a point of tension between visibility and invisibility, an intentionally marginal position that remained slippery and undefined. The venue's move from its underground location to a much more visible one does not come with a more straightforward identity or purpose, however, because new tensions replace old ones. The Stone has become more overtly public, but its new place in a major institution for academic music instruction comes with its own set of contradictions, nestled as it is within a jazz educational culture that, as anthropologist Eitan Wilf argues, is ambivalent about its own existence.[3] A nonprofit organization since its conception, The Stone has now moved from a position calculated to serve music to one more oriented toward serving people.

JAZZ BY DEFAULT

I first visited The Stone on a June evening in 2010, and I found my way inside through a process of elimination. I walked to the intersection where I knew it was located and looked around, deciding that it certainly couldn't be the small green space or one of the convenience stores; therefore, it must be through the unremarkable black door. I paid my twenty-dollar admission fee and settled myself amongst a sparse group of other attendees. Without announcement, a recording began to play. Those of us in the audience heard a chord gently stuck by a solo pianist once every five seconds or so, each one made from the selection of notes B, C, C#, D, and E. Each chord changed only slightly from the one before, maintaining mostly common tones within the already extremely restricted pitch space. After several minutes, Tyshawn Sorey—a composer, drummer, and trombonist—faded out the recording and began to discuss his musical interests, background, and techniques in one of The Stone's regular Monday night seminars, where the audience was invited to interact with and learn from the creators of the music they heard there. Sorey's own work offers a good starting point for grasping the musical culture of the venue, as it represents a fairly broad cross-section of the kinds of sounds and traditions that might be drawn upon there. The excerpt he began with was from *Permutations for Solo Piano*, a sprawling forty-three-minute minimalist meditation that was released on Sorey's 2007 album *That/Not*. The subtle solo piano work is set alongside modernist explorations of extended trombone techniques and drastic dynamic contrasts in works like *Leveled* and *Seven Pieces for Trombone Quartet*. The earlier music that brought Sorey to the attention of New York's new music circles, trio playing with the group Fieldwork featuring saxophonist Steve Lehman and pianist Vijay Iyer, is again different, showing more jazz influence in its use of consistent rhythmic grooves and improvisation. His colleague Lehman declares, "I know of no other young composer so intimately familiar with a manifold of compositional histories that includes the work of Morton Feldman, Elvin Jones, Karlheinz Stockhausen and Anthony Braxton, among many others," listing some of Sorey's many musical models from disparate backgrounds, a list to which Sorey himself adds nonmusicians like comedian Andrew Dice Clay.[4] The result, as Sorey described it in his seminar, is music that is "not jazz, not Western art music, not black music." Though this almost completely unadvertised seminar was sparsely attended—I was one of four or five people in the audience—events like this one would play a role in forming the future relationship between The Stone and The New School. After moving to the university setting, seminars became credit-bearing classes that laid groundwork for the whole venue's move.

Sorey's manner of describing his work by pointing out what it isn't models a useful way of thinking about The Stone's role in the New York jazz scene, as his ambivalence toward the word "jazz" as a label for his music is shared by Zorn and many of the other artists featured at the venue. Understanding Zorn's own work as a composer and performer is perhaps the best method of clarifying the type of musical culture he has sought to support with the creation, maintenance, and eventual transformation of this venue that contributes to the New York City jazz scene without fully embracing a jazz identity. While the labels jazz, classical, radical Jewish music, performance art, rock, underground, Downtown, new music, free improvisation, and many more can at times be successfully used to describe aspects of Zorn's music making and the culture of The Stone, they are just as often ineffective. Calling the venue, in both its incarnations, a physical home for Zorn's musical community is ultimately more accurate and useful. The simplest and most common way of describing John Zorn's music, and the manner he tends to choose himself, is to concede that existing labels do not easily encapsulate his remarkably eclectic and diverse career. As a preface to a rare interview (Zorn has a notorious antipathy for the press), Bill Milkowski encourages readers to "think of John Zorn, the American composer, alto saxophonist and conceptualist, as a juggler" who "keeps aloft a plethora of radically different projects while also heading up his own label (Tzadik) and acting as artistic director at The Stone."[5] Among the musical traditions being juggled in this analogy, jazz is an important one. While Zorn does not identify himself as a jazz musician, thinking of the current jazz community in a broad sense without considering his role in it would be as difficult as neatly tucking him within the genre's boundaries. For example, in order to convey Zorn's ascendance in New York City's downtown scene in the late 1970s, long-time *Village Voice* new music columnist Kyle Gann charted a "shift of Downtown activity away from classically trained composers to jazz-based musicians."[6] Yet, in his interview with Milkowski for the magazine *JazzTimes*, Zorn commented, "I thought of myself as more of a classical musician who then got involved with different kinds of players. But the music is not jazz music, it's not classical music, it's not rock music. It's a new kind of music that was loved by people like yourself and other writers who were on that scene in the late '70s to early '80s....But where can you write about this music that you love? What are the outlets? The only outlets were jazz magazines."

In Zorn's own estimation, he has become a "jazz musician" to critics by default, not because he necessarily plays or composes jazz but because his work is perceived as fitting better in existing jazz discourse and infrastructure than in any other pre-established sphere. As he sees it,

> Even though it didn't belong in that tradition [jazz] or in that format, it was the only format that there was. So I feel like that created a deep misunderstanding in what this music is. People started judging this new music with the standards of jazz, with the definitions of what jazz is and isn't, because stories about it appeared in jazz magazines. And now I'll do a gig at the Marciac Jazz Festival and I'll get offstage and Wynton Marsalis will say, "That's not jazz." And I'll say, "You're right! But this is the only gig I've got, man. Give me another festival and I'll play there."[7]

While Marsalis, the cultural figurehead of jazz conservatism and gatekeeping, and Zorn, a living symbol of the avant-garde, agree that Zorn's music is not jazz, its consistent inclusion in the jazz world has by now made it an essential point of reference—Zorn and his colleagues have come to represent the border between contemporary jazz and a yet-to-be-defined something else.

Zorn's path to becoming a central figure of music's margins began with a childhood in New York City during the 1950s and '60s, during which he was already exposed to musical styles as diverse as Western classical composition lessons with Leonardo Balada and playing bass in a surf rock band. After attending college in the Midwest and spending a brief period on the West Coast, Zorn returned to New York in the mid-1970s and became a part of the musical culture George Lewis refers to as "Downtown II." In general, "downtown" musicians are associated with the informal, countercultural loft scene that emerged during the 1960s in lower Manhattan, and the term places "downtown" in contrast to the major repertory ensembles of Lincoln Center dubbed "midtown" and the high modernist academics of "uptown." Lewis's division into "Downtowns I and II" reflects some of the musical diversity of this geographically and culturally similar scene. The "Downtown I" generation was made up of experimentalist and minimalist composers like John Cage, La Monte Young, and Philip Glass. "Downtown II" composer-performers like Zorn, coming to prominence a decade or so later, performed in similar spaces and with a similarly oppositional stance to the more institutionalized art music world while tending to favor a musical style more rooted in improvisation in general and jazz in particular than that of their "Downtown I" predecessors, a distinction linked to influences like Zorn's exposure to the Black Artist Group (BAG) and the Association for the Advancement of Creative Musicians (AACM).[8]

Zorn attended Webster College in St. Louis, where he began to play saxophone and encountered the experimentalist work of the BAG and AACM, artists who would influence not only his music making but also the manner of presentation he would later adopt at The Stone. While his interest in composition began earlier, Zorn remembers his first serious work as a performer beginning in his late teens, recalling that, "at eighteen or nineteen I started studying jazz saxophone." He elaborated by saying, "It was exactly what I needed to do at that time. I needed to be exposed to the black jazz scene in Chicago, AACM, and BAG in St. Louis: Anthony Braxton, Leo Smith."[9] Significantly, the two organizations and two musicians that Zorn names were part of an interconnected musical community in the Midwest that had just as contentious a relationship to the word "jazz" as Zorn himself does, despite his use of the genre marker to describe them in this passage. Both saxophonist Braxton and trumpeter Smith were members of the Chicago-based AACM, a group with which the BAG of St. Louis had overlapping membership. In his extensive writing on the AACM, Lewis emphasizes the careful consideration founding musicians put into structuring and naming their organization. Through numerous meetings and discussions, they ultimately decided to promote what they called original music or creative music—not jazz, per se. Based on his observation of tapes of early meetings, Lewis reports that, "in direct contradiction to the overwhelming majority of critical commentary on the AACM, terms such as 'new jazz,' 'the avant-garde,' or 'free jazz' were seldom, if ever, used in the discussions."[10] The members of the AACM, although often interested and trained in jazz, considered their experimental music to be distinct from it. Some of the concern surrounding genre labels was rooted in issues of race. According to Lewis, the assumption that work by AACM musicians is necessarily jazz is especially problematic because of the racialized boundaries it creates between different bodies of experimental music, a gesture that "comes bundled with an attempt to discursively revoke the mobility of the musicians themselves." He continues by noting that, unlike their black counterparts, "musicians of other ethnicities have historically been free to migrate conceptually and artistically without suffering charges of rejecting their culture and history."[11] Lewis goes on to offer two reviews by the same writer, one of which celebrates Zorn's ability to "transcend categories."[12] In describing Braxton, an African American saxophonist and AACM member who strongly influenced Zorn's approach to the instrument, the reviewer asserts, "however much he may resist categories, Mr. Braxton's background is in jazz."[13] As a white musician, Zorn can successfully escape boundaries that black musicians cannot.

I point out these racial inequalities not to undermine Zorn's achievements or suggest that he is immune to racially based attacks—indeed, he says he has been accused by black colleagues of being a "cultural imperialist" for "ripping off the blues"—but to express the power and desirability of the position he has established for himself on the margins of a musical tradition.[14] Zorn has access to jazz as a point of reference for the creation of musical meaning, but he also has the flexibility to escape it. Work that has a clear relationship to jazz history, like his 1989 recording project with fellow saxophonist Tim Berne based on the music of Ornette Coleman called *Spy vs Spy*, benefits from jazz's growing art music prestige and communicates to audiences through a familiar landmark. Yet, by declaring himself "not a jazz musician," Zorn is free to depart from Coleman's work without being held accountable for betraying tradition or simply not succeeding in jazz. Jazz gives significance to the project, and fitting into the music's margins rather than its body gives Zorn options and opportunities to experiment with unorthodox sounds and techniques.

It is through his manipulation of boundaries that Zorn has created spaces for his music, both metaphorically and physically. In his 2008 study of Zorn's work, musicologist John Brackett summarizes what he calls "Zorn's musical poetics" not in terms of specific sounds or compositional techniques, which are indeed extremely diverse, but as reflective of a consistent attitude he refers to as a "tradition of transgression." Acknowledging that the many musicians, artists, and thinkers Zorn names as influences vary remarkably, Brackett also points out a general commonality among them: They are "the marginalia of the avant-garde" in their respective fields. As an example, Brackett points to Zorn's interest in surrealism as an avant-garde movement. He writes, "Most of Zorn's surrealist influences are drawn from the work of individuals who operated at the margins of surrealism. For instance, in Zorn's compositional output there are no works dedicated to Dalí, Aragon, Magritte, or other 'mainstream' figures typically associated with surrealism. Instead, figures like Bataille and Artaud appear prominently...individuals who were both 'expelled' from the surrealist circle by [André] Breton."[15] While the surrealists themselves were on the margins of mainstream thought and art, Zorn is more attracted to the work of Georges Bataille, an outsider to the core of the surrealist movement founded by André

Breton, than by its better-known representatives. After reading Bataille, Zorn composed his string quartet *The Dead Man*, inspired by a Bataille short story of the same name, and the liner notes to his *Black Box* quote Bataille at length.[16] Indeed, it is from Bataille that Brackett draws a definition of transgression that he employs throughout his analysis of Zorn's music. From this perspective, Brackett argues, transgression represents not so much a matter of crossing boundaries between two traditionally separate fields as of existing in and expanding those boundaries themselves: "Zorn doesn't seek to topple and replace one set of aesthetic/ideological/discursive structures with another. Instead, he chooses to work within the nearly imperceptible spaces of seemingly opposed structures, an attitude and practice I will describe as *transgressive*."[17] Zorn's transgression does not create synthesis between existing styles or codify a new set of artistic guidelines—it relies on the guidelines set by others as a means of entering an undefined marginal space. With the establishment of The Stone, Zorn created a physical site that embodied his musical and philosophical modes of transgression, a musical space existing in the margins. With the venue's move, he has shifted The Stone from one margin to another, continuing to push back against stable categorization and mainstream identity.

HIDING AND SEEKING

Although The Stone can be conceptualized as occupying many different margins, including the musical space between the traditional and the radical as explored by Brackett, the original Stone's placement at a point of tension between visibility and invisibility is particularly germane to understanding the significance of its physical move from Alphabet City to The New School. In the preface to a book Zorn published in 2007, two years after opening the original Stone location, he wrote, "To survive in this world of distractions and adversity, good music has gone underground, becoming more invisible than ever. It is always there, but to find it one has to make an effort.... Although [underground artists] live in this world and suffer its rules in various ways and to different degrees, they are for the most part outsiders. But they are not outsiders looking in. They are outsiders looking *out*—toward a beautiful new world of truth and beauty."[18] This passage reveals both Zorn's attraction to invisibility and his utopian aspirations for art that fosters a brighter future. Despite his relatively high profile in experimental music circles, Zorn chose to keep the old Stone largely hidden from the world for self-preservation, but he also claimed the art presented there had the power to contribute to a better world.

Peggy Phelan's theory of the unmarked offers one explanation for how The Stone's underground status, its voluntary disenfranchisement, could be maintained as desirable. Essentially, Phelan questions the assumption that greater visibility necessarily leads to greater political power, suggesting that, for example, "If representational visibility equals power, then almost-naked young white women should be running Western culture."[19] Phelan argues that outsiders may access a different route to creating meaning by remaining outside, invisible, or without label:

> I am not suggesting that continued invisibility is the "proper" political agenda for the disenfranchised, but rather that the binary between the power of visibility and the impotency of invisibility is falsifying. There is real power in remaining unmarked; and there are serious limitations to visual representation as a political goal.[20]

Without denying limited visibility's problematic nature in efforts to assert political power, Phelan suggests greater visibility does not guarantee a more positive position with regard to the dominant culture. She continues by saying, "Visibility is a trap...it summons surveillance and the law; it provokes voyeurism, fetishism, the colonialist/imperial appetite for possession. Yet it retains a certain political appeal." Because of the problems of relying on visibility, Phelan suggests making an effort to read the significance of not just what is easily seen but also the things we cannot directly observe. Using photography as a metaphor, she writes, "the words I have lined up here attempt to (re)develop the negative, not in order to produce a clearer print, but rather to see what it would mean to use the negative itself as a way of securing belief in one's self-image."[21] Phelan's suggestion to "(re)develop the negative," to consider the possible meanings of the aspects of representation that remain unseen, unheard, or immaterial, offers another way of reading musical practices at The Stone in terms of what they don't do, and that reading can bring Zorn's aspirations for social change and his avoidance of mainstream exposure and practical labels into more meaningful contact. As Zorn phrased it in a recent interview about The Stone's move, "That was just my aesthetic. Keeping things underground, keeping them hard to find was a way of protecting the artist and the music, and putting the audience through a certain vetting process where they have to actually make an effort to find the place."[22] Zorn, however, has recalibrated the balancing point between invisible self-preservation and the need to affect change in a broader world since The Stone's opening fourteen years ago. In 2017, he said, "In the climate we now exist in—in this political, economic and social climate—it's time for artists to step up and make a statement....And maybe that needs to involve a more visible place."[23]

There is no denying that existing in the original Stone's negative space places certain boundaries around its power to contribute to or alter musical culture on a large scale. Zorn cultivates "incomprehension" as a response to his music by persistently pushing it away from attempts at linguistic labels, relying on the benefits of being on the undefined fringes of his art world.[24] Barbara Kirschenblatt-Gimblett explains how this strategy has been a part of avant-garde artistic practices for quite some time, making a tradition of being nontraditional and therefore inaccessible to conventional explanation or description: "Values derived from the historical avant-garde before World War II and from experimental performance during the postwar period...offer keys to the special pleasures afforded by the incomprehensible and, beyond pleasure, to the importance of making audiences experience, rather than interpret, what they see."[25] Kirschenblatt-Gimblett acknowledges this enticing idea of the immediacy of an encounter between art and its audience, yet she also insists on the importance of "challeng[ing] the idea that art does not mediate. That it speaks directly. Or, that when art speaks, it does so in a universal 'non-language.'"[26] In the end, Zorn's efforts to remain as unmarked as possible form their own kind of frame through which the music at The Stone has been interpreted, and defining his project through the negative reduces one type of vulnerability only to replace it with another. By trying to remain on the outside, radical, independent, and unnamed, Zorn loses control of the discursive box in which others place The Stone.

In his work on the experimental music scene in New York City during the mid-1960s, Benjamin Piekut makes the argument that, indeed, much of the discourse that has made experimentalism into a recognizable category has come from the scholars that stepped into this open interpretive space. He writes, "There is no imaginary space where sounds and an 'experimental spirit' meet up and sort themselves into a tradition. They require human organizers to group them together, and because sounds cannot articulate arguments for themselves, the scholar must engage in acts of translation, the rendering of differences into equivalence."[27] Piekut describes the musical practices now referred to as experimentalist as "a grouping, not a group," that has "[come] into being *through* conflict and disagreement."[28] In his analysis, many of Zorn's precursors in the last half-century of avant-garde music making in New York are thought of collectively despite their individual commitments to breaking away from categorization because of the discourses that have been built around them. "To explain what experimentalism has been, one must attend to its fabrication through a network of discourses, practices, and institutions. This formation is the result of the combined labor of scholars, composers, critics, journalists, patrons, performers, venues, and the durative effects of discourses of race, gender, nation, and class. The continuing performance of this network—and not an experimental 'ethos' or 'spirit'—explains the extension of experimentalism through time."[29]

Music, whether intentionally labeled or interpreted by its creator or not, is never fully autonomous from the cultural networks that surround it. Zorn's choice to discuss his work through a language of what it is not cannot prevent others from deciding what it is.

As Judith Butler argues, "We ascribe an agency to language, a power to injure, and position ourselves as the objects of its injurious trajectory." Submitting to language makes us vulnerable, yet Butler goes on to suggest that it also provides both an identity and an opportunity to define that identity: "One is not simply fixed by the name that one is called. In being called an injurious name, one is derogated and demeaned. But the name holds out another possibility as well: by being called a name, one is also, paradoxically, given a certain possibility for social existence, initiated into a temporal life of language that exceeds the prior purposes that animate that call. Thus the injurious address may appear to fix or paralyze the one it hails, but it may also produce an unexpected and enabling response."[30] To be named brings one into existence and all its possible futures. Butler's solution to the application of damaging labels is not to resist their use but to alter their meaning by taking on that use.

> To take up the name that one is called is no simple submission to prior authority, for the name is already unmoored from prior context, and entered into the labor of self-definition. The word that wounds becomes an instrument of resistance in the redeployment that destroys the prior territory of its operation.[31]

By denying labels and descriptions of music, leaving it to communicate not—as Kirschenblatt-Gimblett reminds us—with true immediacy, but with a lack of words that holds its own suggestive powers, musicians might achieve a certain freedom from language, but they sacrifice the power of self-definition and, with it, a place in the discourse that would pertain to them. Zorn's choice to move The Stone into both a more visible location and an institutional partnership is a step in the direction of self-definition, a step toward more intentionally and legibly performing a place in an existing network. This change reorients the mission of the venue from a stance that strives to serve music itself to one that leverages that music to serve a broader community.

SERVING MUSIC IN THE EAST VILLAGE

The Stone opened its doors in 2005 bearing the name of longtime downtown music supporters Irving and Stephanie Stone, a pair Michael Heller refers to as "the city's most ardent and ever-present supporters of experimental music starting in the 1970s."[32] In addition to honoring important supporters of the scene, this name marks the venue as connected to its neighborhood and community, placing it as a continuation of loft jazz culture extending back decades in the same part of the city. Although the original Stone location could not be deemed a loft by architectural standards, the ethos of Zorn and his associates echoed a local loft jazz culture that "generally focused on the creative possibilities enabled by the presence of large, raw spaces. By emphasizing the liberatory potential of blank space, rather than the nostalgic echoes of industrial place, organizers stressed underlying values of reclamation and community-building."[33] Though this restaurant-turned-music-space was small and dark rather than large and bright like the former industrial lofts sought by Manhattan artists in earlier decades, its treatment as an empty container in which to build an artistic community bears a likeness to established attitudes toward space and art making in the neighborhood. The space's policies were designed to keep music at the center of experience there, even if that meant audience members had to sacrifice certain conveniences and comforts that they might normally have expected from a music venue. To begin with, prospective listeners had to find out about—and find—a venue that relied primarily on its own website and word-of-mouth for advertising. While waiting in line to attend shows, it was not uncommon for passersby to approach me to ask what went on in the practically unmarked building, as not so much as a listing of that evening's performer appeared outside. Listeners were also held responsible for arriving on time. In addition to the lack of advance ticket sales for the limited seating (a couple of cushions for sitting on the floor were handed out after the seventy-four chairs were filled), the volunteers handling admission often prioritized avoiding disruptions over expanding the size of the audience. Jazz critic Howard Mandel describes his first attempt at attending a performance at The Stone as follows: "The first time, I couldn't find its tiny sign on a dark door, then was discouraged by a greeter-with-attitude from entering midperformance, told there'd be a second cover charge to hear the second act of the night. The Stone's spartan policies also put me off. There's no drinking (water, much less booze), no snacks, and the audience sits in rows of flimsy chairs. It's all about the music and musicians.... It's very respectful, but not relaxing or sociable."[34] As Mandel's account suggests, the original Stone presented music not as a service to the audience—the audience was responsible for submitting to the needs of the music. For example, in addition to the lack of food, drink, and comfortable chairs, a frequently mentioned hazard of summertime Stone performances was the use of a single window-box air conditioner, routinely turned off as performances began so that its noise did not interfere with the music. When pianist Sylvie Courvoisier's group Lonelyville performed on a hot June night in 2010, the musicians were sharing a handkerchief to wipe away sweat between tunes until violinist Mark Feldman eventually asked the volunteer at the door to turn the air conditioner back on, regardless of noise. This small lapse in principles was met with the grateful applause of equally sweaty audience members stuck to plastic seats.

Audience responses to the space in the form of online reviews demonstrate how The Stone's policies led to the formation of a self-selecting audience willing to put the needs of the music above its own. For example, the aforementioned lack of air conditioning kept some first-time audience members from returning for a second show. As one online reviewer put it, "Though I would be willing to check it out again in the winter, I don't think I would want to go in the summer again, to quietly suffocate in the stuffy room with little fresh air. But I suppose you go for the music, anyway."[35] Another found the lack of amenities "sterile," commenting that the absence of recorded music between sets and fact that photography and beverages were not allowed in the venue would continue to detract from its "good potential" until "whoever runs this place loosens up a bit."[36] While most reviews mentioned discomfort or inconvenience in one way or another, a core audience for the venue appeared to either find these drawbacks insignificant compared to the musical experience or even consider the absence of typical club perks a significant advantage. One listener said, "From what I remember, The Stone is one windowless room that is cramped and smells like a sweaty body when full. I can't imagine it being the ideal place to sit back and listen to smooth jazz; however, it seemed to work well for the show I saw/heard. In fact, I think the extreme discomfort of the space added to the aura of the art performance."[37] Reviewers like this one indicated through their commentary that the sense of enduring some unpleasant features of the space heightened their overall enjoyment of performances by framing them as extremely important. In this description, a style of music intended for easy listening like smooth jazz is considered inappropriate for The Stone, but experiencing "art" there is worth a certain level of suffering. Another review states, "As far as performance venues go, The Stone is purely a no-frills establishment—and that's what makes it so great. It's literally just a room with some folding chairs. No stage, no bar, no distractions."[38] In addition to appreciating the absence of anything to distract the audience from the music, several reviewers commented on the intimacy of the space and the fact that the audience seemed united in an intention to focus on the music. One wrote, "We went to see Fred Frith and Laurie Anderson, waiting with coffees in the cold for 45 minutes once we had paid the admission. The space was small and chaotic, but I loved the atmosphere. Everyone in attendance was so excited and respectful of the performance which I think the venue 100% adds to."[39] Small trials like waiting outside in winter weather became both badges of honor that proved the dedication of listeners.

Another form of sacrifice for the sake of music Zorn built into the original Stone was committing to self-sufficiency through the avoidance of outside funding. As Amanda Scherbenske describes the old location prior to the transition, "The Stone modifies the typical funding model of a not-for-profit cultural center. Rather than combining private, public, and ticket-sale revenue, it subsists on time and talent donation, private financial contribution, and spatial subsidy (rent below market rate)."[40] The Stone's website proclaimed, "We receive no grants, and give 100% of our nightly revenue to the musicians." Instead, the space was maintained through the sale of its music in the form of "rent party" benefits, regular fundraising concerts of improvised music in which Zorn and his collaborators donated their time and music, the sale of a series of CDs recorded there, and low rent prices based in Zorn's friendship with building owner Ela Dopazo. To supplement these fundraisers, donations were accepted, but the transparency provided by listing the names of donors on the website showed that nearly all donors are private individuals, including some musicians who performed there.[41] Scherbenske writes, "The language [used to describe patronage on the website] is suggestive of survival and subsistence, a move that distances the Stone from greed, commercialization, and related capitalist associations. These actions instrumentalize ideology: they suggest that patronage is individual rather than corporate, privilege community formation over institutionalization, and evade the Stone's participation in the arts as economy."[42] While the venue on one hand celebrated its economic role by highlighting its policy for compensating musicians, its fundraising rhetoric also suggests a lack of participation in capitalist systems. Giving money to The Stone was painted as a form of resistance through which a community with shared artistic values could be self-supporting in the face of rising rents in a changing neighborhood; paradoxically, money given represented, in part, the belief that money should not be central to the project of creating and performing music. By limiting the role of other agencies and corporations in their presentation of music and avoiding framing it as an entertaining service, The Stone maintained a high degree of control over artistic content that generated both financial and cultural capital necessary for the venue's subsistence.

Grants are not the only thing The Stone does not accept in maintaining an autonomous musical community—they also "do not accept demos of any kind."[43] Just as potential audience members essentially needed inside information to find the nearly unlabeled and unadvertised venue, musicians needed connections to The Stone's community in order to perform there because of the curatorial system of booking, a system that continues in the new location. Curating is simultaneously open-ended and exclusive. Pianist Sylvie Courvoisier, who curated The Stone for a month in 2010, explained the process of becoming a curator by simply saying, "John asks people to curate." Once selected, Courvoisier and her spouse and cocurator, violinist Mark Feldman, were free to book any musicians they chose. She said the bookings "went fast" because they "know so many musicians," and they decided to emphasize their own instruments by primarily choosing other pianists and string players from among their circle of friends and musical collaborators.[44] Like most curators, they also featured themselves, performing as a duo for both sets one evening, in a quartet with bassist Thomas Morgan and drummer Gerry Hemingway another, and with the ensemble Lonelyville later in the month. They also appeared individually with many of the other musicians they hired, with Courvoisier performing on five additional sets and Feldman on three.

The tastes and connections of each curator led to significant shifts in the musical offerings of The Stone, playing off the idea of curation in art galleries and museums by turning monthly or weekly musical programming into a unified collection or exhibition. While Courvoisier and Feldman presented a month of piano and strings, material offered just the previous month took an entirely different form. Curator Henry Kaiser kicked off May 2010 with a duo performance for guitar and balloon twisting performed by himself and accompanist "Cookie the Clown" that he announced under the heading of this enthusiastic nod to eclecticism: "Curated by Henry Kaiser / A special week of events curated by the legendary experimental guitarist, research diver, filmmaker Henry Kaiser. Included will be his first-ever performance with a NY comedian also named Henry Kaiser, some unlikely pairings, a lecture on Antarctica and plenty of guitar fireworks."[45] Each curator brings a distinct flavor to the venue when granted the freedom to design a week's or month's programming, essentially crafting a personalized subset of the new music community and tying it together at The Stone. For example, Alicia Svigals, former violinist for the band the Klezmatics, based her month's choices around three different groups to which she belongs by choosing "all kinds of fiddlers, women instrumentalists and Jewish music" after Zorn told her, "Go for it, just book the stuff you like."[46]

Given the fact that musicians choose each other to perform at The Stone, it is not surprising that they are often in the audience as well as on stage. Courvoisier says that in addition to playing and curating there, she attends a lot of her colleague's performances, like those of trumpeter Peter Evans, guitarist Elliott Sharp, and electronics specialist Ikue Mori.[47] The musicians Courvoisier hired also came out to hear each other—clarinetist Chris Speed played with the Ben Perowsky Quartet early in the month and returned to the venue as an audience member for drummer Jim Black's trio performance a couple weeks later, and Black himself came back to hear pianist Craig Taborn's solo performance another night. Svigals described her feelings about the shows she curated by saying, "When I was all done with the programming, I thought I'd like to move into the place with a sleeping bag and see them all. I programmed a lot of people because I want to hear them myself."[48] While the invitation-only curation system makes The Stone more exclusive, it also encourages a sense of community by allowing musicians to choose the music they most want to play and hear and the colleagues with whom they want to work.

There seem to be few limits on the creative use of The Stone by the musicians who work there, and the old space was host to a variety of events that went beyond its regular concert programming. During her month as curator, Laurie Anderson extended the use of the venue as a space for community building by partnering with theater director Anna Brenner in offering what they called the Stone Open House, or SOH, each Sunday afternoon. They summarized these events as follows: "From the practical to the theoretical, SOH will be a place to hang out, drink great coffee, read, listen to unusual presentations and invent alternative ways to live and work. Part think tank, part party, SOH will host a series of presentations that cover a wide range of topics—from the history of boilers to teaching music to dogs. SOH will present a library of must-read books for people interested in expanding in unpredictable ways."[49] Later, composer and pianist Karl Berger carried out a multi-month residency with The Stone Workshop Orchestra, a band that met weekly for rehearsals and performances. Starting in April of 2011, any interested musicians were encouraged to bring instruments and participate, and after a group was established, latecomers were still invited to email Berger about playing with the ensemble. The project culminated in a December concert featuring the ensemble's twenty-nine regular members and an array of guest soloists. These types of open-ended participatory events highlighted The Stone's tenuous balancing act at the border of inclusivity and exclusivity in which a sense of community created through open dialogue and collaboration challenged the closed curatorial system. For thirteen years, this self-supporting community that placed music and artistic freedom at its center remained vibrant despite and because of its place in the largely invisible margins. While the old space is now closed, the community that formed there, including musicians, volunteers, and listeners, established a clear enough ethos and identity to make it possible to conceive of the venue as something that can exist without the physical space in which it originated.

A PURCHASE MADE WITH CULTURAL CAPITAL

Through its uncompromising stance and long-standing presence, the original Stone amassed cultural value that has made it desirable beyond the confines of a former Lower East Side Chinese restaurant. The Stone's new location is indeed more visible in the literal sense of its move to a glass room on a busier street in a denser neighborhood, and it is also more geographically connected to the most concentrated hub of the city's jazz scene. While the Lower East Side has been home to a number of noteworthy jazz venues over the years, including musician-run performance sites in lofts, Slugs' Saloon, the Knitting Factory, and Tonic, by 2017, the old Stone location was more or less alone as a jazz space in its immediate neighborhood. In a press release written at the time of Tonic's closure in 2007 by a group of musicians advocating for public funding for experimental music venues, the neighborhood's situation was described as follows: "Coming on the heels of the closing of CBGC's, Sin-e, Fez, the Continental, and numerous other downtown venues, the closing of Tonic represents the continued shutting down of NYC's hugely important live music experimental jazz, indie, and new music scene.…Tonic is the last new music/indie/avant jazz venue in Manhattan with a capacity above 90, presenting concerts on a nightly basis. It is also the last such venue in the city with the relatively musician friendly policy of paying 75% of the door receipts."[50] While The Stone continued to offer experimental music in the Lower East Side for another decade, it did so on a smaller scale, with less visibility, and with an explicitly independent and nonprofit mission. In its new location, The Stone is within easy walking distance of several of the city's highest-profile clubs, including the Village Vanguard, the Blue Note, the Jazz Standard, and Smalls Jazz Club, as well as a number of other venues that regularly feature live jazz, including the Cornelia Street Café, 55 Bar, and Fat Cat. While the former building stands a half mile from the nearest subway station, The New School address is just around the corner from one station and in close proximity to a couple others, making it easily accessible by several different train lines with connections to various locations uptown and in Brooklyn. The new space is within easy reach for students of not just The New School but also nearby New York University, which boasts a substantial jazz studies degree program.

The residents of The Stone's new neighborhood are significantly more affluent on average than those near the old venue. While the Lower East Side in general is considered to be gentrifying, causing the market value of the building housing the venue to increase four-fold over ten years, the original Stone location is also just a block away from the home of some of the city's poorest residents.[51] For example, Public School 188, which is two tenths of a mile down the street, is surrounded on all sides by public housing projects and had a student population that was, as of 2015, 47 percent homeless.[52] According to 2010 census data, the median household income in the blocks surrounding The New School was just over $100,000 annually, and household incomes around the old Avenue C location were on average more than $20,000 per year lower. Moreover, The New School is surrounded by other census districts that are equally or more affluent, while the old Stone was surrounded by less affluent districts—walking two blocks in any direction from the old Stone brings one to a district with incomes at or below the national median, including places where the median household incomes were as low as $18,000 per year.[53] In addition to the high incomes of local residents that could correlate with disposable income spent on live music, the new Stone location's relative economic prosperity makes it a more appealing destination for tourists and New Yorkers from other neighborhoods, as high-end options for dining and shopping are numerous on all sides and the dense population of tourists and residents creates an atmosphere with an immediate appearance of both vibrant activity and relative safety, a textbook example of what Adam Krims would call integrated, aestheticized space in that it "unites not only the design intensity but also the tourism, cultural regeneration, privatization, personal services, and even the agglomeration of workers in information-dependent production" characteristic of affluent urban neighborhoods in post-Fordist cities.[54]

In addition to moving regular performances at The Stone to The New School, Zorn expanded the venue's offerings to include regular monthly shows in two other places that are, in comparison to the old Stone, significantly more audience-friendly and publicly visible. One location offers a continuation of The Stone's presence on the Lower East Side. Russ & Daughters Cafe, a restaurant that opened in 2014 as an extension of a family-owned Jewish appetizing store that has been in the neighborhood since the early twentieth century, advertises The Stone music series on a poster that reads "Smoked Fish, Pickles, Music Nights." Food and drink specials are offered alongside music with no cover charge, and the series, curated by Zorn, features a number of noteworthy artists associated with the downtown scene, including Bill Frisell and Laurie Anderson. While still on the Lower East Side, Russ & Daughters is part of a street full of high-end restaurants near the Blue Tower luxury condominiums that opened across the street from the former location of Tonic in the same year the club closed due to skyrocketing rents, a very different neighbor than the blocks of housing projects a comparable walk from the old Stone. Zorn's expansion also now reaches across the river to National Sawdust, a twentieth-century sawdust factory converted into a twenty-first-century new music venue in Brooklyn's Williamsburg neighborhood. National Sawdust opened in 2015, nestled amongst coffee shops, restaurants, boutiques, parks along the river, and other music venues in an area noted for both its arts scene and its rapid gentrification since the mid-1990s. The monthly Stone series there features new commissions, which guitarist Julian Lage described during his June 2017 performance as "another word for a dare," highlighting the intersection between The Stone's aesthetic of marginality and National Sawdust's mission to support new work. Inside the venue, a carefully designed performance area offers comfortable seating, clear sight lines, state-of-the-art soundproofing to prevent noise from the street, and a bar that offers extras unavailable at the old music-only Stone.

While The Stone at The New School doesn't provide listeners with cocktails or pickled fish to enjoy alongside the music, it is not without its extras—performances in a university setting have an implicit educational purpose. The New School, a university with around ten thousand total students, houses both the Mannes School of Music and the School of Jazz and Contemporary Music. Zorn has essentially bought space for his venue there, but money was not the currency in play as The Stone moved into the Glass Box Theater rent free. As The New School's executive dean for the performing arts and Dean of Mannes Richard Kessler put it, "the money thing really wasn't the big deal." Instead, Kessler described the experimental, boundary-pushing ethos of The Stone as the value Zorn's venue provided to the university:

> The New School has an extraordinary history, especially in its first thirty to fifty years, connected to experimental artists. Martha Graham taught there, John Cage taught there, Henry Cowell taught there, Erwin Piscator led the dramatic workshop...Brecht was involved in various ways, Tennessee Williams, Frank Lloyd Wright, it's kind of extraordinary....And the Stone and many of the things we're doing with our program...[are] partially intended to reanimate that—for the New School to once again become a center for experimental work and artists of the highest order. So in that case...we thought we were getting something.[55]

While The Stone has access to free space at The New School and continues to give all proceeds to the musicians who perform there, Kessler and others at the university feel that they are gaining enough of The Stone community's experimentalist prestige to make the arrangement worthwhile.

While money may not have been the sole or primary issue that brought The Stone to The New School, it was not absent from discussions of the transition. Indeed, Scherbenske's writing on the Stone draws attention to the venue's long-standing pattern of denying or sidestepping typical relationships between art and money and also using that appearance of autonomy to generate necessary financial support: "At the Stone...affective labor is mobilized for its management to perform community and to highlight its valuation of art as autonomous from economy, downplaying institutionalization and ties to capitalism despite a modus operandi that continuously and deliberately engages with materiality."[56] Leading up to the move in November of 2017, The Stone ran an online crowd-sourced fundraiser, noting in the description that "The Stone is currently running at a $20,000 deficit and will incur more costs with the move to our new location on 13th Street."[57] This suggests that the move to a rent-free location may have been necessary for the venue's long-term survival, but it does not necessarily mean that The Stone gained everything and spent nothing in its transaction with The New School. While both Kessler and Zorn have dismissed laments on the closure of the East Village location as overly romanticizing and nostalgic, some have been sorry to see the old space go. As drummer Greg Fox told journalist Sasha Frere-Jones, "The old Stone, as uncomfortable as it may have been in certain ways, worked. You go in there, you're looking at the stage, there's nowhere else to go, the lights are blacked out, that's it, and that's what makes it work."[58] The venue's closing week in February of 2018 drew large crowds hoping to take in one last show before the move. On a cold, drizzly Saturday night, the second to last on Avenue C, a line was forming outside two hours before the scheduled 8:30 p.m. start time. By 7:45, enough people were in line to fill the venue, including all the cushions on the floor at the musicians' feet and some standing room behind the performance area. A bass player warned audience members to watch out for their eyes when he used his bow, concerned about poking them, and the musicians stepped over listeners' bodies to get on and off the stage. In a decision reflecting the small-scale, community-run nature of the venue, the show simply started early once the audience was packed in. An opening set kicked off a half hour earlier than planned, and, meanwhile, a line continued to grow outside. At the close of the set, Zorn announced that a second, unscheduled set would be performed, and those at the first set were welcomed to stay along with those who had waited outside, "If you pay twenty dollars more. We need the money." The man sitting next to me, who had travelled from Philadelphia for the performance, confessed that although he had thoroughly enjoyed the music, he was ready to leave. The chairs were just too uncomfortable.

While audiences were clearly attached to the old space and its uncompromising, art-focused atmosphere, Zorn was willing to risk any loss of mystique that came with the East Village closure. Shortly after the move, he said, "You know, thirteen years, we had a lot of complaints from artists about the space, about this, about that.... Now that we've closed it, of course, it's a very nostalgic place now, now they're not remembering all of that.... That's bullshit."⁵⁹ Zorn's fierce resistance to this nostalgia was in evidence at the end of the final set of music performed at the old location. He had invited an audience member, Scott Robinson, up to sit in on the last improvisation of the night. Robinson's slide saxophone seemed like an appropriately hybrid and unusual instrument to be the last one to sound in the old space, but Zorn did not draw out the evening to great lengths or linger sentimentally over the end of an era. He spent most of the final performance watching from near the stairs to the green room, playing little, and eventually, as Robinson improvised with closed eyes, Zorn stepped forward to tap him on the arm, indicating that it was time to end the performance and close the venue. After Robinson's final notes, Zorn announced loudly, "Goodbye to The Stone. We will open on Tuesday."

Through his rhetoric at this moment of transition, Zorn separates the geography and community linked in the original Stone; his "we" can both say goodbye to the old space and "open" again two days later. Ten years earlier, guitarist Marc Ribot and musician and activist Rebecca Moore were arrested while performing at Tonic in an act of protest after the space had formally closed with an improvised performance by Zorn the prior evening. For Ribot and similarly minded artist, the specific location of Tonic was one of its essential features. As he wrote, "Those of us involved in the Tonic action...saw the relocation of many clubs to Brooklyn as a geographic and economic marginalization that would hurt rates of pay."⁶⁰ In addition to this economic concern, Ribot called it "culturally barbarous...that the internationally and critically recognized value of this music should be without an adequate, well-advertised, and easily accessible showcase in its place of birth."⁶¹ Downtown music, to Ribot, belonged downtown. At the time, Zorn's underground venue was nearby but largely hidden. When it moved into the light, it also moved out of the neighborhood, suggesting that this music's community is either not geographically grounded in the Lower East Side or no longer has the ability or will to occupy that space.

SERVING THROUGH MUSIC AT THE NEW SCHOOL'S MARGINS

While on the surface a formal institution for musical training and a semihidden experimental artists' space may appear to have little common ground, both entities share The Stone's undercurrent of paradox that comes with exploring the margins of traditionally separate artistic spheres. The School of Jazz and Contemporary Media was one of two research sites informing Eitan Wilf's *School for Cool: The Academic Jazz Program and the Paradox of Institutionalized Creativity*. The central tension Wilf addresses in his consideration of what he terms the *academization* of jazz since the later decades of the twentieth century comes between long-standing conceptions of jazz creativity that valorize individual expression achieved through informal on-the-job training with established masters of the music and a university's "modern rationality, the search for universal and standardized knowledge, and the formalization of rules of action and cognitive schemata that all students ought to follow." As Wilf argues, "the figure of the academically accredited artist generates anxiety and ambivalence because it is neither here nor there; it is a boundary figure that threatens the integrity of both narratives."[62] According to his analysis, The New School's jazz program has both navigated and perpetuated this tension through its employment of "musicians who played with the charismatic past jazz masters to serve as educators in...an attempt to routinize charisma in a permanent organizational structure" despite the risk that "such routinized charisma might occasionally threaten to backfire and undermine the institutional structure itself."[63] Thus, as Zorn, already a "boundary figure" in numerous other ways, enters The New School, he enters yet another marginal space, this time between the formal institution and the real or imagined outside scene. Wilf writes,

> two social forces (out of many) that have led to the rise of academic jazz education in its present form...[are] first, the desire to elevate jazz's traditionally marginal status in the American cultural hierarchy by introducing it into the institutions of high art, including those of music education; and second, the need to create alternative jazz scenes, in lieu of the increasingly nonviable commercial ones.[64]

The Stone's move is linked to both these forces, supporting Wilf's conclusion that, "Put simply, at the present moment jazz programs *are* the reconfigured jazz scenes of the past."[65] What The Stone loses in radical independence and the possible power of invisibility, it trades for, among other things, a higher profile, a direct link to aspiring musicians with the potential to expand its community, and the support and resources of a large-scale institution.

Yet, Zorn's relationship to that institution is characteristically idiosyncratic and murky. Dave Douglas pushed back against a question I posed him suggesting The Stone's move could be neatly categorized in the broader trend of jazz academization, saying, "I have not seen this at any other university or institution. It's a radical experiment."[66] Kessler detailed the unusual nature of the relationship between the institution and the venue that grew from his personal relationship with Zorn. Beginning by describing Zorn's partnering with an institution as "unprecedented," Kessler went on to explain that, "The big deal was, John's not a contract signer.... We had to figure out a way to construct an agreement that essentially would be something that John would be comfortable signing." According to Kessler, the key sticking point for Zorn was,

> a sort of standard partnership clause that [the university] was offering, and it... basically says, if anything would happen that would negatively affect the reputation of the New School in any way, shape, or form as defined by the New School, that the New School basically reserved the right to terminate the partnership at any time. I think it's warranted in many instances. John's never going to sign something like that, and I don't blame him. I think when he looked at it, he saw it as a potential slippery slope towards artistic control.

Thus, Zorn, despite the potential appeal of a new, visible, rent-free performance space, one without the "rodent problems" Kessler noted at the old location, was only interested in partnering with The New School if it could be done on unusual terms, terms allowing him to operate in the university's undefined margins rather than within its standard rules. In Kessler's words, "[W]e had to construct something that basically would blow that [clause] up...And we got it done." Zorn's uncompromising artistic principles and long-standing underground artistic community building appear to have accumulated some power in their undefined invisibility, harnessing what Phelan might call the potential power of the unmarked. Rather than being pulled inside by the power of the institution, this small artist-run community has built up enough strength to successfully pull back, demanding a partnership in which the institution is made radical and experimental by the artists as the artists are institutionalized by the university.

While Zorn's unwillingness to conform to the university's standard procedures temporarily jeopardized the partnership, it also symbolized the qualities of The Stone that made that partnership desirable to The New School. In Kessler's words, "In some ways, I was more interested in The Stone than anything because of the values system that John brings, the idea of The Stone being created to honor, and support, and empower artists, and not to exploit them, and not to put them in a box." If Zorn did not demand an exception to protect artistic freedom, he would create less demand for his presence. Kessler says Zorn's strategy for operating The Stone offers a "critical lesson that we want our students somehow or another to take in.... The beauty of The Stone is, five nights a week... you see it in action." As with informal apprenticeship models that once dominated jazz culture, students learn from established musicians through regular exposure to their professional activities. A new paradox comes in this relationship, however: The Stone as a site of professional music making no longer exists outside the university, making the scene the students work to enter an element of the one they already inhabit. Phelan writes, "Representation follows two laws: it always conveys more than it intends; and it is never totalizing."[67] Performances at the new Stone still represent Zorn's artistic vision of radical independence, but their physical location within a university changes the nature of what Phelan calls its "excess" meaning by framing it as music that teaches a lesson; as Kessler says, "I'm hoping... that it'll begin to have an effect on... ways of thinking about the world around them... for each one of the students. And, hopefully the faculty too." The Stone has become institutionalized with the hope that it will make the visible world more like Zorn's underground, leveraging its mystique as a site of artistic freedom that eludes definition to play a role in defining the artistic ethos of an institution. By spending some of The Stone's cultural capital on real estate at The New School, Zorn traded a largely unseen but easily romanticized place for one with less hidden magic and more visible power, a private culture of serving music to an educational culture of public service.

CHAPTER 5

Reinventing the Recorded at Preservation Hall

The French Quarter in New Orleans puts the city's current tourism-based economy clearly on display. Even the police station advertises its sale of souvenir T-shirts. While some businesses appeal to visitors with their versions of the wild excesses of the city's purported tendency to "laissez les bons temps rouler," like the "stiff" drinks in phallus-shaped cups found in some Bourbon Street bars, others draw customers through appeals to history and tradition, like Walgreens, the ubiquitous American drugstore chain founded in Chicago, which advertises that it has been serving New Orleans since 1938 in an effort to establish a connection to the local. In his study of New Orleans tourism, sociologist Kevin Fox Gotham makes jazz the first item on his list of markers of the New Orleans culture that forms the basis of the city's tourist appeal, along with its "French and Spanish architecture, streetcars, historic neighborhoods, multiplicity of festivals and Mardi Gras, and famous cemeteries."[1] Right in the middle of the French Quarter, a couple blocks away from historic Jackson Square in one direction and just around the corner from the raucous party atmosphere of Bourbon Street in the other sits Preservation Hall. Its visual tourist appeal stems from its patina of age and use, giving it a sense of authenticity that surpasses the bright lights and souvenir shops of Bourbon Street and a worn-in, intimate vibe that contrasts just as sharply with the towering steeples of St. Louis Cathedral. The sign above the door is both unassuming and distinctive, with time-worn lettering on an old trombone case. While the space is clearly well loved and regularly in use, nothing about the exterior is fresh or shiny. Instead, the paint on old shutters has been allowed to weather and fade, the iron work around the door and balcony to show its age. The building's interior follows suit, with simple, worn wooden benches and a crumbling pegboard wall in the back of the room with a visible line at shoulder height left by the countless listeners who have leaned against it. While preservation is in the venue's very name, the physical space makes clear that the passage of time continues to subtly shape a venue with roots in the past that has, nonetheless, kept moving through the present.

The month of June more or less marks low tide for New Orleans tourism—in fact the *Lonely Planet* travel guide's month-by-month breakdown of popular events, festivals, and parades in the city skips June altogether while highlighting annual opportunities for travellers during the other eleven months of the year.[2] Yet, as I approached Preservation Hall on a humid, ninety-degree Sunday evening in 2018 with the June sun still beating down on St. Peter Street, I found a substantial line of sweaty tourists lined up awaiting a 6 p.m. show, the second of five sets that would be performed that evening. Some armed with plastic cups of cold beer purchased at a neighboring bar, most patrons waited for half an hour or more in the heat before entering the small performance space, a 620-square-foot room cooled only by ceiling fans, not air conditioning. The Hall accommodates a crowd of around one hundred people at full capacity; that night, many audience members stood, some packed tightly on benches, and others seated on rows of cushions on the floor. The room was dimly lit, giving a spectral quality to the Noel Rockmore portraits of former Hall musicians that line the walls. There is no stage; the band forms in front of windows coated in enough historic dust to make them opaque, on the same wood floor as its audience. The front line sat in wooden chairs with red cushions that look like they could have been borrowed from a grandmotherly dining room. There's an upright piano and a bare-bones drum set with a big bass drum, and there are no music stands or trappings of amplification beyond the occasional modest bass amp. Like many earlier sets, this one attracted families with children in addition to adults of all ages, from a group of twenty-somethings on a girls' road trip to a retired couple who sprung for $50 reserved seats and came ready with requests of their favorite Louis Armstrong tunes. Bandleader and pianist Rickie Monie assumed a nonlocal crowd in his verbal introduction to the set, assuring us, "When you go home, you can tell people" about the history of the eighteenth-century building and more than fifty-year-old venue in which we were gathered. The forty-five-minute set contained a healthy dose of New Orleans chestnuts, including "Down by the Riverside," "Basin St. Blues," and, because the requester was willing to chip in the $10 prescribed by the sign hanging over the bandstand, "When the Saints Go Marching In." After the set was a break and time to turn over to the second band of the evening, who would play the 8, 9, and 10 p.m. sets, following the schedule running 360 days of the year. In a city that has at least 11 million visitors annually and aggressively markets jazz as a central aspect of its local identity, the Hall sees an average of nearly three thousand visitors a week.[3]

There is certainly plenty of competition from other jazz presenters for the attention of New Orleans's many tourists. In the nearby Marigny neighborhood, Frenchmen Street is lined with music clubs, including Snug Harbor, a mainstay of the city's more postbop-leaning jazz where members of the Marsalis family have been heard regularly, as have touring artists like New York–based singer Karrin Allyson and other popular New Orleans musicians like Galactic's Stanton Moore, who leads a jazz trio when not working with his popular jam band, and Herlin Riley, former drummer for the Jazz at Lincoln Center Orchestra. Across the street is the Spotted Cat, a popular club featuring primarily early jazz, and a number of other jazz-centric music spaces like the Maison, d.b.a., and Blue Nile. Around the corner from Preservation Hall on Bourbon Street are several other jazz clubs, including Fritzel's European Jazz Pub, the Jazz Playhouse, and Maison Bourbon, which ties itself to its storied neighbor with a sign proclaiming the space "dedicated to the preservation of jazz." Jazz can also be heard on riverboats docked nearby, ready for pleasure cruises on the Mississippi, at a jazz museum run by the National Park Service where a band of park rangers performs, at the newly renovated New Orleans Jazz Market, home to the New Orleans Jazz Orchestra, and outdoors as part of the city's many festivals and parades. Yet, in some ways, the Hall's competition is what helps to create its unique appeal. As historian J. Mark Souther wrote of its location amongst noisy Bourbon Street neighbors, "the wilder the French Quarter became, the more authentic Preservation Hall seemed."[4]

To describe how Preservation Hall "seems" draws into question easy assumptions about the space as a crucible of jazz from the early days of the twentieth century. While a tourist may see its weathered facade in the city that advertises itself as the birthplace of jazz and draw fanciful conclusions about a young Louis Armstrong coming of age there, the venue opened in 1961 as a site of revival and extension for early jazz traditions with proprietors rooted in the culture of jazz record collecting. While its name suggests an unbroken line to the birth of jazz, that line is anything but straight; Preservation Hall in many ways has created a culture of live, local music making from a part-remembered, part-recorded, part-imagined past, and tracing that past will involve a side trip away from New Orleans to the homes of predominantly white, college-educated record collectors in the Northeast. Preservation Hall is a physical and social realization of the scene records suggested to these non–New Orleanian listeners, now a place in which live presence and musical mentorship take precedence over the reproduction of early jazz as heard on record, despite the essential role those records played in the establishment of the venue. Like the Village Vanguard, this small venue built a local and eventually international audience in part through the relationship between jazz records and a specific urban place, but in this case, the records came first. This chapter begins by exploring the relationship between jazz record collecting and early jazz revivals with particular attention to how these two phenomena and their interconnections have been shaped by race. I will then return focus to Preservation Hall itself in order to show how the venue's relationship to its location in New Orleans has eclipsed the records that inspired it in determining contemporary musical practices there. Once a site for reanimating the sounds and careers of New Orleanian African American recording artists, the Hall now continues its tradition of showcasing the next generations of local black voices in a new landscape of increased tourism and post-Katrina gentrification.

RECORDS, REVIVALS, AND RACE

Preservation Hall was established not by native New Orleanians, but by a young white couple from the Northeast named Allan and Sandra Jaffe who shared a love of early African American jazz records, and while its name suggests the maintenance of an existing musical style, the venue's early days were as much about creating a scene as preserving one. Travelling for their honeymoon in 1961, the Jaffes made their way to New Orleans in search of live jazz as they had heard it in recording. As Allan remembered it in 1969,

> We were so disappointed. We had expected to find a lot more music here in town. I guess we had the Folkways series. It had just come out shortly before we came down here, maybe around six months before....I really thought

that all these people were still playing and it was relatively easy to get to hear them.⁵

In essence, Perseveration Hall emerged as the Jaffes' response to the gulf between the early jazz of the record-collecting world and the live scene in New Orleans. Jaffe describe the venue as turning out "probably the way someone from out-of-town pictures what a place in New Orleans should look like."⁶ When they did not find the live performance scene that records led them to imagine, they sought to build it.

While efforts to foster jazz performance in the style of its early New Orleans practitioners have never completely disappeared, they have waxed and waned at various times throughout the past century, and understandings of what it means to play traditional New Orleans jazz have been equally malleable. The notion of early New Orleans jazz as a music at risk of extinction emerged alongside the music's first major rival, the popular swing music that became emblematic of the 1930s and '40s. As Bruce Boyd Raeburn points out, the idea that jazz styles could have varying degrees of cultural value arose as a part of the conflict over "hot" and "sweet" music during the 1930s as newer swing began to eclipse the popularity of early jazz. "The idea that one kind of jazz might be considered more authentic than another did not exist among New Orleans musicians when the idiom was first coalescing, in the years from 1896 to 1917; 'hot' record collectors in major urban capitals such as New York and Paris developed it later, in the 1930s."⁷ From the 1930s to the mid-1940s, early jazz styles, particularly those deemed "hot" by fans, critics, and scholars enjoyed a vogue as the "real" insider's jazz. While a specific definition of "hot" music was never quite arrived at, the concept, by general consensus, had as much to do with context and perceived intentions as it did with sound. As far as "hot" collectors were concerned, a record grew warmer through musical factors such as improvisation and discernable blues influence, but also based on its rarity, the date of the recording, and the record and band's points of origin. As Andrew Berish notes, the term also "had strong racial connotations. Describing a band as 'hot' was another way of saying that the music was played in, or at least approximated, a black style."⁸ As the disciplines of jazz history and discography emerged in earnest toward the end of the 1930s, the older, blacker, and closer to New Orleans a record was, the more highly it was valued, and the "hotter" the music was considered.

Paul Lopes describes the role of the emerging hot record-collecting community of the 1930s as a major factor in the transition from a general perception of jazz as a popular music in the 1920s to a firm belief in its high art status by the 1950s. "Most collectors...preferred the black jazz vernacular as performed before its cultivation by professional musicians. These self-proclaimed 'jazz enthusiasts' in the 1930s and 1940s became the first critics, producers, and consumers of an emerging jazz art world."[9] What the word *jazz* meant to the average American of the 1920s and what today's jazz listeners generally think of as the authentic jazz of that decade are not necessarily the same. During the period between World War I and the Great Depression, the so-called "Jazz Age," jazz was very broadly defined. As Lopes describes, "While many small 'jazz bands' performed a black vernacular style of music from the Delta Region of New Orleans, jazz music in the 1920s encompassed not only this style but syncopated dance music, blues music, piano rags, and virtually any tune 'jazzed up' by musicians."[10] Much of what the broad American public knew to be jazz during the 1920s was influenced by black vernacular music in one way or another, but it was not necessarily identical to it. In fact, what is now commonly thought of as the most authentically artistic jazz of that era was seen by many at the time as needing improvement in order to reach the status of true art. While playing in a jazzy manner became increasingly useful for professional players who sought marketability, Lopes points out that keeping jazz influences to a minimum was not an uncommon choice. "White professional musicians distanced themselves from non-professionals and the pure vernacular in emphasizing their 'legitimate' techniques of music making. Constantly referring to the cacophonous noise and primitive techniques of non-professionals, white professional musicians prided themselves on cultivating vernacular jazz in their orchestras."[11] In the mid-1920s, Paul Whiteman, not Louis Armstrong, was called "The King of Jazz," despite the fact that many jazz writers since that time have denied Whiteman's status as a jazz musician, writing off the enormous popularity of his "sweet" rather than "hot" music as a commercial and therefore nonjazz phenomenon. As Stephanie Doktor argues, "Rejecting these historical facts—that Whiteman performed and recorded jazz—reflects an age-old investment in defining 'real' jazz outside of a commercial sphere....By excluding Whiteman, historians and critics create a distorted version of the racial history of black music and its exploitative relationship to the marketplace."[12]

It was not until the vogue for record collecting in the 1930s that "hot" jazz came to be revered, but once it was, dedicated collectors amassed, cataloged, discussed, and enjoyed enormous libraries of records. One such collection, amassed by a cornetist and bandleader living in the Northeast during the second half of the twentieth century and later maintained by his surviving relatives, contains over 84,000 ten-inch 78-rpm records, the majority of which date from before 1942. The collection is so vast that its owners designed and built their home with the records in mind, devoting a separate floor of their house to the enormous library of music. They have shared the collection with people seeking old recordings for a variety of reasons, from individuals looking for records made by their relatives to documentary makers for the Discovery Channel and PBS. Ken Burns consulted with the family while gathering recordings for his much-discussed 2000 series, *Jazz*. They have also provided records for rereleases of early jazz on LP or CD, providing better copies or missing recordings for collections by artists like Bessie Smith and Sidney Bechet.[13]

During a visit to their home, the collectors directed my attention to a particular shelf, the portion of their collection they call the "A-Case." It contains all the most valuable records, those that could be sold for the highest prices. One of them explained how records were chosen for that shelf, saying, "Records are like stamps. Their value is very subjective. It depends on how rare they are [and] what condition they're in." Another added "how good the performance is" to the list of determining factors. To demonstrate what they meant, they pulled a record from the A-Case at random and then looked up details about it in Brian Rust's discography, *Jazz Records, 1897–1942, 78 Quarterly*, and a few other reference sources they had on hand. The record was made by New Orleanian trombonist and cornetist Merritt Brunies and his Friar's Inn Orchestra for the Autograph label in Chicago in 1925. One side contained a version of *Clarinet Marmalade* and the other *Flag That Train to Alabam'*, both performed by a typical early jazz ensemble of cornet, clarinet, trombone, and rhythm section in an improvised polyphonic style. The collectors attributed the record's high value to its obscurity. As they said, in addition to being an example of relatively scarce "early black music," this particular record was never produced in large quantities. "There weren't too many Autographs printed, so it's a rare label," one said, and the Merritt Brunies record we were listening to was now one of "two or three of them in existence in the world."

The preference for rare recordings and obscure tunes, shared by record collectors and bands that base their repertoire on collecting, shapes the way the musical 1920s are recreated. Rather than bringing back the songs and sounds of groups like Paul Whiteman's that dominated the style many listeners knew as jazz in the 1920s, which the music collectors would later dub "sweet" instead of "hot," today's early jazz audiences tend to be presented with music that was less well known in its own time but is more highly regarded now. The effect is akin to a photographic negative of 1920s jazz: the music that was most popular at the time, since disregarded as derivative and commercial, fades into the background as the less frequently recorded, less mass-produced music tied closely to black vernacular styles is emphasized in its place.

Yet, this veneration of black early jazz by the culture of record collecting has not manifested in African Americans dominating the live early-jazz scene in the United States. Since the 1940s Dixieland revival, a large proportion of early jazz players and listeners have been white, despite the fact that revivalists considered documenting the creations of African American artists to be at the core of their work. As jazz historian, clarinetist, and New Orleans transplant Samuel Charters remembers, "There was...throughout the beginnings of the revival, a clearly demarcated color line. The young enthusiasts who journeyed to New Orleans to record veteran musicians were emotionally committed to recording African American musicians."[14] While the older New Orleans players involved in the movement were predominantly black, the young musicians playing in revival bands typically were not, a situation that persists in many traditional jazz bands throughout the country. As a traditional jazz performer and writer active since the late 1960s, Tex Wyndham writes that he has frequently been asked, "Why aren't more Black musicians playing Dixieland?"[15] He believes that a substantial part of the answer to that question lies in early jazz's lack of commercial viability in most markets, a notion that is corroborated by the personal experiences of Charters as an early jazz player in New Orleans during the mid-twentieth century. Charters's consideration of this issue from the perspective of a white revivalist in New Orleans warrants quotation at length:

> I played in revival bands for many years, and for us even the dizzying heights of ordinary union scale were beyond our ambitions. We would have welcomed any African American musicians who chose to join us, but it was not until the 1990s that I met any young black musicians who felt easy enough with the New Orleans past to join the bands. If the groups were generally composed entirely of white musicians, it was because during these years there were no young African American musicians that any of us knew who elected to play New Orleans–style jazz. In addition to whatever misgivings they might had had [sic] about the complicated racial dynamic of the revival,

they realized, quite sensibly, that there was no way to make a living being a part of it. In their enthusiasm, the white bands made every effort to hire veteran black New Orleans musicians whenever they had some economic support, and for many of the New Orleans veterans there were years of extensive tours appearing as the featured soloist with a young revival band. The young black musicians I encountered had a visceral response to the new sounds and challenges of bop, to Miles Davis and John Coltrane. The New Orleans idiom was something they left to us.[16]

The issue of what it means for black musicians to have "left" unprofitable early jazz to white musicians in the middle decades of the twentieth century is far from simple, as can be seen in Charters's allusions to musical and social trends in the passage above. In returning to a consideration of the cultural place of this style in the late 1930s, we will find a tangled web of economic, political, social, and musical factors that brought white musicians and fans like the Jaffes toward the early jazz repertoire as black performers and audiences grew farther and farther away from it.

Patrick Burke's study of New York City's 52nd Street jazz scene in the 1930s and 1940s offers insight into the treatment of early jazz during the swing era and burgeoning bebop movement, giving a glimpse of trends in early jazz performance and consumption that would eventually come to characterize the music's later life in much of the United States, including New Orleans. Burke points out that, from the very beginning of the New York club scene, race was a significant factor in how musicians and audiences understood early jazz, and white professional players were drawn to it because of the perceived racial differences it represented to them. "At the Onyx club, the first jazz venue on 52nd Street, young, white, male musicians strove to reject the perceived banality and pretense of mainstream pop music in favor of what they saw as the more open, vital expression to be found in African American jazz. The improvisatory creativity of jazz allowed these musicians to enact an ideal of masculine independence and self-determination that contrasted with the restrictions and limitations imposed by the music business in which they worked."[17] The Onyx Club, which opened sometime between 1927 and 1930, became a space in which white musicians frustrated by commercially oriented performance during the day could enjoy greater musical freedom as African American–styled improvisers in a recreational atmosphere in the evenings. Because of largely segregated working conditions in the music industry at that time, however, white players' ideas about black players were not formed through the direct, personal contact of performing together regularly in a professional context. As Burke argues, "Because the white musicians of the Onyx did not often work formally with black musicians, there were not many situations in which they dealt with blacks professionally, and there were thus few opportunities for white musicians to perceive African Americans as fellow professionals engaged in a formal system of labor. To play black, then, both personally and musically, was a way for the musicians at the Onyx to assume an identity that was both distinctly masculine and free from labor restraints."[18] Already by the early 1930s, then, white musicians had adopted early jazz as a noncommercial music that was considered more expressive because it was not a part of their controlled working lives. Yet, for black musicians who were not often allowed to work in more lucrative recording jobs, 52nd Street functioned quite differently. Over time, there was a growing presence of black musicians on the street. They were not, however, seeking the same relaxed, recreational atmosphere appreciated by the first white players at the Onyx Club whose primary professional obligations took place elsewhere. As Burke describes, "Although black musicians saw 52nd Street as a valuable professional opportunity, they did not necessarily view it as a place to spend their free time, as some white musicians did."[19]

Meanwhile, as the big-band swing movement gained widespread commercial appeal, white musicians used some of the street's small clubs, particularly Jimmy Ryan's, as places to retreat to what they saw as more artistically authentic earlier jazz styles. "Some musicians chose to play on 52nd Street precisely because it still seemed to offer an alternative to the world of commercial swing. This reasoning seems to have been most common among white musicians, who were the immediate heirs of the equation of authentic jazz and anticommercialism that had informed 52nd Street's musicians throughout the 1930s."[20] While white musicians were drawn to African American early jazz styles out of respect for what they considered superior musical qualities and artistic freedoms when compared to more mainstream popular music, it was playing mainstream popular music in recording studios during the day that made it possible to indulge in the less financially stable world of 52nd Street's tiny clubs at night. Unfortunately for the black musicians they modeled themselves on while acting out fantasies in their recreational nightlives, the anticommercial atmosphere of 52nd Street clubs translated into financial insecurity for black players who did not have access to participation in less artistically ideal but more lucrative work.

As bebop came to dominate first 52nd Street and eventually jazz in general, perceptions of early jazz as a pure, expressive, noncommercial music became increasingly problematic. By the late 1940s, when Bunk Johnson was known to sit in with New Orleans–style groups at Jimmy Ryan's, early jazz was defined by its overwhelmingly white, middle-class, college-educated supporters in opposition to the bebop played by the younger generation of black musicians. Fans who came to see Johnson were interested in what Burke refers to as a "historical exhibit" in which a working-class black man with hands callused from physical labor displayed what was viewed as his "direct connection to the supposed folk origins of jazz."[21] In other clubs in the same neighborhood, beboppers fought against these stereotypes of African Americans as a noble but simple people to be revered and protected by the white intelligentsia by infusing their music with a startling, challenging, and unprecedented level of rhythmic and harmonic complexity. This dynamic complicates Charters's description of early jazz being "left" to white players by a generation of black musicians who were uninterested in pursing it. The more early jazz was romanticized as a vernacular music best played by untutored, "natural" players in an anticommercial spirit, the less accessible it was for young African American musicians who sought serious recognition and compensation for their musical abilities.[22] If the early jazz repertoire can be seen as "left" to white revivalists, it was left not simply as a gift or legacy but as yet another musical realm that was not equally available to black professional players. While the impulse of the revivalists was ostensibly a noble one, to protect and valorize music they loved that originated in a community with fewer economic and social opportunities, the possibility of maintaining early jazz as the expression of an oppressed folk culture would rely on the continued oppression of that culture. It would also rely on the continued willingness of working-class African American amateur musicians to perform in a way that mirrored the expectations and values set up for jazz by a well-meaning but ultimately paternalistic community of economically and educationally privileged white men. As Burke describes, pursuing bebop instead of early jazz allowed African American jazz players of the 1940s to do work "grounded in the intellectual prerogatives of artistic modernism rather than a clichéd notion of black musicians as irrational, spontaneous creators."[23] While it would border on exaggeration to say that early jazz was simply stolen by white players, the rhetoric surrounding this music in the 1940s coupled with contemporary politics of race negated the possibility of the repertoire being equally shared. In this context, it is perhaps no surprise that when the Jaffes arrived in

New Orleans a decade after Charters, they had difficulty finding live performances of early jazz by African American New Orleanians.

A PLACE TO WORK

In collaboration with other jazz enthusiasts, the Jaffes set out to create a venue in which African American musicians with ties to the early New Orleans jazz scene of the preswing era could regularly perform and be compensated for their work. Historian J. Mark Souther writes that, "Preservation Hall's greatest contribution to the jazz revival lay in providing steady employment to forgotten, downtrodden New Orleans jazz players, many of whom lived in dire poverty in the sunset of their lives."[24] He notes that from the Depression years up to the 1960s, "few musicians could find steady employment," and, "for many of the city's best musicians, like Paul Barbarin, leaving New Orleans afforded the only hope of realizing their full potential."[25] In the twenty-first century, Paul Barbarin's great nephew, trombonist Lucien Barbarin, had multiple regular gigs in New Orleans, including frequent appearances at Preservation Hall, where he performed from the 1980s until his death in 2020. Souther states, "Preservation Hall succeeded beyond the wildest imagination of its founders. It fed off the spectacular rise in tourism beginning in the 1960s, the ascendant American penchant for seeking the nation's cultural roots, and the increasing rarity of old jazzmen."[26] While Allan Jaffe, who ran the Hall with Sandra from the 1960s up until his death in 1987, might not have intended or expected it, the venue has outlived both him and the musicians he originally sought to support and feature, eventually becoming a center for subsequent generations of predominantly African American New Orleans musicians. From one perspective, the Jaffes' intervention in the New Orleans scene could be viewed as another paternalistic or exploitative use of aging African American musicians by white outsiders in an increasingly viable tourist economy. Indeed, the Jaffes' son Ben, who has taken over operations of the venue, has heard his critics call it "Plantation Hall" and "The Old Folks' Home," remarks he finds especially frustrating given that the bulk of his family's income derived from his father's real estate investments, not the Hall itself, which has at times operated at a deficit.[27] Yet Souther argues that in New Orleans, "predictably, African Americans did not always rush to embrace cultural preservation initiatives that either ignored or exploited them, yet ultimately they began to reclaim a degree of control over the public presentation of jazz. In building commercial demand for the art form, tourism set jazz apart from its cultural and spatial moorings and laid the foundation for the biracial grassroots interest in brass bands, street processions, and the preservation of local sites of jazz history, in turn creating a sustainable cultural resource that enriched the community even as it furthered tourism development."[28] Indeed, the date that Allan Jaffe noted as the anniversary of the Hall was not a celebration of the first time music was played there but the date that they started to pay their roster of locally based African American musicians union-scale wages.[29] Nearly sixty years later, saxophonist and third-generation New Orleans musician Calvin Johnson described the venue's significance by saying, "Preservation Hall is one of the last holdouts for true New Orleans jazz. It's one of the last venues where you're going to see black musicians, black local musicians, perform daily. That's big."[30]

The late career of "Sweet Emma" Barrett exemplifies the type of change that the Jaffes's efforts to provide steady employment could render. Despite the enthusiasm of post–World War II jazz revivalists, Barrett, once a member of the Original Tuxedo Jazz Orchestra, a group that also boasted Louis Armstrong, Joe Oliver, and many other New Orleans jazz greats among its alumni, was only working about once per week in the years leading up to the opening of the Hall.[31] In contrast, during the first ten months of 1963, around two years after the Jaffes took on the venue, Barrett was performing about twice as much. Union records show Barrett playing seventy-six gigs from January through October that year, and thirty-nine of those were at Preservation Hall.[32] She also played regularly at other venues, including the Royal Orleans Hotel and Dixieland Hall, the latter of which was the longest-running example of what Charles Suhor called Preservation Hall's "many imitators" during the 1960s, a list of venues that included Perseverance Hall, Icon Hall, the Dixieland Coffee Shop, and Mahogany Hall.[33] No other venue featured her as frequently as Preservation Hall itself, however. Thus the Hall provided roughly half of Barrett's work opportunities directly, and it indirectly contributed even more through the other venues that sought to emulate it. Born in 1897, Barrett was already in her mid-sixties by the time the Hall opened, and the income she was able to earn there during the last two decades of her life constituted a significant part of her livelihood. After suffering a stroke in 1967 that paralyzed the left side of her body, Barrett continued to perform at Preservation Hall, one-handed and seated in her wheelchair. Her final performance took place at the Hall around two weeks before her death in 1983.[34]

Although Preservation Hall did not turn a profit during its first two years of existence or in the years immediately following Hurricane Katrina, it has now successfully provided employment for musicians playing jazz in the style of early New Orleans practitioners for nearly sixty years. Souther writes, "Preservation Hall proved so successful, in fact, that in later years young musicians, who had come of age during the height of the civil rights struggle and associated Dixieland with segregation, hard times, and Uncle Tom mentality, became inspired to take up the traditional style of playing."[35] In part, the venue's financial viability has relied on its presentation of a touring band that has both spread the reputation of the Hall and earned considerable income for the musicians and the venue outside New Orleans. Tom Sancton broke down the financial picture for Preservation Hall musicians at the time of the venue's fiftieth anniversary in 2011 as follows:

> Few members of the touring band would complain about being exploited. They work an average of 150 travel days a year, at $550 a day. That comes to $82,500, plus what they make on other engagements when they're not on the road. That's more than the average college professor or recent law-school graduate makes....The nightly pay is considerably less at the hall itself—$125 for sidemen, $150 for the leader—but that's far better than the average French Quarter remuneration. There is no question that Preservation Hall has raised the standard of living of the musicians who play there.[36]

When Ben Jaffe took over the Hall in the 1990s, he was deeply concerned about the future of the venue as musicians of Barrett's generation disappeared from the scene, but the space continues to function as a hub of New Orleans jazz and source of steady employment for local musicians.

PLAYING WITH TRADITION

Just as recordings shaped the Jaffes' vision for Preservation Hall as a venue, the role of old records in contemporary live performances of early jazz is often central. Yet, given the strong dose of heritage that comes from the venue as a place, performers at the Hall can move away from the exact sounds of recorded early jazz without losing their apparent connections to history. Outside of New Orleans, one of the most prominent musicians specializing in early jazz is Vince Giordano, leader of the New York–based Nighthawks. In addition to regular live performances at a midtown Manhattan restaurant and club called Iguana, Giordano's band has been featured in numerous period film and television scores, including *The Aviator*, *Café Society*, and *Boardwalk Empire*. Giordano first encountered jazz through his grandmother's record collection and eventually amassed a substantial jazz collection of his own that includes both records and over 60,000 scores related to his interest in early big band arrangements. Musicologist Gretchen Carlson writes about what she calls "dual authenticity" in Giordano's approach to jazz repertoire of the 1920s and '30s, a combination of striving for sonic accuracy in historical recreation through a jazz corollary of historically informed performance practice with a desire to simultaneously cultivate experiential accuracy through the cultivation of an entertaining atmosphere that evokes the excitement of the Jazz Age for its twenty-first century audience.[37] Carlson explains that, "Giordano leans toward having his musicians perform 'accurate' solos—rather than personally expressive ones—by providing them with solo notation."[38] To ensure his version of authenticity in his band's performances, Giordano encourages band members to read from notated transcribed solos or to improvise in a way that avoids conventions of postbop styles. Saxophonist Mark Lopeman explained that he "tries to stick to elaborations on the 1, 3, and 5 of the chords, avoiding upper extensions and 'out' playing," and clarinetist Dan Levinson described needing to "forget about swing and bebop and all the subsequent permutations of post-1934 jazz" in order to improvise appropriate solos for the Nighthawks.[39] The aim is to recreate live, or in the heightened fidelity of a twenty-first century recording, the kind of performances that are documented on Jazz Age records.

Given that the founders of Preservation Hall shared Giordano's interest in records and created a venue in which the aging creators of those records and their peers could continue to play, it might be reasonable to expect that a performance by the Nighthawks and one by a representative Preservation Hall ensemble would sound markedly similar. Yet a 2018 performance satisfying an audience member request for "Struttin' with some Barbeque" led by Rickie Monie did not dance along in the loping two-beat feel that opens Louis Armstrong's 1927 Hot Five recording or include soloists reading from careful transcriptions of Armstrong's improvisations. Indeed, like Armstrong's own later versions of the tune, this performance engaged with the post-1934 musical world that Giordano's band studiously ignores by employing a driving four-beat swing feel through a walking bass line and syncopated ride cymbal pattern and freshly improvised solos. Indeed, an Armstrong tune need not even have originated in the 1920s or the early jazz style to warrant preservation at Preservation Hall. Anne Dvinge names a handful of specific pieces she observed during her 2010 fieldwork there, but she calls "What a Wonderful World" specifically the "pièce de résistance" of the venue, not "St. James Infirmary" or "Li'l Liza Jane," which she also mentions as being commonly played.[40] Unlike the other two pieces, which both originated at least as early as the term "jazz" in the first decades of the twentieth century and have long held a place in the traditional New Orleans repertoire, "What a Wonderful World" struck me as an outlier in Dvinge's list as it was first recorded by Armstrong in 1967, six years after the Hall was established. In its original guise, it has very little to do with the typical stylistic features associated with historical New Orleans jazz practices. It is a pop ballad, arranged with orchestral strings in a gently lilting 6/8 meter quite foreign to the syncopated rhythms of early New Orleans style. There is no collective improvisation, nor any wind instruments or sustained improvisation, not even Armstrong's trumpet playing, featured in the original recording of "What a Wonderful World." The tune became a hit single in Europe before catching on in the United States, where it wouldn't break the Billboard Hot 100 until its use in the film *Good Morning Vietnam* in the late 1980s, more than a decade after Armstrong's death. While it is Armstrong's most popular song in the present—it has around 170 million Spotify plays while his next most played track has just under 100 million—the song has little relationship to most of the specific musical traits that made Armstrong an icon of early New Orleans jazz.

Alongside repertoire choices at the Hall that draw on a broad historical spectrum of locally significant material, the Preservation Hall Jazz Band (PHJB), the touring ensemble linked to the venue, has openly embraced a twenty-first-century musical identity. The choice to cultivate an updated sound spurred controversy and some division in the Hall's musical community. In 2011, Sancton noted the tension around the touring band's aesthetic: "Trumpeter Wendell Brunious...along with other ex–band members, including banjoist Don Vappie and clarinetist Michael White...quit the group after falling out with Ben Jaffe over personal and artistic differences....'You don't need to re-invent the wheel—you just have to roll the one you have. In the field of traditional jazz, Ben already had the biggest wheel.'"[41] Conversely, musicologist Sarah Suhadolnik argues that the band's "strategy of performing across a range of musical contexts is deeply engrained," pointing to their "evocation of a constructed past, as opposed to the exact replication of specific performance practices" as a long-held trait of the ensemble's approach.[42] Jaffe's interest in leading an ensemble that looks to more than early

New Orleans jazz for inspiration is evident in the group's 2017 album, *So It Is*, which is entirely made up of original compositions rather than 1920s evergreens, and in the band's many collaborations with popular artists, including the rock group My Morning Jacket and singers Tom Waits and Robert Plant. As Jaffe points out, however, there are precedents for these kinds of stylistic juxtapositions reaching back to the band's early days. As he puts it, "In 1968, the PHJB was on the same bill as the Grateful Dead at the Fillmore. What I'm doing is just a continuation of what's been done in New Orleans for years."[43]

Daily performances in the Hall maintain a more conservative aesthetic than the hybridized performance and recording projects of the touring band, but they, too, embrace elements of post-1930s jazz practices that artists like Giordano avoid when aiming to recreate the sonic past. Calvin Johnson, a New Orleans musician who grew up listening to music at Preservation Hall and went on to perform there regularly himself describes "staying within the genre...[of] New Orleans traditional jazz" and spending time during his own practice working "to get as close to this vocabulary as possible," yet he also acknowledges departures from performance practices of the past in shows at the Hall today.[44]

> I know from an outsider it seems that it's a restrictive and scripted environment, but it's truly not. And one of the beautiful things about the Hall is that when we knock a song down, that song can go in any direction....Because we allow the music to remain organic, the music is living, and the music breathes, and the music lives in real time. And you'd be surprised how many times I've stretched and went into like some tenor Coltrane sheets of sound kind of vibes at the Hall, but the people—at that point, the people are so invested in it, because they came on that ride with me from the beginning of the song. You know, we started "St. James Infirmary," but by the time it's my solo, the band is screeching and hooting and hollering, and I'm playing all these harmonics and overtones and everything, and the crowd is dancing and hooting and hollering with me because they understand how it was put together.

Johnson emphasizes that while the practices of the musicians performing at the Hall are rooted in early New Orleans jazz and maintain connections to repertoire and styles associated with the past, they remain open to musical developments from other times and places.

In attending multiple sets at Preservation Hall, I found that most performances followed a fairly similar formal template that suited both the musicians' needs to come together successfully without rehearsal and to respond spontaneously to requests and the need of the audience of tourists, many of whom had little knowledge of jazz, for a relatively accessible listening experience. Any given song was likely to begin with a performance of the head in polyphonic collective improvisation followed by a series of individual solos. The solos did not tend to make enormous demands on the attention spans of nonspecialist listeners in that they were almost all one or two choruses long, and if a second chorus was performed, variety and interest were created both visually and sonically halfway through as the soloist stood up for their second chorus and nonsoloist horn players added background figures. I was struck by Johnson's performance of Sidney Bechet's "Georgia Cabin" not because it confounded these regular formal expectations but for the extent to which his choices as an improviser differed from the simple melodic paraphrasing of Bechet's approach to this tune. I asked Johnson about his use of chromatic harmony and bebop-inflected phrasing, and he told me,

> In New Orleans we don't really—I know it's weird, because we play so many genres, but in New Orleans, we don't think genre-based. We just think musically based. And I know that's kind of difficult to explain, but when I play a song like that, I mean I'm hearing it from Bechet's perspective, but I'm also hearing everything that I've ever learned from a gospel bandstand, everything that I've ever learned from a folk bandstand, everything I've ever learned from a classical bandstand, everything I've ever learned from a brass band bandstand, all that comes into the pot, you know?

Johnson describes the music at Preservation Hall as having a New Orleans aesthetic not because of strict adherence to specific early jazz techniques but in part because of its relationship to its listeners. Johnson had moved to New York shortly before the time of our interview, and he contrasted what he saw as New York– and New Orleans–based conceptions of performance in terms of audience engagement:

> New Yorkers, they don't talk to the audience; they don't engage the audience...So they kind of weeded out the audiences, so now...you're really just left with...the true hardcore aficionados or the former musicians. And in New Orleans...the music and the people still have a symbiotic relationship. And we are not trying to reinvent the wheel....What the elders are doing when they hit the bandstand is they're trying to maintain...the integrity of music while still making the music palatable for people. I'll just give you a prime example. We can swing, and we can play changes, and people can dance. Now, if I was to get on the bandstand and if I was to play "You are My Sunshine," how many people you think on planet Earth or in America know that song?...Now a New Orleans approach is going to hit the bandstand and say, "We're going to play this song in 4/4 at a moderate tempo, and

we're going to engage the audience because we know that they know this." And at that point, if you're maintaining your integrity, it's going to translate to the music, and you can play all the changes you want over it, and people are gonna "oo" and "ah" and get up and dance as you're spitting all of your substitutions. As compared to a non–New Orleanian's approach is to say, "Hey, man, I have a cool arrangement of 'You are My Sunshine' in seven, and we're gonna start on a Phrygian chord." And it's like, man, what the fuck, you just totally removed the accessibility that the people would have to this song because you just wanted to satisfy your own artistic hunger.

In Johnson's description of New Orleans performances, space for individual artistic expression emerges once audience engagement is achieved. Through the lens of Carlson's dual authenticity model, while Giordano strongly values accurate sonic recreations of the past in seeking to create an authentic 1920s atmosphere, Johnson's balance of historical accuracy and experiential accuracy leans more toward the latter, making the relationship between musicians and listeners more important to a traditional New Orleans aesthetic than a specific approach to jazz improvisation.

RELATIONSHIPS TO HISTORY

Alongside geographic location, one of the main factors that allows Preservation Hall musicians to present their audiences with convincing renderings of traditional New Orleans jazz without directly recreating or limiting themselves to the musical language of the 1920s is the way that they establish relationships to earlier generations of New Orleans musicians; they are rooted, in other words, in both heritage and place. As musicians are introduced at the Hall, it is not unusual for their family history to be pointed out, with bandleaders directing the attention of the audience to players who are third-, fourth-, and even fifth-generation New Orleans musicians. In addition to familial relationships, Johnson stresses the importance of mentor relationships at the Hall:

> The Hall serves as the place where a mentee can find a mentor. . . . That's one thing that I can't stress enough about the Hall is that every musician that you see there had a mentor. More than one. And that's . . . still one of the differentiations about New Orleans. New Orleans, old school New Orleans, doesn't give a fuck about what school you went to, how many changes you can play—you gotta have a mentor. If you don't have a mentor, you're not reading the right materials.

Johnson recounts stories of both receiving and giving mentorship at the Hall, differentiating it from the kind of jazz education one might receive at one of the schools detailed in chapter three in part through the familial nature of bonds between older and younger players. In addition to feeling like he has "dozens of fathers" because of his musical relationships with older New Orleans musicians, Johnson says,

> I'm a third-generation New Orleans musician. I started hanging in Pres Hall when I was about six years old. My uncle, Ralph Johnson...was the Hall's clarinetist for the last twenty years of his life. So that bench on the side? That's where me and a whole bunch of my homies grew up, literally on that bench watching the elders play. And then we would go in the back with them, and they would say, "What you been sheddin' on?" It would be a conversation; they'd always treat us like grown men, and then eventually they would let us sit in on the last set. And we would sound like shit, but that's part of the process. And they allowed us to engage the process and engage the music.

Later, when Johnson began performing professionally as a part of the band, more established musicians continued to shape his learning process on the job:

> I'm sitting down next to my elders...and their repertoire far exceeds what I was able to take in in thirty years, you know. They've been gigging longer than I've been alive. So the first few months that I was sitting on that bandstand, I used to carry a sheet of paper with me, and every time somebody called a tune that I didn't know, which was basically every other tune, I wrote it down. I wrote it down, and then at the end of every gig, when I was at home doing my daily practice or rehearsing, I was pulling up these tunes, I was transcribing solos, I was transcribing melodies, I was learning forms and learning changes, so that when I went to the bandstand next week, I was prepared. Naturally, when your elders know that you are trying to get it, that you're trying to tread water, it's more of a baptism by fire. They're not going to call those same tunes again the next week, because you know them now [laughs]. That defeats the purpose of you being in an institution like Preservation Hall which is all about perpetuating the music across generations, you dig?

Johnson's process involved using older jazz recordings to study technical details of the music, but the specific repertoire he explored through records and individual practice was determined through his professional relationships and experiences at Preservation Hall, and he sees himself filling a role in the perpetuation of a venue-specific repertoire and aesthetic as he learns from older generations, performs, and teaches younger generations.

The Hall's role in mentoring young musicians has, to a certain extent, been formalized through the service mission of the Preservation Hall Foundation, the nonprofit education and outreach organization launched through the venue in 2011. The announcement preceding every set at the Hall lets patrons know that they are contributing to this service through a portion of their ticket price. The mission of the nonprofit is to "protect, preserve, and perpetuate" New Orleans jazz through a variety of programs, including music instruction in local public schools and juvenile detention facilities, educational workshops at the Hall, community concerts, and programs that provide instruments to aspiring musicians. Johnson worked as a teaching artist for the foundation and described it as another means of connecting young musicians with professional mentors at Preservation Hall. He offered an anecdote about a student he met through the foundation's public school outreach program who had recently been accepted at the local performing arts high school as an example of how the "Foundation was the bridge...to the Hall."

> When I first met him, in August of 2018...he was playing trombone. He only knew about three major scales. Then me and him started sitting down... and then his eyes started to light up, his ears started to open. So then he just became obsessed with the trombone, and so...within that year I got him from knowing three scales to transcribing Slide Hampton, Steve Turre, J. J. Johnson. But then it got to the point to where he was begging his daddy— and this is one of the differences between a teacher and a mentor—he was begging his daddy to come down to the Hall to sit in with the band so much, his dad called me up and said, "Man, I just can't do it. I'm a single father. I can't bring him out there three nights a week."...So then it came to the point where I was picking him up, and I was bringing him home, and toward the latter part of that, it wasn't even all me. Then he got cool with the trombonist, with Craig Klein, in the band. Then Craig would come pick him up on Saturday mornings, and he would hang by Craig's house and shed on pedal tones and long tones and stuff all day, and then Craig would bring him to all of his gigs, and by the time I would get to the Hall with him, he would tell me, "Man, this is my fourth sit-in of the day."

Johnson's story shows how a student, even one encountering Preservation Hall at an elementary level of musicianship, could become a part of the venue's musical community through mentorship.

In contrast, Johnson noted that highly trained musicians without personal relationships connecting them to the Hall do not necessarily find immediate acceptance or success in the venue. Johnson described an encounter with a performer from out of town with two degrees in jazz as an example:

> You call any song under the sun, he's gonna play it. "Along Came Betty," "In Walked Bud"—call "Countdown," he'll play "Cherokee" in all twelve keys and he'll go back and forth between 4/4 and 12/8 you know? And then, we

get up there, and he played with us, and we called "Bogalusa Strut." Now, you're a musician—five wants to go to one....The whole song is five-one. He couldn't get it. We were standing there shouting to him for like eight choruses, "Five, one. Five, one." He couldn't get it. The reason he couldn't get it is because school—and this is why I've never really been a fan of school, because when you hit like jazz school, for example, they start you off with things like, "Hey man, you gotta transcribe this Bird, 'Blues for Alice.'" Okay. That's almost like sitting a person down and saying I'm going to start you on geometry. I think you need to start this person off on the times tables. You know, so he came there, and he's sitting down with us, not saying that we're playing just simple arithmetic, but we're playing building blocks here. I mean, because the music is cumulative. First came Jelly Roll, then Armstrong, then swing, then bebop, you see what I'm saying? Like, bebop didn't come first, and then they went back, you know? So, it was just like these young cats come here, and they have a total misconception of what the music really is, and then when they finally come to the Hall, just to be frank, they roll their nose up at the Hall. They think we're playing some old music, until they get up there on the bandstand and literally get their asses handed to them like they've never got it before. Yeah, it's one thing for you to go sit in with a group of your peers where you're playing, you know, "Night in Tunisia" in thirteen and you get piped. But it's another thing when you get up there and we're just playing "You are My Sunshine" and you can't even hit a one chord.

Johnson emphasizes the importance of learning the music and culture of the Hall in person in order to successfully participate in performances there, even for performers like the one described above who have formal credentials and considerable performance experience in bebop and later styles:

> You see those same cats, they start to come back week after week. And then they get hip; then they try to connect with someone in the band. Then they try to do what? Get a mentor. You see what I'm saying? It's like, after college, after they hit the scene, then they realize that they don't know shit. So then they try to get a mentor. But then, once again, that's the beautiful thing about the Hall, and the people that are at the Hall: we're not trying to step on anybody or discourage anybody. If you want it, all you got to do is come around.

From Johnson's perspective, the performance practice of Preservation Hall emerges from not 1920s records or specific musical techniques but a combination of geography and personal connection; successfully playing at the Hall is contingent on "coming around," on spending time at the space learning the local culture and connecting with established mentors.

SERVING NEW ORLEANS, AND SERVING IT TO VISITORS

In addition to young musicians who come around to learn to play in the style associated with the venue, the Hall relies on the many out-of-town visitors who make the space financially viable. The success and longevity of Preservation Hall as a venue is rooted in its marketability as a valuable tourist experience. The proprietors and musicians of the Hall have found a niche that draws a consistent audience through the way they have leveraged local culture and jazz history to create a feel-good experience on multiple levels, an enjoyable entertainment that is also legible as a public service and a unique engagement with New Orleans as a place. As Raeburn described the venue even prior to the creation of the nonprofit foundation,

> What the founders of Preservation Hall gained was the same insight that has sustained the collector independents and the revivalists of the 1940s: "noncommercial" music could find a market when correctly presented. The lack of appurtenances at the Hall—the absences of alcohol, air-conditioning, and luxurious appointments—reminded the audience that it was the music that mattered. Whether the bands were playing "authentic" jazz in the manner of its first practitioners was seemingly beside the point and, at best, debatable... It was the *expectation* that they were that kept the audiences clamoring for more. New Orleans-style jazz, like Plymouth Rock, had intrinsic appeal as a touchstone of the American experience. Audiences believed that what they were hearing was authentic, and therefore profound, because that was what they wanted. Yet in the final analysis, it was the musician's power to generate joy and move audiences that made such belief possible.[45]

In the past decade, Preservation Hall audiences have moved even further in the direction of purchasing a product that is framed as valuable and yet noncommercial. Preperformance announcements draw attention to the venue's history and the musicians' relationships to the past, and they also remind patrons that they are, by purchasing tickets, contributing to a nonprofit foundation with a mission of continuing to support the music and musicians of the venue and spread their reach to new audiences and future generations. While there are many venues in New Orleans where one could hear jazz, the Hall differentiates itself through history and service.

Appeals to public service and historical preservation have a unique weight in the post-Katrina New Orleans landscape, and understandings of what it means to revive, protect, or restore New Orleans culture for both residents and the visitors that play a large role in economically sustaining the city are intensely intertwined with issues of race. As Gotham lays out, economic and population declines in New Orleans since the 1960s brought about a series of demographic shifts that set the stage for the disproportionate impact of Hurricane Katrina on the city's large African American community.

> The region's class inequalities interlock with racial inequalities. In 1960, whites made up 62.6 percent of the city's population, and blacks were 37.2 percent. As of the 2000 census, blacks made up 66.7 percent of the Central City's population, and whites were 26.6 percent. In 2005, blacks made up 84 percent of the city's poor population, with a high percentage living in segregated neighborhoods....The black poverty rate was more than three times higher than the white poverty rate (35 percent compared with 11 percent)....As a result, by the time Katrina came ashore, New Orleans had become a place of glaring racial and class inequalities, a place where poor African Americans were segregated and spatially isolated from the rest of the population.[46]

Katrina led to a massive drop in the New Orleans population, but, as of 2018 Census Bureau estimates, the metro area has rebounded to 95 percent of its prestorm size. The demographic make-up of that population, however, is much different than it was before the storm. In terms of race, the Hispanic and Asian populations have grown while both black and white populations remain smaller than pre-Katrina numbers. The difference between the population loss for the two groups is staggering: while there are presently around 8,600 fewer whites living in New Orleans than there were in 2005, there are an estimated 94,245 fewer African Americans. While the number of African Americans in the city had been increasing in the years following the hurricane, growth more or less flatlined by its tenth anniversary, and the black population of New Orleans decreased from 2017 to 2018.[47] The black population that has remained in, returned to, or moved into the city is also faced with intensified versions of some of the problems faced by pre-Katrina residents. While wages have not increased, the process of rebuilding the city has come with a wave of gentrification that has brought a 30 percent increase in average rent prices, and neighborhoods have become more racially segregated.[48] As journalist Ben Casselman describes, "Housing costs in parts of New Orleans now rival those in expensive coastal cities like Boston and New York, despite typical incomes that are far lower. New Orleans ranks among the worst cities in the country for housing affordability; 37 percent of renters spend more than half their pre-tax income on rent and utilities."[49] The impact of these economic pressures has hit the African American community disproportionately; Casselman writes that "fully 35 percent of black men under 25 in New Orleans are neither working nor in school, compared with 5 percent of white men in that age group," factors that contribute to the city's shrinking African American population as more young residents look to other cities for better economic opportunities.

Johnson describes post-Katrina shifts in the demographics of the New Orleans jazz scene as mirroring those of the city at large. "Now the...demographics of the city, and the socioeconomic numbers of the city, are so different to where African Americans are...losing a lot of numbers....And even more so, we are no longer the...majority population of musicians. Nor are we the club owners. So, the Hall serves [as] a very significant place because once again this is where local African Americans can be seen and heard and earn a wage."

He went on to contrast Preservation Hall with the nearby clubs on Frenchman Street, saying, "Most places on Frenchman Street do not hire black bands, black-led bands, black local bands. This is just what it is. New Orleans is a very racist place." The artist pages of the websites for Preservation Hall and the Spotted Cat, a popular Frenchman Street club, do indeed show significantly different demographics. On the Preservation Hall page, there are roughly twice as many black artists as white artists pictured, a ratio that mirrors the population of the city, and the Spotted Cat page is the opposite, showing approximately two all-white bands for each one that includes people of color.[50] Johnson relates the predominance of white musicians at the Spotted Cat to New Orleans's tourist economy:

> Patrons come down to New Orleans, just being frank, they don't want to see African Americans. Because first of all, the typical patron travelling to New Orleans is not African American....Think about it from the tourist perspective: You get off a plane, you don't know anything. All you know is what you saw on the TV show *Treme*....So then you take a club like the Spotted Cat on Frenchman Street that never has a cover charge...and historically always an all-white band....If people go to a foreign place, you would think that they would want to engage the local scene, but in actuality when people go to foreign places, they look for things that are comforting. So when Caucasians come from wherever they come from in America and they come to New Orleans, they are looking for something that's familiar to them. And also, being frank, when a white person hears a white person play music, they relate to that easier than if they hear me play it, because this white person is playing it in the exact same accent in which they like to hear. That's just how it goes.

Johnson's observations from his lived experience in the context of New Orleans tourism align with general trends in the appeal of familiarity to tourists described by psychological researchers. For example, a recent study concludes that "tourists in general prefer to meet compatriots and *not* local people when they travel to countries that are unknown to them," and "although most tourists seem to think about themselves that they are novelty seekers, most people still prefer an optimal balance of novelty and familiarity in their tourist experiences."[51] While Preservation Hall has always prioritized the work of local African American performers, considering its practices through the lens of tourism also raises questions about the display of black musicians to predominantly white visitors by white club owners, however well intentioned and however economically beneficial to the musicians who have performed there. Although the constellation of factors differentiating the tourist experiences on offer at Preservation Hall in comparison to other New Orleans jazz venues is multifaceted and complex, Johnson's perceptions of the role of race in the hiring practices and tourist appeal of local clubs speak to broader shared concerns in New Orleans about racial inequities highlighted or magnified by the post-Katrina rebuilding process and new landscape of tourism in the area.

Within this context, Preservation Hall's claims to heritage and community service offer important frames for the venue as it promotes itself to potential visitors. With its version of musical heritage rooted in mentorship rather than live reproduction of the sounds of early jazz records and its history as a sixty-year-old space founded by outsiders seeking to valorize a hundred-year-old local musical idiom, the Hall is an embodiment of Kirshenblatt-Gimblett's pithy assertion, "Memory is not reclaimed. It is produced."[52] In many ways, it has become a New Orleans jazz institution by creating space for the local jazz culture that, to the minds of tourists like Allan and Sandra Jaffe themselves, seemed to or ought to exist. Through its growth and the development of its touring ensemble and foundation, the Hall continues to push for the realization of an idealized New Orleans jazz culture.

Epilogue

On closing night at the old Stone in Alphabet City, John Zorn sat at the back of the room talking with friends before the venue's final set began. He asked someone if she wanted a souvenir, and she requested a lamp on the table near the door with a shade made from folded paper triangles. Zorn offered jokingly to sign it and said, "That's going to be at the Whitney in twenty years when they recreate The Stone." Despite the fact that Zorn himself was in the process of recreating The Stone across town at the New School, taking not just his community of musicians but also the photographs from the walls and the exact same number of chairs with him, his quip suggests that his venue will follow in the footsteps of other New York jazz spaces, disappearing from the live scene only to reappear as sculptures in museums, like Jason Moran's rendering of the Savoy Ballroom.

Indeed, a display of The Stone at the Whitney Museum of American Art would reflect many of the trends observable in live jazz performance spaces in the twenty-first century. The increased presence and scope of institutions, especially those like the Whitney, that are supported by donors who, through their sponsorship, designate them as providers of important but noncommercial services is significantly shaping the present landscape of live jazz. In fact, a little over a year after Zorn prophesized his lamp's future value, the Whitney opened an exhibition of Moran's sculptures including one of Slugs' Saloon, a venue that once operated about a block away from the former location of The Stone.[1] As part of the exhibition, a concert series made up of nine events was performed on the recreated stages inside the museum. Meanwhile, within a mile or two in either direction, regular performances carried on at the new Stone inside the New School and at Dizzy's Club inside Jazz at Lincoln Center, two more versions of small jazz clubs rebuilt to live in large-scale, nonprofit institutions.

Going to the trouble of recreating an old world of small jazz clubs inside a new landscape of nonprofit institutions demonstrates the role of heritage in contemporary performances of live jazz. Returning to Zorn's lamp, the suggestion that it belongs in a museum is also a suggestion that it holds a special connection to the past—until February 2018, it simply made light, but now it could have a second life in which it also makes heritage, and that heritage is key to its value. So many of the live performances documented in the previous chapters build heritage into the present, including Fred Hersch's interpretations of standard tunes, Robert Glasper's homage to Miles Davis, and the Eastman Jazz Ensemble's memorization of Ellington. As Preservation Hall makes explicit, maintaining jazz heritage has become central to the mission of numerous twenty-first-century jazz presenters. While live performance is a central strategy for preserving jazz heritage, educational programming is also ubiquitous in contemporary jazz. Just as the Whitney offers classes and school programming as part of its mission of collecting, preserving, interpreting, and exhibiting American art, jazz performances and formal jazz education now regularly go hand in hand. To teach people what jazz is, why it is important, and how to play it has become a larger and larger part of the operation of a typical jazz venue, a shift that frames the music not as entertainment but instead as personal and societal enrichment. The places in which jazz is performed give shape to the sounds they contain, defining the music's present as well as current understandings of its past and its potential value for the future.

Notes

INTRODUCTION

1. Paul Lopes, *The Rise of a Jazz Art World* (Cambridge: Cambridge University Press, 2002), 216.
2. Reproduced in *Keeping Time: Readings in Jazz History*, ed. Robert Walser (New York: Oxford University Press, 1999), 333.
3. Martin Williams, *The Jazz Tradition* (Oxford: Oxford University Press, 1970) and *Jazz Heritage* (Oxford: Oxford University Press, 1985).
4. Scott DeVeaux, "Constructing the Jazz Tradition: Jazz Historiography," *Black American Literature Forum* 25, no. 3 (Autumn 1991): 526.
5. Barbara Kirschenblatt-Gimblett, *Destination Culture: Tourism, Museums, and Heritage* (Berkeley: University of California Press, 1998), 156.
6. Kirschenblatt-Gimblett, *Destination Culture*, 150.
7. Kirschenblatt-Gimblett, 150.
8. Peggy Phelan, *Unmarked: The Politics of Performance* (New York: Routledge, 1993), 6–7.
9. Kirschenblatt-Gimblett, *Destination Culture*, 76.
10. Philip Auslander, *Liveness: Performance in a Mediatized Culture* (London and New York: Routledge, 1999); Jason Stanyek and Benjamin Piekut, "Deadness: Technologies of the Intermundane," *The Drama Review* 54, no. 21 (Spring 2010): 14–38.
11. [Christi Jay] Christopher J. Wells, "'Go Harlem!' Chick Webb and His Dancing Audience during the Great Depression" (PhD diss., University of North Carolina at Chapel Hill, 2014).
12. Darren Mueller, "The Ambassadorial LPs of Dizzy Gillespie: *World Statesman* and *Dizzy in Greece*," *Journal of the Society for American Music* 10,

no. 3 (August 2016): 239–69; "Quest for the Moment: The Audio Production of *Ellington at Newport*," *Jazz Perspectives* 8, no. 1 (October 2014): 2–23.

13. Tim Cresswell, *Place: An Introduction* (Hoboken: John Wiley & Sons, 2014), 19.

14. Cresswell, *Place*, 70–71.

15. Edward S. Casey, "How to Get from Space to Place in a Fairly Short Stretch of Time: Phenomenological Prolegomena," in *Senses of Place*, ed. Steven Feld and Keith H. Basso (Santa Fe: School of American Research Press, 1996, distributed by the University of Washington Press), 26.

16. Casey, "How to Get from Space to Place," 24.

17. George Lipsitz, *How Racism Takes Place* (Philadelphia: Temple University Press, 2011).

18. Lipsitz, *How Racism Takes Place*, 20.

19. Doreen Massey, *Space, Place, and Gender* (Minneapolis: University of Minnesota Press, 1994), 153.

20. Adam Krims, *Music and Urban Geography* (New York: Routledge, 2007), xxix.

21. Krims, *Music and Urban Geography*, xxxi.

22. Andrew Berish, "Space and Place in Jazz," in *The Routledge Companion to Jazz Studies*, ed. Nicholas Gebhardt, Nichole Rustin-Paschal, and Tony Whyton (New York: Routledge, 2019), 155.

23. David Ake, *Jazz Matters: Sound, Place, and Time since Bebop* (Berkeley: University of California Press, 2010), 7. Italics in original.

24. Philip Bohlman and Goffredo Plastino, eds., *Jazz Worlds / World Jazz* (Chicago: University of Chicago Press, 2016); Alex Rodriguez, "Making the Hang in Chile at Thelonious, Lugar de Jazz," *Jazz and Culture* 3, no. 1 (Spring/Summer 2020): 45–70.

25. Andrew Berish, *Lonesome Roads and Streets of Dreams: Place, Mobility, and Race in Jazz of the 1930s and '40s* (Chicago: University of Chicago Press, 2012), 6.

26. Patricia Price, *Dry Place: Landscapes of Belonging and Exclusion* (Minneapolis: University of Minnesota Press, 2004), xiii.

CHAPTER 1

1. Matthew Kassel, "As the Village Vanguard Turns 80, It Remains New York's Most Cherished Jazz Club," *The Observer*, February 17, 2015.

2. Ethan Iverson, interview with the author, July 29, 2009.

3. Ashley Kahn, "After 70 Years, the Village Vanguard Is Still in the Jazz Swing," *Wall Street Journal*, February 8, 2005.

4. Kassel, "As the Village Vanguard Turns 80."

5. Georgina Born, ed., *Music, Sound and Space: Transformations of Public and Private Experience* (Cambridge: Cambridge University Press, 2013), 16.

6. Born, *Music, Sound and Space*, 21.

7. Born, 19.

8. Barbara Kirschenblatt-Gimblett, "Theorizing Heritage," *Ethnomusicology* 39, no. 3 (Autumn 1995): 369.

9. Steve Schwartz and Michael Fitzgerald, "Chronology of Art Blakey (and the Jazz Messengers)," JazzMF, https://jazzmf.com/art-blakey-chronology-and-the-jazz-messengers/. Schwartz and Alexander use documentation from recordings of the band and announcements of live performances from newspapers and magazines to reconstruct Blakey's itinerary.

10. Performance dates and locations are drawn from venue and musician websites accessed in April 2019. Village Vanguard, www.villagevanguard.com; Antonio Sanchez, www.antoniosanchez.net/tour.html; Joe Lovano, www.joelovano.com/gigs/; Renee Rosnes, https://reneerosnes.com/performances/; Brad Mehldau, www.bradmehldau.com/tour; Mark Turner, markturnerjazz.com/concerts/.

11. Yoshi's, www.yoshis.com/venue-info/, accessed May 27, 2019.

12. Yoshi's, www.yoshis.com/venue-info/; Dakota, www.dakotacooks.com/about/faq/, accessed May 27, 2019; Jacob Kirn, "Jazz at the Bistro to Become $10 Million Education Center, Venue," *St. Louis Business Journal* (May 13, 2014), www.bizjournals.com/stlouis/news/2014/05/13/jazz-at-the-bistro-to-become-10-million-education.html; Dimitriou's Jazz Alley, www.jazzalley.com/www-home/history.jsp, accessed May 27, 2019.

13. Nighttown, "A Unique Cleveland Venue," www.nighttowncleveland.com/about/, accessed May 27, 2019.

14. Kahn, "After 70 Years."

15. Max Gordon, *Live at the Village Vanguard* (New York: St. Martin's Press, 1980), 27.

16. Lewis A. Erenberg, *Steppin' Out: New York Nightlife and the Transformation of American Culture, 1890–1930* (Westport, CT: Greenwood Press, 1981), 252–53.

17. Gordon, *Live at the Village Vanguard*, 61; Lorraine Gordon and Barry Singer, *Alive at the Village Vanguard: My Life In and Out of Jazz Time* (Milwaukee, WI: Hal Leonard, 2006), 106, 143–47.

18. L. Gordon and Singer, *Alive at the Village Vanguard*, 143–47.

19. L. Gordon and Singer, 96–99.

20. L. Gordon and Singer, 201–02.

21. Lopes, *Rise of a Jazz Art World*, 264–65.

22. L. Gordon and Singer, *Alive at the Village Vanguard*, 202.

23. John Howland, "Jazz with Strings: Between Jazz and the Great American Songbook," in *Jazz / Not Jazz: The Music and Its Boundaries*, ed. David Ake, Charles Hiroshi Garrett, and Daniel Goldmark (Berkeley: University of California Press, 2012), 114.

24. James Lincoln Collier, "Mainstream Jazz," Grove Music Online, www.oxfordmusiconline.com.

25. Scott DeVeaux, *The Birth of Bebop: A Social and Musical History* (Berkeley: University of California Press, 1997), 2. Emphasis in original.

26. Alex Stewart, *Making the Scene: Contemporary New York City Big Band Jazz* (Berkeley: University of California Press, 2007), 90.

27. L. Gordon and Singer, *Alive at the Village Vanguard*, 201.

28. Leonard Feather, review of *Waltz for Debby*, *DownBeat*, (April 26, 1962), 36.

29. C. Michael Bailey, review of *The Complete Village Vanguard Recordings, 1961*, by Bill Evans, All About Jazz, November 1, 2005, www.allaboutjazz.com/php/article.php?id=19577.

30. Philip Auslander, *Liveness: Performance in a Mediatized Culture* (London and New York: Routledge, 1999), 51.

31. Travis Jackson, *Blowin' the Blues Away: Performance and Meaning on the New York Jazz Scene* (Berkeley: University of California Press, 2012), 10–11, emphasis in original.

32. Kahn, "After 70 Years."

33. "Birdland History," Birdland, www.birdlandjazz.com, accessed 20 September 2009.

34. Nat Hentoff, "Introduction," in *Live at the Village Vanguard*, by Max Gordon (New York: St. Martin's Press, 1980), 5.

35. L. Gordon and Singer, *Alive at the Village Vanguard*, 204.

36. L. Gordon and Singer, 204, 234.

37. Andy Battaglia, "The Village Vanguard at 80: Legendary New York Jazz Club Is Still Setting the Pace," *The National*, June 18, 2015.

38. Battaglia, "Village Vanguard at 80."

39. Ethan Iverson, "Interview with Jed Eisenman," Do the Math, 2013, https://ethaniverson.com/interviews/interview-with-jed-eisenman/.

40. Sharon Zukin, *Naked City: The Death and Life of Authentic Urban Places* (Oxford: Oxford University Press, 2010), 39.

41. Neil Smith, Betsy Duncan, and Laura Reid, "From Disinvestment to Reinvestment: Mapping the Urban 'Frontier' in the Lower East Side," in *From Urban Village to East Village: The Battle for New York's Lower East Side*, ed. Janet L. Abu-Lughod et al. (Oxford: Blackwell Publishers, 1994), 163.

42. Betsy Schriffman, "America's Most Expensive ZIP Codes 2015," *Forbes*, November 10, 2015.

43. Paul Harris, "New York's Heart Loses Its Beat," *The Guardian*, August 13, 2005.

44. Jackson, *Blowin' the Blues Away*, 90.

45. L. Gordon and Singer, *Alive at the Village Vanguard*, 230; Ethan Iverson, interview with the author, July 29, 2009.

46. Fred Hersch, interview with author, July 28, 2009. All quotations of Hersch are drawn from this source unless otherwise specified.

47. *Let Yourself Go: The Lives of Fred Hersch*, directed by Katja Duregger, (Aha! DVD, 2008).

48. For a detailed study of the many New York City jazz clubs that coexisted with the Vanguard in the mid-twentieth century, see Patrick Burke, *Come in and Hear the Truth: Jazz and Race on 52nd Street* (Chicago: University of Chicago Press, 2008.)

49. Since our interview, Hersch has appeared at a Jazz at Lincoln Center venue, but not Dizzy's Club Coca Cola specifically. He played a concert entitled "Fred Hersch and Friends: Intimate Moments" at a space called the Appel Room in January of 2016, his first appearance at Jazz at Lincoln Center as a bandleader. Unlike the jazz club atmosphere of Dizzy's Club Coca Cola, which more directly mirrors and therefore competes with the Vanguard, the Appel

Room is a concert hall setting that offers jazz performances in a context reminiscent of a classical chamber music format.

50. For transcriptions and a more detailed analysis, see my article "Fred Hersch at the Village Vanguard: The Sound of Jazz Heritage at New York's Oldest Jazz Club," *Journal of the Society for American Music* 12, no. 4 (November 2018): 449–76.

51. As recorded by The Fred Hersch Trio, *Live at the Village Vanguard* (Palmetto Records PM2088, 2002).

52. In the 9 p.m. sets on July 22 (recorded for NPR) and July 25 (attended by the author) and the 11 p.m. set on July 26 (attended by the author), a total of twenty-seven performances included seven standards, ten jazz compositions, and ten Hersch originals. Each set contained at least two and no more than four of each type of tune.

53. Recorded July 22, 2009 for live broadcast by NPR, www.npr.org/event/music/106776373/fred-hersch-trio-live-at-the-village-vanguard?refresh=true, accessed September 13, 2016.

54. See my article "Fred Hersch at the Village Vanguard" for a more detailed analysis.

55. Ethan Iverson, interview with the author, July 29, 2009. All subsequent quotations of Iverson are from this source unless otherwise noted.

56. Jason Koransky, "And Now for Something Completely Different," *DownBeat* 71, no. 5 (May 2004), 8.

57. David Adler, "The Bad Plus: Honoring Great Music," *DownBeat* 70, no. 4 (April 2003), 26.

58. 9 p.m. set, July 29, 2009 (attended by author).

59. L. Gordon and Barry Singer, *Alive at the Village Vanguard*, 226, 48–50, 232.

60. Will Friedwald, "Woman at the Vanguard," *Wall Street Journal*, January 2, 2013.

61. Christian McBride, on "All Things Considered," National Public Radio, broadcast October 22, 2015; partial transcript available at www.npr.org/2015/10/22/450908686/why-everyone-wants-to-record-live-at-the-village-vanguard.

CHAPTER 2

1. John F. Kennedy Center for the Performing Arts, https://www.kennedy-center.org/Pages/VirtualTour/FoyerSouth, accessed June 4, 2019.

2. Fred Kaplan, "This Kennedy Center Director Is Making Performance Art out of Jazz. Can He Bring Fans Along?" *The Washington Post*, November 2, 2017, https://www.washingtonpost.com/lifestyle/magazine/how-the-kennedy-centers-director-of-jazz-is-redefining-the-national-cultural-center/2017/11/01/aa687370-af5c-11e7-be94-fabb0f1e9ffb_story.html?utm_term=.09d5343d82f2.

3. Kaplan, "This Kennedy Center Director Is Making Performance Art."

4. Kaplan.

5. Kaplan.

6. Peter Watrous, "Good News for Jazz, with a Big Caveat," *New York Times*, August 18, 1991: 23.

7. Watrous, "Good News for Jazz."

8. Sheila Rule, "Lincoln Center's Menu of Jazz Is Quadrupled," *New York Times*, May 28, 1992: C14.

9. Bill Milkowski, "Expanding the Mission: Jazz at Lincoln Center," *JazzTimes*, supp. Jazz Education Guide, 2000: 43.

10. For lengthy critiques of JALC, see Stuart Nicholson, *Is Jazz Dead? (Or Has It Moved to a New Address)*, (New York: Routledge, 2005) and Eric Nisenson, *Blue: The Murder of Jazz* (New York: St. Martin's Press, 1997).

11. Peter Applebome, "A Jazz Success Story with a Tinge of the Blues," *New York Times*, September 22, 1998: E1.

12. Giovanni Russonello, "At 30, What Does Jazz at Lincoln Center Mean?" *New York Times*, September 17, 2017, https://www.nytimes.com/2017/09/13/arts/music/jazz-at-lincoln-center-30th-anniversary.html.

13. Ben Ratliff, "Jazz Flexes New Muscles in Lincoln Center Schedule," *New York Times*, January 30, 1997: C14; Applebome, "A Jazz Success Story," E1.

14. James C. McKinley, Jr., "Just One Bishop at Jazz Church of High Purity," *New York Times*, December 7, 2012, https://www.nytimes.com/2012/12/09/arts/music/wynton-marsalis-holds-reins-at-jazz-at-lincoln-center.html?mtrref=www.google.com.

15. Russonello, "At 30."

16. Eric Porter, *What Is This Thing Called Jazz? African American Musicians as Artists, Critics, and Activists* (Berkeley: University of California Press, 2002), 288.

17. Applebome, "A Jazz Success Story," E1.

18. Rafi Zabor and Vic Garbarini, "Wynton vs. Herbie: The Purist and the Crossbreeder Duke It Out," *Musician* 77 (March 1985), reprinted in *Keeping Time: Readings in Jazz History*, ed. Robert Walser (New York: Oxford University Press, 1999), 339–51, quotations from 343–44.

19. Ann S. Faulkner, "Does Jazz Put the Sin in Syncopation?," *Ladies' Home Journal*, August 1921: 16.

20. Marty Khan, *Straight Ahead: A Comprehensive Guide to the Business of Jazz (Without Sacrificing Dignity or Artistic Integrity)* (Tucson, AZ: Outward Visions, 2004), 19.

21. Khan, *Straight Ahead*, 10.

22. Wynton Marsalis with Geoffrey C. Ward, *Moving to Higher Ground: How Jazz Can Change Your Life* (New York: Random House, 2008), xiv–xv, 38.

23. Dale Chapman, *The Jazz Bubble: Neoclassical Jazz in Neoliberal Culture* (Berkeley: University of California Press, 2018), 14.

24. Chapman, *The Jazz Bubble*, 12–14.

25. Stanley Crouch, liner notes to *Jazz at Lincoln Center Presents: The Fire of the Fundamentals*, Columbia CK 57592, 1994.

26. In 2013 JALC began providing a list of Hall of Fame nominees rather than a list of inductees, and additions to the Hall of Fame began to be chosen through an online popular vote. This shift may have come as a response to

critiques of the earlier model of strict control over new Hall of Fame musicians by JALC alone. The names-nominating committee members and criteria for nomination are provided on the JALC website, accessed July 9, 2014, http://academy.jalc.org/hall-of-fame/. The online Hall of Fame interactive website that once included history, recordings, and photographs is no longer maintained.

27. Tracy McMullen, *Haunthenticity: Musical Replay and the Fear of the Real* (Middletown, CT: Wesleyan University Press, 2019), 98.

28. Stewart, *Making the Scene*, 62.

29. Nicholson, *Is Jazz Dead?*, 69.

30. Stanyek and Piekut, "Deadness," 15.

31. Stanyek and Piekut, 14.

32. Stanyek and Piekut, 17–18.

33. Stanyek and Piekut, 18.

34. Nichole Rustin-Paschal, *The Kind of Man I Am: Jazzmasculinity and the World of Charles Mingus Jr.* (Middletown, CT: Wesleyan University Press, 2017), 5.

35. Alyn Shipton, *Fats Waller: The Cheerful Little Earful* (London: Continuum, 1988), 3.

36. "The Music of Fats Waller," recorded April 17, 2010, Jazz at Lincoln Center Archives.

37. Judy Carmichael, phone interview with the author, June 6, 2010. All subsequent quotations of Carmichael are from this source unless otherwise noted.

38. "Fats Waller: A Handful of Keys," recorded April 17, 2010, 7:30 p.m. set.

39. "Fats Waller."

40. Dick Hyman, phone interview with the author, June 1, 2010. All subsequent quotations of Hyman are from this source unless otherwise noted.

41. Billie Jean King with Kim Chapin, *Billie Jean* (New York: Harper & Row, 1974), 103. After a tournament advertising men's prizes totaling $25,000 while women were to split only $2,000 in winnings, King and eight other women left the U.S. Lawn Tennis Association to establish the first independent women's tennis tour in 1971, the first step toward more equitable playing opportunities and compensation for women players. The Pacific Coast Championships raised the women's prize from $2,000 to $9,000 three days prior to the tournament in response to the women's complaints. The tournament was still boycotted by King and the other eight women who started the Virginia Slims tour.

42. King, *Billie Jean*, 165.

43. King, 169–70; James Pipkin, "Life on the Cusp: Lynda Huey and Billie Jean King" in *Impossible to Hold: Women and Culture in the 1960s*, ed. Avital Bloch and Lauri Umansky (New York: New York University Press, 2005), 55.

44. Pipkin, "Life on the Cusp," 55.

45. Billie Jean King, speech as host during the Mary Lou Williams Centennial on November 14, 2009. Transcribed from a recording of the concert housed at the Jazz at Lincoln Center library. All subsequent quotations of King are from this source unless otherwise noted.

46. D. Antoinette Handy, "First Lady of the Jazz Keyboard," *The Black Perspective in Music* 8, no. 2 (Autumn 1980): 203.

47. Handy, "First Lady," 204.
48. Tammy L. Kernodle, *Soul on Soul: The Life and Music of Mary Lou Williams* (Boston: Northeastern University Press, 2004), 2.
49. Kernodle, *Soul on Soul*, 82.
50. Kernodle, 182.
51. Guest performers like the two additional pianists in the Mary Lou Williams performance are features of most programs. For example, the Bill Evans tribute later that season included a total of six extra players along with the regular orchestra. New arrangements of important works not originally for big band are also commonplace. At the Evans concert, nearly all the pieces performed by the big band were new arrangements of Evans's compositions and recorded performances originally for piano trio.
52. JALC sidestepped Williams's avant-garde music in much the same manner as it did her sacred works. While King briefly mentioned her collaboration with Cecil Taylor as an important aspect of Williams's all-inclusive resume at the beginning of the concert, none of Williams more dissonant experiments from the 1960s and '70s made the cut in the musical programming. Another track from the original *Black Christ of the Andes* release called "A Fungus Among Us" is an example of some of Williams's more free jazz-tinted composing and playing. Its asymmetrical phrasing, unpredictable and dissonant harmonies, and flexible approach to time clearly relate to other free jazz experiments of the 1960s, and the omission of this work and all others like it again serves to keep the picture presented of Williams clear of the more controversial or niche-oriented margins of jazz history.
53. John A. Tynan, "Natural Flow: The Bill Evans Trio," *DownBeat*, June 17, 1965: 20.
54. David Ake, *Jazz Cultures* (Berkeley: University of California Press, 2002), 99.
55. Ingrid Monson, *Freedom Sounds: Civil Rights Call Out to Jazz and Africa* (New York: Oxford University Press, 2007), 12.
56. Monson, *Freedom Sounds*, 106.
57. Monson, 89.
58. Monson.
59. Peter Pettinger, *Bill Evans: How My Heart Sings* (New Haven: Yale University Press, 1998), 62.
60. Miles Davis with Quincy Troupe, *Miles: The Autobiography* (New York: Simon & Schuster, 1989), 221.
61. Pettinger, *Bill Evans*, 63.
62. Pettinger, 131.
63. Martin Williams, review of *Sunday at the Village Vanguard* by the Bill Evans Trio in *DownBeat*, March 1, 1962: 32.
64. Tynan, "Natural Flow," 21.
65. Paul Allen Anderson, "'My Foolish Heart': Bill Evans and the Public Life of Feelings," *Jazz Perspectives* 7, no. 3 (2013): 218.
66. Nat Hentoff, review of *The Jazz Workshop* by George Russell, *Down-*

Beat, August 8, 1957: 26; Dom Cerulli, review of *Brandeis University Festival*, *DownBeat*, August 7, 1958: 22.

67. Hentoff, review of *New Jazz Conceptions*, *DownBeat*, March 21, 1957: 24–25.

68. Don DeMichael, review of *Portrait in Jazz* by Bill Evans, *DownBeat*, September 15, 1960: 24. Italics in original.

69. DeMichael, review of *Interplay* by Bill Evans, *DownBeat*, July 18, 1963: 20–21.

70. Pete Welding, review of *Undercurrent* by Bill Evans and Jim Hall, *DownBeat*, November 22, 1962: 30–32.

71. Bill Charlap, speech as host during the Bill Evans concert on May 15, 2010. Transcribed from a recording of the concert housed at the Jazz at Lincoln Center library. All subsequent quotations of Charlap are from this source unless otherwise noted.

72. *Blue in Green* by Bill Evans, arranged by Ted Nash, located at the Jazz at Lincoln Center library.

73. Chapman, *Jazz Bubble*, 12.

74. Farah Jasmine Griffin, *If You Can't Be Free, Be a Mystery: In Search of Billie Holiday* (New York: Free Press, 2001), 143.

75. Herman S. Gray, *Cultural Moves: African Americans and the Politics of Representation* (Berkeley: University of California Press, 2005), 4.

76. Gray, *Cultural Moves*, 47.

77. Gray, 52. Emphasis in original.

78. Chapman, *Jazz Bubble*, 12.

79. Kaplan, "This Kennedy Center Director."

80. Giovanni Russonello, "After a Scandal, the New Orleans Jazz Market Rises Again," *New York Times*, May 28, 2019, https://www.nytimes.com/2019/05/28/arts/music/new-orleans-jazz-market.html.

81. Russonello, "After a Scandal."

82. Russonello.

83. McKinley, "Just One Bishop."

84. Howard Reich, "A Jazz Nexus Takes Shape in San Francisco," *Chicago Tribune*, May 16, 2011, https://www.chicagotribune.com/entertainment/ct-xpm-2011-05-16-ct-live-0517-jazz-san-francisco-20110516-story.html.

85. Nate Chinen, "As Open as the Genre It Celebrates," *New York Times*, January 26, 2013, https://www.nytimes.com/2013/01/26/arts/music/at-sfjazz-center-a-genres-boundaries-are-flexible.html.

86. Chinen, "As Open as the Genre."

87. Reich, "A Jazz Nexus."

88. Chinen, "As Open as the Genre."

89. Chinen.

90. Chinen.

91. Sam Whiting, "SFJazz Hits High Note at 5-Year Mark," *SFGate*, July 9, 2018, https://www.sfgate.com/music/article/SFJazz-hits-high-note-at-5-year-mark-13051418.php#item-85307-tbla-5.

92. David Fricke, "Branford Marsalis' Secret," *JazzTimes*, June 3, 2019,

https://jazztimes.com/features/interviews/branford-marsalis-secret/; Wynton Marsalis quoted by Eugene Holley, Jr., "Wynton Marsalis: Jazz Messenger," *Ebony*, September 4, 2012, https://www.ebony.com/entertainment/interview-wynton-marsalis-jazz-messenger-552/2/.

93. "The Art of Sampling: How Robert Glasper Sampled Miles Davis on 'Ghetto Walking,'" https://pudding.cool/2017/03/sampling/.

94. Monica Poling, "Hitting a High Note," *Bespoke Concierge*, June 23, 2014, www.bespokemagazineonline.com/hitting-high-note/; "Audience," www.bespokemagazineonline.com/about/.

95. See Chapman, *Jazz Bubble*, 157–77, for an analysis of urban redevelopment and the closure of jazz clubs in the Fillmore District.

96. Mike Greensill quoted by Whiting, "SFJazz Hits High Note."

97. Whiting, "SFJazz Hits High Note."

98. Phone interview with the author, June 18, 2019.

99. Owen Courrèges, "Irvin Mayfield's Jazz Market and the Forced Gentrification of Central City," *Uptown Messenger*, June 8, 2015, http://uptownmessenger.com/2015/06/owen-courreges-irwin-mayfields-jazz-market-and-the-forced-gentrification-of-central-city/.

CHAPTER 3

1. Ken Prouty, *Knowing Jazz: Community, Pedagogy, and Canon in the Information Age* (Jackson: University of Mississippi Press, 2012), 47.

2. Paul Berliner, *Thinking in Jazz: The Infinite Art of Improvisation* (Chicago: University of Chicago Press, 1994), 37.

3. Berliner, *Thinking in Jazz*, 55.

4. Sherrie Tucker, *Swing Shift: "All-Girl" Bands of the 1940s* (Durham: Duke University Press, 2000), 109.

5. Dan Murphy, "Jazz Studies in American Schools and Colleges: A Brief History," *Jazz Educators Journal* 26 (1994): 34.

6. Ake, *Jazz Matters*, 144–49.

7. Prouty, *Knowing Jazz*, 46.

8. Dick Hebdige, *Subculture: The Meaning of Style* (London: Taylor & Francis Group, 1981), 12–13.

9. M. J. Toswell, *Today's Medieval University* (Kalamazoo, MI: ARC Humanities Press, 2017).

10. Paul W. Gooch, *Course Correction: A Map for the Distracted University* (Toronto: University of Toronto Press, 2019), 216.

11. Gooch, *Course Correction*, 222.

12. Gooch, 223, 225.

13. Henry Kingsbury, *Music Talent & Performance: Conservatory Cultural System* (Philadelphia: Temple University Press, 1988), 35.

14. Bruno Nettl, "Heartland Excursions: Exercises in Musical Ethnography," *The World of Music* 34, no. 1 (1992), 29.

15. Gary W. Kennedy, "Jazz Education," in *The New Grove Dictionary of Jazz*, 2nd ed., ed. Barry Kernfeld, *Grove Music Online, Oxford Music Online*,

www.oxfordmusiconline.com/subscriber/article/grove/music/J602300, accessed September 28, 2011.

16. Philip Anson, "Summertime and the Listening Is Not Always Easy," *Globe and Mail*, August 15, 1998: C10.

17. Andrew Alter, "Gurus, Shishyas and Educators: Adaptive Strategies in Post-Colonial North Indian Music Institutions," in *Music Cultures in Contact: Convergences and Collisions*, ed. Margaret J. Kartomi and Stephen Blum (Sydney: Currency Press, 1994), 165.

18. Alter, "Gurus, Shishyas and Educators," 163.

19. Nicholson, *Is Jazz Dead*, 100–01.

20. Nicholson, 116.

21. John P. Murphy, "Beyond the Improvisation Class: Learning to Improvise in a University Jazz Studies Program," in *Musical Improvisation: Art, Education, and Society*, ed. Gabriel Solis and Bruno Nettl (Urbana: University of Illinois Press, 2009), 172–184.

22. Ake, *Jazz Matters*, 103.

23. Ake, 103.

24. Ake, 115.

25. Ake, 116.

26. Pete Madsen, telephone interview with the author, October 22, 2019. All quotations of Madsen are from this source unless otherwise noted.

27. Kevin Eagan, Ella Bara Stolzenberg, Joseph J. Ramirez, Melissa C. Aragon, Maria Ramirez Suchard, and Sylvia Hurtado, *The American Freshman: National Norms Fall 2014* (Los Angeles: Higher Education Research Institute), 2014; Michael A. Wilner, "Are Students Who Go Far Away to College More Likely to Study Abroad?" *New York Times* (blog), June 10, 2013, https://thechoice.blogs.nytimes.com/2013/06/10/are-students-who-go-far-away-to-college-more-likely-to-study-abroad/?_r=0; Nicholas Hillman and Taylor Weichman, *Education Deserts: The Continued Significance of 'Place' in the Twenty-First Century*, Viewpoints: Voices from the Field (Washington, DC: American Council on Education, 2016).

28. Hillman and Weichman, *Education Deserts*, 3.

29. Niraj Chokshi, "Map: The States College Kids Can't Wait to Leave," *Washington Post* (blog), June 5, 2014, www.washingtonpost.com/blogs/govbeat/wp/2014/06/05/map-the-states-college-kids-cant-wait-to-leave/.

30. Ake, *Jazz Cultures*, 123.

31. Mike Van Bebber, interview with the author, May 6, 2010. All subsequent quotations of Van Bebber are from this source unless otherwise noted.

32. Bill Dobbins, interview with the author, April 15, 2010. All subsequent quotations of Dobbins are from this source unless otherwise noted.

33. Gabriel Solis, "Genius, Improvisation, and the Narratives of Jazz," in *Musical Improvisation: Art, Education, and Society*, ed. Solis and Bruno Nettl (Urbana: University of Illinois Press, 2009), 97.

34. The ensemble continued to feature works by student composers and arrangers in addition to the Ellington music they performed.

35. Tim Craig, interview with the author, May 4, 2010. All subsequent quotations of Craig are from this source unless otherwise noted.

36. Kenneth Prouty, "Canons in Harmony, or Canons in Conflict: A Cultural Perspective on the Curriculum and Pedagogy of Jazz Improvisation," *Research and Issues in Music Education* 2, no. 1 (September 2004), www.stthomas.edu/rimeonline/vol2/prouty.htm, accessed September 28, 2011.

37. Ake, *Jazz Cultures*, 119.

38. Ake, 113.

39. Nicholson, *Is Jazz Dead?*, 109.

40. Tommy Poole, phone interview with the author, October 22, 2019. All subsequent quotations of Poole are from this source.

41. Kate Duncan, phone interview with the author, November 15, 2019. All subsequent quotations of Duncan are from this source.

42. Prouty, *Knowing Jazz*, 71

43. McMullen, *Haunthenticity*, 98.

CHAPTER 4

1. The Stone, www.thestonenyc.com, accessed June 2010. For analyses of other artist-run experimental music spaces operating during the same period as The Stone at its original location, see Alan Stanbridge on the now-closed venue Somewhere There in Toronto ("Somewhere There: Contemporary Music, Performance Spaces, and Cultural Policy," in *People Get Ready: The Future of Jazz Is Now!*, ed. Ajay Heble and Rob Wallace [Durham: Duke University Press, 2013], 184–96) and Amanda Scherbenske on Ibeam, a space in Brooklyn ("On the Production of Alternative Music Places: Im-materiality, Labor, and Meaning," *Popular Music and Society* 41, no. 4 [2018]: 408–23).

2. Larry Blumenfeld, "John Zorn Is Rolling The Stone from Avenue C to The New School," *The Village Voice*, March 6, 2017, https://www.villagevoice.com/2017/03/06/john-zorn-is-rolling-the-stone-from-avenue-c-to-the-new-school/.

3. Eitan Y. Wilf, *School for Cool: The Academic Jazz Program and the Paradox of Institutionalized Creativity* (Chicago: University of Chicago Press, 2014).

4. Kurt Gottschalk, "Tyshawn Sorey," All About Jazz, August 16, 2009, http://www.allaboutjazz.com/php/article.php?id=33674, accessed November 22, 2011.

5. Bill Milkowski, "John Zorn: The Working Man," *JazzTimes*, May 2009, http://jazztimes.com/articles/24597-john-zorn-the-working-man, accessed November 25, 2011. For information on Zorn's relationship with the press, see See Howard Mandel, "Musicians Dread Words," *Jazz Beyond Jazz*, March 2, 2008, http://www.artsjournal.com/jazzbeyondjazz/2008/03/musicians_dread_words.html#more, accessed November 25, 2011.

6. Kyle Gann, *Music Downtown: Writings from the* Village Voice (Berkeley: University of California Press, 2006), 12.

7. Bill Milkowski, "John Zorn: The Working Man," *JazzTimes*, May 2009, http://jazztimes.com/articles/24597-john-zorn-the-working-man, accessed November 25, 2011.

8. George E. Lewis, *A Power Stronger than Itself: The AACM and American Experimental Music* (Chicago: University of Chicago Press, 2008), 331.

9. Edward Strickland, *American Composers: Dialogues on Contemporary Music* (Indianapolis: Indiana University Press, 1991), 129, 138.
10. Lewis, *A Power Stronger than Itself*, 98.
11. Lewis, xl–xli.
12. John Rockwell, "As Important as Anyone in His Generation," *New York Times*, February 21, 1988: sec. 2 p. 27.
13. Rockwell, "Jazz: Two Braxton Programs," *New York Times*, April 23, 1982: C32.
14. Strickland, *American Composers*, 130.
15. John Brackett, *John Zorn: Tradition and Transgression* (Bloomington: Indiana University Press, 2008), xx.
16. Brackett, *John Zorn*, 21.
17. Brackett, xx.
18. John Zorn, *Arcana II: Musicians on Music* (New York: Hips Road, 2007), v.
19. Phelan, *Unmarked*, 10.
20. Phelan, 6.
21. Phelan, 5.
22. Larry Blumenfeld, "John Zorn Is Rolling The Stone from Avenue C to The New School," *The Village Voice*, March 6, 2017, https://www.villagevoice.com/2017/03/06/john-zorn-is-rolling-the-stone-from-avenue-c-to-the-new-school/.
23. Blumenfeld, "John Zorn Is Rolling The Stone."
24. Cole Gagne, *Soundpieces 2: Interviews with American Composers* (Metuchen, NJ: Scarecrow Press, 1993), 525.
25. Kirschenblatt-Gimblett, *Destination Culture*, 223.
26. Kirschenblatt-Gimblett, 245.
27. Benjamin Piekut, *Experimentalism Otherwise: The New York Avant-Garde and Its Limits* (Berkeley: University of California Press, 2011), 15.
28. Piekut, *Experimentalism Otherwise*, 6, 11.
29. Piekut, *Experimentalism Otherwise*, 7.
30. Judith Butler, *Excitable Speech: A Politics of the Performative* (New York: Routledge, 1997), 1–2.
31. Butler, *Excitable Speech*, 163.
32. Michael Heller, *Loft Jazz: Improvising New York in the 1970s* (Berkeley: University of California Press, 2017), 137.
33. Heller, *Loft Jazz*, 13.
34. Howard Mandel, "Who What Where Why Jazz: Jazz Great John Zorn's The Stone Club," *New York Press* (September 7, 2005), http://www.nypress.com/article-12018-jazz-who-what-where-why.html, accessed November 26, 2011.
35. "J.K.," review of The Stone, September 1, 2011, http://www.yelp.com/biz/the-stone-new-york, accessed November 26, 2011.
36. "addrockride," review of The Stone, February 11, 2011, http://maps.google.com, accessed November 26, 2011.
37. "Elite '11," review of The Stone, February 5, 2009, http://www.yelp.com/biz/the-stone-new-york, accessed November 27, 2011.

38. "Dave K.," review of The Stone, February 16, 2010, http://www.yelp.com/biz/the-stone-new-york, accessed November 27, 2011.
39. "Molly T.," review of The Stone, April 11, 2011, http://www.yelp.com/biz/the-stone-new-york, accessed November 27, 2011.
40. Scherbenske, "On the Production," 416.
41. The Stone, http://thestonenyc.com, accessed December 6, 2011.
42. The Stone, http://thestonenyc.com.
43. The Stone, http://thestonenyc.com.
44. Sylvie Courvoisier, interview with the author, June 22, 2010.
45. The Stone, calendar, http://thestonenyc.com/calendar.php?month=-19, accessed December 6, 2011.
46. George Robinson, "Romancing The Stone," *The Jewish Week*, March 30, 2007: 45.
47. Sylvie Courvoisier, interview with the author, June 22, 2010.
48. Robinson, "Romancing The Stone."
49. The Stone, calendar, http://thestonenyc.com/calendar.php?month=-10, accessed December 7, 2011.
50. Marc Ribot, "Days of Bread and Roses," in *People Get Ready: The Future of Jazz Is Now!*, ed. Ajay Heble and Rob Wallace (Durham: Duke University Press, 2013), 148.
51. Scherbenske, "On the Production," 420.
52. Elizabeth A. Harris, "Where Nearly Half of Pupils Are Homeless, School Aims to Be Teacher, Therapist, Even Santa," *New York Times*, June 6, 2016, https://www.nytimes.com/2016/06/07/nyregion/public-school-188-in-manhattan-about-half-the-students-are-homeless.html.
53. United States Census Bureau, https://www.census.gov/censusexplorer/censusexplorer.html, accessed January 28, 2019.
54. Krims, *Music and Urban Geography*, xxxi.
55. Richard Kessler, phone interview with the author, August 31, 2018. Subsequent quotations of Kessler are drawn from the same source unless otherwise indicated.
56. Scherbenske, "On the Production," 410.
57. Help the Stone Start Its Next Chapter, https://www.generosity.com/community-fundraising/help-the-stone-start-its-next-chapter, accessed November 30, 2017. The fundraising campaign was successful, bringing in over $30,000, mostly through relatively small individual gifts. Donors included people active in the New York jazz scene, like Village Vanguard manager Jed Eisenmann and musicians Peter Evans and Sylvie Courvoisier.
58. Sasha Frere-Jones, "Heart of Stone," *Artforum*, April 2, 2018, https://www.artforum.com/music/sasha-frere-jones-on-the-closing-of-the-stone-s-second-street-location-74880.
59. Frere-Jones, "Heart of Stone."
60. Ribot, "Days of Bread and Roses," 143.
61. Ribot, 150.
62. Wilf, *School for Cool*, 10.
63. Wilf, 87.
64. Wilf, 17.

65. Wilf, 52.
66. Dave Douglas, email correspondence with the author, May 27, 2017.
67. Phelan, *Unmarked*, 2.

CHAPTER 5

1. Kevin Fox Gotham, *Authentic New Orleans: Tourism, Culture, and Race in the Big Easy* (New York: New York University Press, 2007), vii.
2. Lonely Planet, "New Orleans in Detail: Month by Month," https://www.lonelyplanet.com/usa/new-orleans/planning/month-by-month/a/nar/7d2b68b5-987f-404b-a449-ac406cc2f0b5/362207, accessed September 18, 2019.
3. At present, New Orleans visitor numbers are highly contested due to a recent change in who counts tourists for the city and how those numbers are determined. The more conservative count by the University of New Orleans (UNO) puts 2017 visitors at around 11 million while the Virginia-based D. K. Shifflet and Associates estimates 17.7 million. Some of the discrepancy can be accounted for by the UNO practice of only counting visitors who come from more than fifty miles away while Shifflet counts day trips from neighboring towns. See Tyler Bridges, "How Many Visitors Come to New Orleans Each Year? Depends Whom You Ask—And What Counts," *New Orleans Advocate*, March 9, 2019, https://www.nola.com/news/article_378c4c08-8c5a-58e5-b4cb-e3f852f5fba9.html. The Preservation Hall Foundation reports over 150,000 annual visitors at the Hall, https://www.preshallfoundation.org/whoweare.
4. J. Mark Souther, "Making the 'Birthplace of Jazz': Tourism and Musical Heritage Marketing in New Orleans," *Louisiana History: The Journal of the Louisiana Historical Association* 44, no. 1 (Winter 2003): 53.
5. Allan Jaffe, Hogan Jazz Archive Oral Histories Collection, HJA-033, Tulane University Special Collections, April 16, 1969.
6. Jaffe, Hogan Jazz Archive.
7. Bruce Boyd Raeburn, *New Orleans Style and the Writing of American Jazz History* (Ann Arbor: University of Michigan Press, 2009), 1–2.
8. Berish, *Lonesome Roads*, 14.
9. Paul Lopes, *The Rise of a Jazz Art World* (Cambridge: Cambridge University Press, 1992), 159–60.
10. Lopes, *Rise of a Jazz Art World*, 49.
11. Lopes, 55.
12. Stephanie Doktor, "'Sweet' Jazz and Luckies: How a White Man Sold Black Music to White People," paper presented at the Conference of the American Musicological Society, Boston, November 2019.
13. Interview with the author, December 18, 2009. The collectors' names and specific location have been removed to protect their privacy. All subsequent quotations relevant to the collection are from this source.
14. Samuel Charters, *A Trumpet around the Corner: The Story of New Orleans Jazz* (Jackson: University of Mississippi Press, 2008), 341.
15. Tex Wyndham, *Texas Shout: How Dixieland Jazz Works* (Seattle: Light, Words, & Music, 1997), 111.
16. Charters, *A Trumpet around the Corner*, 352.

17. Patrick Burke, *Come in and Hear the Truth: Jazz and Race on 52nd Street* (Chicago: University of Chicago Press, 2008), 14.
18. Burke, *Come in and Hear the Truth*, 30.
19. Burke, 122.
20. Burke, 123.
21. Burke, 185–86.
22. Bebop is another form of jazz often discussed in terms of anticommercial values, but, as work by Scott DeVeaux suggests (see *The Birth of Bebop*), the rhetoric surrounding bop served more to link the music to concepts of high art than to actually remove it from systems of commercial exchange. After the initial popularity of the Dixieland revival, early jazz followed a path to the near complete commercial obsolescence outside New Orleans described by Wyndham (see *Texas Shout*) while bebop enjoyed a period of reasonable economic viability throughout the 1950s and '60s that continues to some extent in the present day.
23. Burke, *Come in and Hear the Truth*, 158.
24. J. Mark Souther, *New Orleans on Parade: Tourism and the Transformation of the Crescent City* (Baton Rouge: Louisiana State University Press, 2006), 115.
25. Souther, *New Orleans on Parade*, 104.
26. Souther, 116.
27. Tom Sancton, "Hall That Jazz," *Vanity Fair*, December 9, 2011, https://www.vanityfair.com/culture/2012/01/preservation-hall-201201.
28. Souther, *New Orleans on Parade*, 103.
29. Jaffe, Hogan Jazz Archive.
30. Calvin Johnson, Jr., phone interview with the author, June 18, 2019.
31. Souther, *New Orleans on Parade*, 109.
32. American Federation of Musicians Local 174-496, HJA-001, Tulane University Special Collections.
33. Charles Suhor, "Jazz in New Orleans in the 1960s," *Jazz Archivist* 10, no. 2 (May–December 1995), 7.
34. John Pope, "'Sweet Emma' Barrett, Jazz Musician, Is Dead," *Times-Picayune*, January 29, 1983.
35. Souther, *New Orleans on Parade*, 116.
36. Sancton, "Hall That Jazz."
37. Gretchen Carlson, "Jazz Goes to the Movies: Contemporary Jazz Musicians' Work at the Intersections of the Jazz and Film Art Worlds," (PhD diss., University of Virginia, 2016), 69–139.
38. Carlson, "Jazz Goes to the Movies," 108.
39. Carlson, 107–08.
40. Anne Dvinge, "Pride at Preservation Hall: Tourism, Spectacle, and Musicking in New Orleans Jazz," in *Creating and Consuming the American South*, ed. Martyn Bone, Brian Ward, and William A. Link (Gainesville: University Press of Florida, 2015), 171.
41. Sancton, "Hall That Jazz."
42. Sarah Suhadolnik, "Navigating Jazz: Music, Place, and New Orleans," (PhD diss., University of Michigan, 2016), 139–40.

43. Sancton, "Hall That Jazz."

44. Johnson, interview with the author. All subsequent quotations of Johnson are from this source.

45. Raeburn, *New Orleans Style*, 257. Emphasis in original.

46. Gotham, *Authentic New Orleans*, 16–17.

47. The Data Center, "Who Lives in New Orleans and Metro Parishes Now?" October 10, 2019, https://www.datacenterresearch.org/data-resources/who-lives-in-new-orleans-now/?utm_source=twitter&utm_medium=post&utm_campaign=optimism.

48. Jenn Bently, "Pushed Out: The Changing Demographics of New Orleans," *Big Easy Magazine*, February 11, 2019, https://www.bigeasymagazine.com/2019/02/11/pushed-out-the-changing-demographics-of-new-orleans/.

49. Ben Casselman, "Katrina Washed Away New Orleans's Black Middle Class," *FiveThirtyEight*, August 24, 2015, https://fivethirtyeight.com/features/katrina-washed-away-new-orleanss-black-middle-class/.

50. As of October 2019, the artist page for Preservation Hall (http://preservationhall.com/hall/player-bios/) contains sixteen photos of individual musicians who appear black and eight who appear white, along with two ensemble photos, both of which are majority black. The Spotted Cat page (https://www.spottedcatmusicclub.com/bands) has primarily group photos; twenty individuals appear to be all white while twelve appear to be racially mixed or black.

51. Svein Larsen, Ktharina Wolff, Rouven Doran, and Torvald Ogaard, "What Makes Tourist Experiences Interesting," *Frontiers in Psychology* 10 (August 2019), doi:10.3389/fpsyg.2019.01603.

52. Kirshenblatt-Gimblett, *Destination Culture*, 187.

EPILOGUE

1. For more on Moran's Slugs' sculpture, see Kimberly Hannon Teal, "Jazz, Space, and Labor: Mixed Media Aestheticization of Work Songs in Jason Moran's STAGED," *Jazz Research Journal* 13/1–2 (2019), 93–109.

Bibliography

Adler, David. "The Bad Plus: Honoring Great Music." *DownBeat*, vol. 70, no. 4 (April 2003): 26.
Ake, David. *Jazz Cultures*. Berkeley: University of California Press, 2002.
———. *Jazz Matters: Sound, Place, and Time since Bebop*. Berkeley: University of California Press, 2010.
Alter, Andrew. "Gurus, Shishyas and Educators: Adaptive Strategies in Post-Colonial North Indian Music Institutions." In *Music Cultures in Contact: Convergences and Collisions*, edited by Margaret J. Kartomi and Stephen Blum, 158–68. Sydney: Currency Press, 1994.
Anderson, Paul Allen. "'My Foolish Heart': Bill Evans and the Public Life of Feelings." *Jazz Perspectives*, vol. 7, no. 3 (2013): 205–49.
Anson, Philip. "Summertime and the Listening Is Not Always Easy." *Globe and Mail*, August 15, 1998.
Applebome, Peter. "A Jazz Success Story with a Tinge of the Blues." *New York Times*, September 22, 1998.
Auslander, Philip. *Liveness: Performance in a Mediatized Culture*. London and New York: Routledge, 1999.
Battaglia, Andy. "The Village Vanguard at 80: Legendary New York Jazz Club Is Still Setting the Pace." *The National*, June 18, 2015.
Bently, Jenn. "Pushed Out: The Changing Demographics of New Orleans." *Big Easy Magazine*, February 11, 2019.
Berish, Andrew. *Lonesome Roads and Streets of Dreams: Place, Mobility, and Race in Jazz of the 1930s and '40s*. Chicago: University of Chicago Press, 2012.
———. "Space and Place in Jazz." In *The Routledge Companion to Jazz Studies*,

edited by Nicholas Gebhardt, Nichole Rustin-Paschal, and Tony Whyton, 153–62. New York: Routledge, 2019.

Berliner, Paul. *Thinking in Jazz: The Infinite Art of Improvisation*. Chicago: University of Chicago Press, 1994.

Blumenfeld, Larry. "John Zorn Is Rolling The Stone from Avenue C to The New School." *The Village Voice*, March 6, 2017.

Bohlman, Philip, and Goffredo Plastino, eds. *Jazz Worlds / World Jazz*. Chicago: University of Chicago Press, 2016.

Born, Georgina, ed. *Music, Sound and Space: Transformations of Public and Private Experience*. Cambridge: Cambridge University Press, 2013.

Brackett, John. *John Zorn: Tradition and Transgression*. Bloomington: Indiana University Press, 2008.

Bridges, Tyler. "How Many Visitors Come to New Orleans Each Year? Depends Whom You Ask—And What Counts." *New Orleans Advocate*, March 9, 2019.

Burke, Patrick. *Come in and Hear the Truth: Jazz and Race on 52nd Street*. Chicago: University of Chicago Press, 2008.

Butler, Judith. *Excitable Speech: A Politics of the Performative*. New York: Routledge, 1997.

Carlson, Gretchen. "Jazz Goes to the Movies: Contemporary Jazz Musicians' Work at the Intersections of the Jazz and Film Art Worlds." PhD diss., University of Virginia, 2016.

Casey, Edward S. "How to Get from Space to Place in a Fairly Short Stretch of Time: Phenomenological Prolegomena." In *Senses of Place*, edited by Steven Feld and Keith H. Basso, 13–52. Santa Fe: School of American Research Press, 1996. Distributed by the University of Washington Press.

Cerulli, Dom. Review of *Brandeis University Festival*. *DownBeat*, August 7, 1958.

Chapman, Dale. *The Jazz Bubble: Neoclassical Jazz in Neoliberal Culture*. Berkeley: University of California Press, 2018.

Charters, Samuel. *A Trumpet around the Corner: The Story of New Orleans Jazz*. Jackson: University of Mississippi Press, 2008.

Chinen, Nate. "As Open as the Genre It Celebrates." *New York Times*, January 26, 2013.

Courrèges, Owen. "Irvin Mayfield's Jazz Market and the Forced Gentrification of Central City." *Uptown Messenger*, June 8, 2015.

Cresswell, Tim. *Place: An Introduction*. Hoboken: John Wiley & Sons, 2014.

Davis, Miles, with Quincy Troupe. *Miles: The Autobiography*. New York: Simon & Schuster, 1989.

DeMichael, Don. Review of *Portrait in Jazz* by Bill Evans. *DownBeat*, September 15, 1960.

———. Review of *Interplay* by Bill Evans. *DownBeat*, July 18, 1963.

DeVeaux, Scott. *The Birth of Bebop: A Social and Musical History*. Berkeley: University of California Press, 1997.

———. "Constructing the Jazz Tradition: Jazz Historiography." *Black American Literature Forum*, vol. 25, no. 3, Literature of Jazz Issue (Autumn, 1991): 525–56.

Doktor, Stephanie. "'Sweet' Jazz and Luckies: How a White Man Sold Black Music to White People." Paper presented at the Conference of the American Musicological Society, Boston, November 2019.
Dvinge, Anne. "Pride at Preservation Hall: Tourism, Spectacle, and Musicking in New Orleans Jazz." In *Creating and Consuming the American South*, edited by Martyn Bone, Brian Ward, and William A. Link. Gainesville: University Press of Florida, 2015.
Eagan, Kevin, Ella Bara Stolzenberg, Joseph J. Ramirez, Melissa C. Aragon, Maria Ramirez Suchard, and Sylvia Hurtado. *The American Freshman: National Norms Fall 2014*. Los Angeles: Higher Education Research Institute, 2014.
Erenberg, Lewis A. *Steppin' Out: New York Nightlife and the Transformation of American Culture, 1890–1930*. Westport, CT: Greenwood Press, 1981.
Feather, Leonard. Review of *Waltz for Debby*. *DownBeat*, April 26, 1962: 36.
Fricke, David. "Branford Marsalis' Secret." *JazzTimes*, June 3, 2019.
Friedwald, Will. "Woman at the Vanguard." *Wall Street Journal*, January 2, 2013.
Gagne, Cole. *Soundpieces 2: Interviews with American Composers*. Metuchen, NJ: Scarecrow Press, 1993.
Gann, Kyle. *Music Downtown: Writings from the* Village Voice. Berkeley: University of California Press, 2006.
Gooch, Paul W. *Course Correction: A Map for the Distracted University*. Toronto: University of Toronto Press, 2019.
Gotham, Kevin Fox. *Authentic New Orleans: Tourism, Culture, and Race in the Big Easy*. New York: New York University Press, 2007.
Gordon, Lorraine, and Barry Singer. *Alive at the Village Vanguard: My Life In and Out of Jazz Time*. Milwaukee, WI: Hal Leonard, 2006.
Gordon, Max. *Live at the Village Vanguard*. New York: St. Martin's Press, 1980.
Gray, Herman S. *Cultural Moves: African Americans and the Politics of Representation*. Berkeley: University of California Press, 2005.
Griffin, Farah Jasmine. *If You Can't Be Free, Be a Mystery: In Search of Billie Holiday*. New York: Free Press, 2001.
Handy, D. Antoinette. "First Lady of the Jazz Keyboard." *The Black Perspective in Music*, vol. 8, no. 2 (Autumn 1980): 194–214.
Hannon Teal, Kimberly. "Fred Hersch at the Village Vanguard: The Sound of Jazz Heritage at New York's Oldest Jazz Club." *Journal of the Society for American Music*, vol. 12, no. 4 (November 2018): 449–76.
———. "Jazz, Space, and Labor: Mixed Media Aestheticization of Work Songs in Jason Moran's *STAGED*." *Jazz Research Journal*, 2020.
———. "Posthumously Live: Canon Formation at Jazz at Lincoln Center through the Case of Mary Lou Williams." *American Music*, vol. 34, no. 2 (Winter 2015): 400–22.
Harris, Elizabeth A. "Where Nearly Half of Pupils are Homeless, School Aims to Be Teacher, Therapist, Even Santa." *New York Times*, June 6, 2016.
Harris, Paul. "New York's Heart Loses Its Beat." *The Guardian*, August 13, 2005.

Hebdige, Dick. *Subculture: The Meaning of Style*. London: Taylor & Francis Group, 1981.
Heller, Michael. *Loft Jazz: Improvising New York in the 1970s*. Berkeley: University of California Press, 2017.
Hentoff, Nat. "Introduction." In *Live at the Village Vanguard*, by Max Gordon (New York: St. Martin's Press, 1980).
———. Review of *The Jazz Workshop* by George Russell. *DownBeat*, August 8, 1957.
———. Review of *New Jazz Conceptions*. *DownBeat*, March 21, 1957.
Hillman, Nicholas, and Taylor Weichman. *Education Deserts: The Continued Significance of 'Place' in the Twenty-First Century*. Viewpoints: Voices from the Field. Washington, DC: American Council on Education, 2016.
Holley, Eugene, Jr. "Wynton Marsalis: Jazz Messenger." *Ebony*, September 4, 2012.
Howland, John. "Jazz with Strings: Between Jazz and the Great American Songbook." In *Jazz/Not Jazz: The Music and Its Boundaries*, edited by David Ake, Charles Hiroshi Garrett, and Daniel Goldmark, 144. Berkeley: University of California Press, 2012.
Jackson, Travis. *Blowin' the Blues Away: Performance and Meaning on the New York Jazz Scene*. Berkeley: University of California Press, 2012.
Kahn, Ashley. "After 70 Years, the Village Vanguard Is Still in the Jazz Swing." *Wall Street Journal*, February 8, 2005.
Kaplan, Fred. "This Kennedy Center Director Is Making Performance Art out of Jazz. Can He Bring Fans Along?" *The Washington Post*, November 2, 2017.
Kassel, Matthew. "As the Village Vanguard Turns 80, It Remains New York's Most Cherished Jazz Club." *The Observer*, February 17, 2015.
Kernodle, Tammy L. *Soul on Soul: The Life and Music of Mary Lou Williams*. Boston: Northeastern University Press, 2004.
Khan, Marty. *Straight Ahead: A Comprehensive Guide to the Business of Jazz (Without Sacrificing Dignity or Artistic Integrity)*. Tuscon, AZ: Outward Visions, 2004.
King, Billie Jean, with Kim Chapin. *Billie Jean*. New York: Harper & Row, 1974.
Kingsbury, Henry. *Music Talent & Performance: Conservatory Cultural System*. Philadelphia: Temple University Press, 1988.
Kirschenblatt-Gimblett, Barbara. *Destination Culture: Tourism, Museums, and Heritage*. Berkeley: University of California Press, 1998.
———. "Theorizing Heritage." *Ethnomusicology*, vol. 39, no. 3 (Autumn, 1995): 367–80.
Koransky, Jason. "And Now for Something Completely Different." *DownBeat*, vol. 71, no. 5 (May 2004): 8.
Krims, Adam. *Music and Urban Geography*. New York: Routledge, 2007.
Larsen, Svein, Ktharina Wolff, Rouven Doran, and Torvald Ogaard. "What Makes Tourist Experiences Interesting." *Frontiers in Psychology*, vol. 10 (August 2019), doi: 10.3389/fpsyg.2019.01603.

Lewis, George E. *A Power Stronger than Itself: The AACM and American Experimental Music*. Chicago: University of Chicago Press, 2008.
Lipsitz, George. *How Racism Takes Place*. Philadelphia: Temple University Press, 2011.
Lopes, Paul. *The Rise of a Jazz Art World*. Cambridge: Cambridge University Press, 2002.
Mandel, Howard. "Who What Where Why Jazz: Jazz Great John Zorn's The Stone Club." *New York Press*, September 7, 2005.
Marsalis, Wynton, with Geoffrey C. Ward. *Moving to Higher Ground: How Jazz Can Change Your Life*. New York: Random House, 2008.
Massey, Doreen. *Space, Place, and Gender*. Minneapolis: University of Minnesota Press, 1994.
McKinley, James C., Jr. "Just One Bishop at Jazz Church of High Purity." *New York Times*, December 7, 2012.
McMullen, Tracy. *Haunthenticity: Musical Replay and the Fear of the Real*. Middletown, CT: Wesleyan University Press, 2019.
Milkowski, Bill. "Expanding the Mission: Jazz at Lincoln Center." *JazzTimes*, supp. Jazz Education Guide, 2000.
———. "John Zorn: The Working Man." *JazzTimes*, May 2009.
Monson, Ingrid. *Freedom Sounds: Civil Rights Call Out to Jazz and Africa*. New York: Oxford University Press, 2007.
———. *Saying Something: Jazz Improvisation and Interaction*. Chicago: University of Chicago Press, 1996.
Mueller, Darren. "The Ambassadorial LPs of Dizzy Gillespie: *World Statesman* and *Dizzy in Greece*." *Journal of the Society for American Music*, vol. 10, no. 3 (August 2016): 239–69.
———. "Quest for the Moment: The Audio Production of *Ellington at Newport*." *Jazz Perspectives*, vol. 8, no. 1 (October 2014): 2–23.
Murphy, Dan. "Jazz Studies in American Schools and Colleges: A Brief History." *Jazz Educators Journal*, vol. 26 (1994): 34–38.
Murphy, John P. "Beyond the Improvisation Class: Learning to Improvise in a University Jazz Studies Program." In *Musical Improvisation: Art, Education, and Society*, eds. Gabriel Solis and Bruno Nettl. Urbana and Chicago: University of Illinois Press, 2009.
Nettl, Bruno. "Heartland Excursions: Exercises in Musical Ethnography." *The World of Music*, vol. 34, no. 1 (1992): 8–34.
Nicholson, Stuart. *Is Jazz Dead? (Or Has It Moved to a New Address)*. New York: Routledge, 2005.
Nisenson, Eric. *Blue: The Murder of Jazz*. New York: St. Martin's Press, 1997.
Pettinger, Peter. *Bill Evans: How My Heart Sings*. New Haven: Yale University Press, 1998.
Phelan, Peggy. *Unmarked: The Politics of Performance*. New York: Routledge, 1993.
Piekut, Benjamin. *Experimentalism Otherwise: The New York Avant-Garde and Its Limits*. Berkeley: University of California Press, 2011.
Pipkin, James. "Life on the Cusp: Lynda Huey and Billie Jean King." In *Impos-

sible to Hold: Women and Culture in the 1960s, edited by Avital Bloch and Lauri Umansky. New York: New York University Press, 2005.

Poling, Monica. "Hitting a High Note." *Bespoke Concierge*, June 23, 2014.

Pope, John. "'Sweet Emma' Barrett, Jazz Musician, Is Dead." *Times-Picayune*, January 29, 1983.

Porter, Eric. *What Is This Thing Called Jazz? African American Musicians as Artists, Critics, and Activists*. Berkeley: University of California Press, 2002.

Price, Patricia. *Dry Place: Landscapes of Belonging and Exclusion*. Minneapolis: University of Minnesota Press, 2004.

Prouty, Ken. "Canons in Harmony, or Canons in Conflict: A Cultural Perspective on the Curriculum and Pedagogy of Jazz Improvisation." *Research and Issues in Music Education*, vol. 2, no. 1 (September 2004).

———. *Knowing Jazz: Community, Pedagogy, and Canon in the Information Age*. Jackson: University of Mississippi Press, 2012.

Raeburn, Bruce Boyd. *New Orleans Style and the Writing of American Jazz History*. Ann Arbor: University of Michigan Press, 2009.

Ratliff, Ben. "Jazz Flexes New Muscles in Lincoln Center Schedule." *New York Times*, January 30, 1997.

Reich, Howard. "A Jazz Nexus Takes Shape in San Francisco." *Chicago Tribune*, May 16, 2011.

Ribot, Marc. "Days of Bread and Roses." In *People Get Ready: The Future of Jazz Is Now!*, edited by Ajay Heble and Rob Wallace. Durham: Duke University Press, 2013.

Robinson, George. "Romancing The Stone." *The Jewish Week*, March 30, 2007.

Rockwell, John. "As Important as Anyone in His Generation." *New York Times*, February 21, 1988.

———. "Jazz: Two Braxton Programs." *New York Times*, April 23, 1982.

Rodriguez, Alex. "Making the Hang in Chile at Thelonious, Lugar de Jazz." *Jazz and Culture*, vol. 3, no. 1 (Spring/Summer 2020): 45–70.

Rule, Sheila. "Lincoln Center's Menu of Jazz Is Quadrupled." *New York Times*, May 28, 1992.

Russonello, Giovanni. "After a Scandal, the New Orleans Jazz Market Rises Again." *New York Times*, May 28, 2019.

———. "At 30, What Does Jazz at Lincoln Center Mean?" *New York Times*, September 17, 2017.

Rustin-Paschal, Nichole. *The Kind of Man I Am: Jazzmasculinity and the World of Charles Mingus Jr.* Middletown, CT: Wesleyan University Press, 2017.

Sancton, Tom. "Hall That Jazz." *Vanity Fair*, December 9, 2011.

Scherbenske, Amanda. "On the Production of Alternative Music Places: Immateriality, Labor, and Meaning." *Popular Music and Society*, vol. 41, no. 4 (2018): 408–23.

Schriffman, Betsy. "America's Most Expensive ZIP Codes 2015." *Forbes*, November 10, 2015.

Shipton, Alyn. *Fats Waller: The Cheerful Little Earful*. London: Continuum, 1988.

Smith, Neil, Betsy Duncan, and Laura Reid. "From Disinvestment to Reinvestment: Mapping the Urban 'Frontier' in the Lower East Side." In *From Urban Village to East Village: The Battle for New York's Lower East Side*, edited by Janet L. Abu-Lughod et al., 149–68. Oxford: Blackwell Publishers, 1994.

Solis, Gabriel. "Genius, Improvisation, and the Narratives of Jazz." In *Musical Improvisation: Art, Education, and Society*, edited by Gabriel Solis and Brun Nettl, 90–102. Urbana: University of Illinois Press, 2009.

Souther, J. Mark. "Making the 'Birthplace of Jazz': Tourism and Musical Heritage Marketing in New Orleans." *Louisiana History: The Journal of the Louisiana Historical Association*, vol. 44, no. 1 (Winter 2003): 39–73.

———. *New Orleans on Parade: Tourism and the Transformation of the Crescent City*. Baton Rouge: Louisiana State University Press, 2006.

Stanbridge, Alan. "Somewhere There: Contemporary Music, Performance Spaces, and Cultural Policy." In *People Get Ready: The Future of Jazz Is Now!*, edited by Ajay Heble and Rob Wallace, 184–96. Durham: Duke University Press, 2013.

Stanyek, Jason and Benjamin Piekut. "Deadness: Technologies of the Intermundane." *The Drama Review*, vol. 54, no. 21 (spring 2010).

Stewart, Alex. *Making the Scene: Contemporary New York City Big Band Jazz*. Berkeley: University of California Press, 2007.

Strickland, Edward. *American Composers: Dialogues on Contemporary Music*. Indianapolis: Indiana University Press, 1991.

Suhadolnik, Sarah. "Navigating Jazz: Music, Place, and New Orleans." PhD diss., University of Michigan, 2016.

Suhor, Charles. "Jazz in New Orleans in the 1960s." *Jazz Archivist*, vol. 10, no. 2 (May–December 1995).

Toswell, M. J. *Today's Medieval University*. Kalamazoo, MI: ARC Humanities Press, 2017.

Tucker, Sherrie. *Swing Shift: "All-Girl" Bands of the 1940s*. Durham: Duke University Press, 2000.

Tynan, John A. "Natural Flow: The Bill Evans Trio." *DownBeat*, June 17, 1965.

Walser, Robert, ed. *Keeping Time: Readings in Jazz History*. New York: Oxford University Press, 1999.

Watrous, Peter. "Good News for Jazz, with a Big Caveat." *New York Times*, August 18, 1991.

Welding, Pete. Review of *Undercurrent* by Bill Evans and Jim Hall. *DownBeat*, November 22, 1962.

Wells, [Christi Jay] Christopher J. "'Go Harlem!' Chick Webb and His Dancing Audience during the Great Depression." PhD diss., University of North Carolina at Chapel Hill, 2014.

Whiting, Sam. "SFJazz Hits High Note at 5-Year Mark." *SFGate*, July 9, 2018.

Wilf, Eitan Y. *School for Cool: The Academic Jazz Program and the Paradox of Institutionalized Creativity*. Chicago: University of Chicago Press, 2014.

Williams, Martin. *Jazz Heritage*. Oxford: Oxford University Press, 1985.

———. *The Jazz Tradition*. Oxford: Oxford University Press, 1970.

———. Review of *Sunday at the Village Vanguard* by the Bill Evans Trio. *DownBeat*, March 1, 1962.

Wyndham, Tex. *Texas Shout: How Dixieland Jazz Works*. (Seattle: Lights, Words, & Music, 1997.
Zorn, John. *Arcana II: Musicians on Music*. New York: Hips Road, 2007.
Zukin, Sharon. *Naked City: The Death and Life of Authentic Urban Places*. Oxford: Oxford University Press, 2010.

Index

acoustic mainstream jazz, 24
Adler, David, 45–46
aesthetics of marginalization, 5
African American expressive culture, 7–8
Ake, David, 9, 75, 95, 101, 102, 105, 111
Allen Room at JALC, 64, 68
Alphabet City (East Village, Manhattan), 173. *See also* Stone, The: original location
Anderson, Laurie, 77–78, 86, 134, 137
Anderson, Paul, 45, 47
Applebome, Peter, 56–57
apprenticeship, 119; informal apprenticeship system, 94, 99, 102, 119; the records' apprentices, 105–14
Armstrong, Louis, 2; Preservation Hall and, 160; "Struttin' with some Barbeque," 160; "What a Wonderful World," 161
Association for the Advancement of Creative Musicians (AACM), 125, 126
Auslander, Philip, 6, 28

Bach, Johann Sebastian, 108
Bad Plus, The, 34, 35, 44–47
Bailey, C. Michael, 28
Barbarin, Lucien, 156
Barbarin, Paul, 156

Barrett, "Sweet Emma," 158
Bataille, Georges, 127–28
bebop, 1–3, 26, 100, 155–56; African Americans and, 156; Bill Evans and, 80; Billie Jean King and, 70; Calvin Johnson and, 163, 167; 52nd Street and, 154–56; Fred Hersch and, 38; overview, 190n22
Bechet, Sidney, 163
Berger, Karl, 137
Berish, Andrew, 9, 10, 150
Berliner, Paul, 94–95
Bilal, 90
Birdland (New York), 19, 31, 34, 48
Black Artist Group (BAG), 125, 126
Black Christ of the Andes (Williams), 72, 73
black masculinity, 64. *See also* jazzmasculinity
blacks. *See* race
Blakey, Art, 19
Bley, Carla, 119
Blue Angel, 23, 31; Max Gordon and, 22–23, 29, 31
Blue Note Records, 23, 27, 48
Born, Georgina, 16–17
Bourbon Street, 146, 148
Brackett, John, 127, 128
Braxton, Anthony, 126, 127

Breton, André, 127–28
Brookmeyer, Bob, 113
Burke, Patrick, 154–56
Burns, Ken, 152. *See also Jazz*
Butler, Judith, 131

capitalism, 62, 135, 141
Carlson, Gretchen, 160, 164
Carmichael, Judy, 65–68
Casey, Edward S., 7
Casselman, Ben, 169–70
Central City, New Orleans, 92
Chapman, Dale, 59–60, 82–83; Wynton Marsalis and, 59–60, 82
Charlap, Bill, 79–81
Charters, Samuel, 153, 154, 156
Cheatham, Doc, 4
Chinen, Nate, 86–87
"Chunka Lunka" (Williams), 72, 73
Coleman, Ornette, 127
Collier, James Lincoln, 26
Coltrane, John, 25, 111; Village Vanguard and, 25, 27, 30
community: (mis)identification of place with, 8. *See also* jazz community
Courrèges, Owen, 92
Courvoisier, Sylvie, 135
COVID-19 pandemic, 12–13; lives lost to, 13
Craig, Tim, 108, 111–13
Cresswell, Tim, 6–7
Crouch, Stanley, 60
cultural capital, 5. *See also under* Stone, The

Dakota (Minneapolis), 20, 21
Davis, Miles, 62; Bill Evans and, 74, 76, 80; concerts and festivals, 88; *Kind of Blue*, 62, 74, 80, 88; Robert Glasper and, 88–90; SFJazz and, 89, 90
deadness and liveness in recording, 6
Dease, Michael, 115
DeMichael, Don, 78–79
democracy, 59
democratic art, jazz as, 59–60, 68, 73–74
design intensity, 9
DeVeaux, Scott, 26
Dobbins, Bill, 107–8, 110–13
Douglas, Dave: John Zorn and, 143, 144;

New School and, 121; and The Stone, 143–44
Downtown I and II, 125
Duncan, Kate, 116–18
Dvinge, Anne, 160–61

Eastman Ellington project, 109–11, 113, 114
Eastman Jazz Ensemble, 107, 108
Eastman School of Music, 106
education. *See* jazz education
Eisenman, Jed, 32
Ellington, Duke, 61, 107–14; celebrations of the birth of, 57, 106; Mary Lou Williams and, 70. *See also* Eastman Ellington project
Erenberg, Lewis, 21–22
Essentially Ellington (JALC educational program), 20, 57
Evans, Bill, 79–81; Bill Charlap and, 79, 80; compositions, 27, 28, 80, 182n51; concerts, 75, 90, 91; descriptions and characterizations of, 74–75, 81; Fats Waller and, 63, 66, 74, 75; Hall of Fame and, 74, 75, 78; in historical and cultural context, 75, 76; honors, 74, 88, 182n51; at the House of Swing, 74–93; introversion, 74, 77, 79–81; JALC and, 75, 79, 81, 88, 90; John Tynan on, 74, 77; Leonard Feather on, 28; masculinity, 77–79, 81; Miles Davis and, 74, 76, 80; physical appearance, 74, 75, 81; race, blacks, and, 76, 77, 79, 81; Village Vanguard and, 27, 28; voice, 80
Evans, Orrin, 46. *See also* Bad Plus, The
Everything's Beautiful (Glasper), 88–90
experimental music, 125–28, 130, 132, 142–43; Benjamin Piekut and, 130–31; John Zorn and, 126–28, 130–31; and The Stone, 122, 128, 138, 140, 142–44 (*see also* Stone, The)

"Fats Waller: A Handful of Keys" (2010 concert in JALC Allen Room), 64–68
Fats Waller Festival (2010), 64–68
Feather, Leonard, 28
Feldman, Mark, 133, 135, 136
feminism, 69; Billie Jean King and, 69–71; Mary Lou Williams and, 71, 73–75
Ferring Jazz Bistro (St. Louis), 20

52nd Street (Manhattan), 154, 155; bebop and, 154–56
For All I Care (The Bad Plus), 45
Fox, Greg, 141
Frederick P. Rose Hall at JALC, 64–65, 85
French Quarter, 146, 148, 159
Frenchman Street, New Orleans, 148, 170
"Fungus Among Us, A" (Williams), 182n52
fusion, 45, 57, 88

Giordano, Vince, 159–60, 164
Glasper, Robert, 88–90
Glass Theater at New School, 122, 140
Gooch, Paul W., 97–98
Gordon, Deborah, 32
Gordon, Lorraine, 23, 25, 27, 30, 32, 48; Blue Angel and, 23; Blue Note Records and, 23, 27, 48; Ethan Iverson and, 34, 35, 47–48; "everything changes," 32, 48; Fred Hersch and, 37–38, 46–48; honors, 32; Kurt Rosenwinkel and, 34; Max Gordon and, 23–25, 27; styles of music and, 47–48; Thelonious Monk and, 23–25; Village Vanguard and, 24–25, 27, 28, 31–35, 37, 38, 47; Wynton Marsalis on, 31–32
Gordon, Max, 24, 30, 31; Blue Angel and, 22–23, 29, 31; finances, 29; Lorraine Gordon and, 23–25, 27; Thelonious Monk and, 23; Village Vanguard and, 21–25, 27, 28, 33, 34
Gotham, Kevin Fox, 146, 168–69
Grammy Awards, 102
Gray, Herman, 82
Greenwich Village, 21, 24, 32, 33, 51; description of, 21–22. *See also* New School; Village Vanguard
Gress, Drew, 40
Griffin, Farah Jasmine, 82

Hall of Fame. *See* Nesuhi Ertegun Jazz Hall of Fame
Hancock, Herbie, 57
"Handful of Keys" (Waller), 68
Harris, Paul, 33
Hebdige, Dick, 96–97
Heidkamp, Konrad, 62
Hersch, Fred: changing keys, 43–44; Ethan Iverson and, 44, 46; fame and honors, 36–38; "food groups," 42; at JALC, 178n49; on jazz, 44; life history, 36, 37; Lorraine Gordon and, 37–38, 46–48; overview, 36–44; performances at Jazz Standard, 38–41; performances at Village Vanguard, 36–38, 50; in Pocket Orchestra, 38–42; songs, 39–44; and today's Village Vanguard, 35–38; on Village Vanguard, 35–38; Village Vanguard and, 50
Holliday, Judy, 22, 34, 35
"hot" jazz, 150–53
"hot" music, 150, 151
House of Swing, 81. *See also under* Evans, Bill
Howland, John, 25–26
Hurricane Katrina, aftermath and social effects of, 159, 168–71
Hyman, Dick, 65–68

"I Wish I Knew" (Warren), 42–43
integrated aestheticized space, 9, 139
integrity, 32
Interplay (Evans), 78–79
invisibility, 122, 128. *See also* visibility
Iverson, Ethan, 34, 35, 44–49; albums, 35; descriptions and characterizations of, 35, 44, 46–47; fame, 35, 45; Fred Hersch and, 44, 46; Lorraine Gordon and, 34, 35, 47–48; Max Gordon and, 35; positions held by, 35; Thelonious Monk and, 46, 49; at Village Vanguard, 15, 34, 35, 47, 50; on Village Vanguard, 15, 47, 48

Jackson, Travis, 28–29, 33
Jaffe, Allan, 149–50, 156–58
Jaffe, Ben, 157, 159, 161–62
Jaffe, Sandra, 149, 150, 156–58
jazz: changing meanings of the term, 151; defining, 2–3, 8, 42, 54, 55, 74, 84, 85, 87, 125, 151; in small slubs, 19–21. *See also* mainstream jazz; *specific topics*
Jazz (2000 documentary miniseries), 49, 56, 152
Jazz Age, 151, 160
Jazz at Lincoln Center (JALC), 54, 55; Bill Evans and, 75, 79, 81, 88, 90; educational programming, 20, 56, 57, 84, 94

Jazz at Lincoln Center *(continued)* (*see also* Essentially Ellington); Fats Waller Festival (2010), 64–68; Fred Hersch at, 178n49; jazzmasculinity and, 64, 68, 79; Kennedy Center and, 52, 54, 84; Marty Khan on, 58; Mary Lou Williams and, 64, 68–69, 72–74, 88, 182n52; performing controlled diversity, 60–64; SFJazz Center and, 83–89; swing music and, 55, 59, 73–76, 83; Wynton Marsalis and, 56–60, 64, 82, 83, 85–87. *See also* Nesuhi Ertegun Jazz Hall of Fame
Jazz at Lincoln Center Jazz Orchestra, 56, 57, 70, 79
jazz community, 94–95, 100–102, 118
jazz education, 94; criticism of, 95–96, 99, 105–6, 109, 111; finding a place, 118–19; historical perspective on, 99; an increasingly (un)popular approach to learning jazz, 99–102; Paul Berliner on, 94–95. *See also* apprenticeship; university jazz education programs
jazz education community, 100–102
jazz education initiatives connected to JALC, 20, 56, 57, 84
jazz institutions, making a case for, 55–60
Jazz Messengers, 19
jazz piano trio, 27–28. *See also specific trios*
jazz-rock fusion, 45, 57, 88
Jazz St. Louis, 20
Jazz Standard (New York), 38–41
jazz standards, 42–44, 125
jazz tradition, boundaries of the, 25–26, 45
jazzmasculinity, 64, 68; JALC and, 64, 68, 79
Jimmy Ryan's, 155, 156
John F. Kennedy Center for the Performing Arts: Billy Taylor at, 52, 54; JALC and, 52, 54, 84; Jason Moran's work at, 53, 54, 83; physical description and overview, 51–52; programs and programming, 51, 52, 83, 84, 93
Johnson, Bunk, 156
Johnson, Calvin, 92, 163–67, 170; mentor relationships and, 164–66; on New Orleans jazz, 162, 163; New Orleans tourism and, 170–71; Preservation Hall and, 158, 162, 164–67; race and, 158, 170, 171
Johnson, James P., 46
Juilliard School, 99

Kahn, Ashley, 21, 30
Kaiser, Henry, 136
Kaplan, Fred, 53
Kassel, Matthew, 16
KC Jazz Club (Kennedy Center), 52
Kennedy, Gary, 99–102
Kernodle, Tammy L., 71
Kessler, Richard: Dave Douglas and, 121; finances and, 140; John Zorn and, 140, 144, 145; on New School, 140, 144, 145; and The Stone, 140, 141, 144, 145
Khan, Marty, 58
Kind of Blue (Davis), 62, 74, 80, 88
King, Billie Jean: Bobby Riggs and, 69, 71; Mary Lou Williams, 69–75, 182n52; overview, 69; women, feminism, and, 69–71, 74
King, David ("Dave"), 45–46. *See also* Bad Plus, The
Kingsbury, Henry, 98
Kirschenblatt-Gimblett, Barbara, 5, 17, 130, 131
Kitt, Eartha, 23
Kline, Randall, 85–87
Krims, Adam, 8–9, 139

LaFaro, Scott, 27, 74, 77, 78
language, agency, and power, 131
Lehmen, Steve, 123
"Light Years" (Hersch), 39, 40
Lincoln Center Jazz Orchestra, 56, 57, 70, 79
Lipsitz, George, 7–8
live albums, 6, 28–30, 91
liveness and deadness in recording, 6
Lopeman, Mark, 160
Lopes, Paul, 3, 25, 150–51
Loyola University New Orleans, 116–18

Madsen, Pete, 103–5
mainstream jazz, 24, 26; borders/boundaries of, 25–27, 45; historical perspective on, 24; Pocket Orchestra and, 38, 40–42; uses of the term, 26;

Village Vanguard and, 16, 22, 24–27, 40–42; willingness to break with the conventions of, 41, 45
Mandel, Howard, 133
Marsalis, Branford, 46–47, 88
Marsalis, Wynton, 53, 60, 76, 83, 84, 93; awards and honors, 57; characterizations of, 46, 57; conservatism, neoliberalism, and, 59, 82, 83; criticism of, 87; critique of popular music, 57–58; Dale Chapman and, 59–60, 82; Ethan Iverson and, 46–47; fame, 57; Herbie Hancock and, 57; JALC and, 56–60, 64, 82, 83, 85–87; Jason Moran and, 52–53; on jazz, 56–59, 125; on Lorraine Gordon, 31–32; moral qualities of jazz and, 58; *Moving to Higher Ground: How Jazz Can Change Your Life*, 58–59, 81; personality, 57; politics and, 59, 60, 82, 83; Randall Kline and, 85; Robert Glasper and, 88–89; swing music and, 53, 59; version of jazz history and values, 56–60, 64, 75, 81; Village Vanguard and, 27, 31–32. *See also* Lincoln Center Jazz Orchestra
masculinity: of Bill Evans, 77–79, 81. *See also* jazzmasculinity
Massey, Doreen, 8
Mayfield, Irvin, 84
McBride, Christian, 50, 115
McMullen, Tracy, 61, 82, 119
Milkowski, Bill, 124
Miner Auditorium, 86, 89–91
Monie, Rickie, 147–48, 160
Monk, Thelonious, 23–26; compositions, 23–24, 26, 43, 46, 49; Ethan Iverson and, 46, 49; Lorraine Gordon and, 23–25; Mary Lou Williams and, 70, 71; performances, 49; at Village Vanguard, 16, 23–25
Monson, Ingrid, 75–76
Moran, Jason, 1, 16, 83; Billy Taylor and, 52; Fred Kaplan and, 53; sculptures, 2, 173; *STAGED*, 1–2, 6; work at Kennedy Center, 53, 54, 83; Wynton Marsalis and, 52–53
Motian, Paul, 27, 47, 74, 77, 78
Mueller, Darren, 6
Murphy, John P., 101

Music and Urban Geography (Krims), 8–9
"Music of Fats Waller, The" (2010 concert in JALC Rose Hall), 64–65

National Sawdust, 139–40
neoclassicism, jazz, 59–60, 82
Nesuhi Ertegun Jazz Hall of Fame, 60–61, 180n26; Bill Evans and, 74, 75, 78; concerts, 61, 63, 64, 73, 75, 81; establishment of, 60; musicians inducted into, 68, 73–75, 78, 79, 180n26
Nettl, Bruno, 98
New Orleans, 168. *See also* Hurricane Katrina; Preservation Hall
New Orleans jazz clubs and Loyola University, 116–17
New School: finances, 138–41; Glass Theater, 122, 140; history, 140; jazz program, 143; John Zorn and, 139, 140, 143–45; location, 138–39; overview, 140; Richard Kessler on, 140, 144, 145; staff, 121; and The Stone, 123, 128, 140–41 (*see also under* Stone, The)
Nicholson, Stuart, 100–101, 113
Nighthawks, 159, 160
Nighttown (Cleveland), 20–21

Oklahoma State University (OSU), 114–17
Omaha, Nebraska, 102–5
Onyx Club, 154, 155

Parker, Ashlin, 102–3
Parker, Charlie, 31, 101, 102
Pettinger, Peter, 76
Phelan, Peggy, 129, 145; on power, 5, 129, 144; on representation, 145; theory of the unmarked, 129, 144; on visibility, 5, 129, 144
Piekut, Benjamin, 62, 130–31
pitch, 111
place, 2, 6–7; heritage and, 97–98; nature of, 7; role in narratives in jazz history, 9. *See also* space; *specific topics*
Pocket Orchestra, 38–42
Poole, Tommy, 114–16
popular music (pop): vs. African American jazz, 154, 155; Wynton Marsalis's critique of, 57–58

power, 63; democracy and shared, 59; language and, 131; Peggy Phelan on, 5, 129, 144; place, space, and, 6–8; of self-definition, 131–32; visibility and, 5, 129, 143–45
power geometry of space and place, 8
Preservation Hall, 13, 146–48; description and characterizations of, 148–49; establishment, 149–50; Kate Duncan on, 116; opening, 12; a place to work, 157–59; playing with tradition, 159–64; relationships to history, 164–67; serving New Orleans, and serving it to visitors, 168–71; tourism and, 146, 147, 157, 158, 162–63, 168, 170, 171; Village Vanguard and, 9, 149
Preservation Hall Jazz Band (PHJB), 161, 162
Price, Patricia, 12
protected place, 97
Prouty, Ken, 94, 95, 111, 118

race: Calvin Johnson and, 158, 170, 171; records, revivals, and, 149–57. *See also under* Evans, Bill; Zorn, John
racial segregation, 7, 91, 154, 169
racialized jazzmasculinity, 64. *See also* jazzmasculinity
racialized space, 7–8
Raeburn, Bruce Boyd, 150, 168
Reich, Howard, 85
replay, 119
representation, laws of, 145
Ribot, Marc, 142
Riggs, Bobby, 69, 71
Roberts, Marcus, 65, 67–68
Robinson, Scott, 142
Rollins, Sonny, 27, 29
Rose, Adonis, 84
Rose Hall at JALC, 64–65, 85
Rosenwinkel, Kurt, 34
Russ and Daughters Café, 139
Russonello, Giovanni, 56, 57, 84
Rustin-Paschal, Nichole, 64

"Saint Martin de Porres" (Williams), 72–73
San Francisco, 54, 86, 91–92. *See also* SFJazz Center
Sancton, Tom, 159, 161

Schoenberg, Loren, 15
School of Jazz and Contemporary Media, 140, 143
segregation, 7, 91, 154, 169
self-definition, 131–32
SFJazz Center, 85–87; characterizations of, 85, 87; creating space and taking space, 90–93; digital membership program, 13; founding and opening, 54, 85; historical perspective on, 83, 92; JALC and, 83–89; Miles Davis and, 89, 90; programming, 84–88, 94; Randall Kline and, 85–87; Robert Glasper and, 88–90
Smith, Leo, 126
Snug Harbor (New Orleans), 20, 116, 148
Solis, Gabriel, 108
Sorey, Tyshawn, 123, 124
Souther, J. Mark, 148, 157–59
space, 1–6; conceptualization of, 16–17; Edward S. Casey on, 7; lineages of thought in the analysis of sound and, 16. *See also* place; *specific topics*
St. Louis, Missouri, 20, 126
STAGED (exhibit), 1–2
Stanyek, Jason, 6, 62
Stewart, Alex, 26–27
Stillwater, Oklahoma, 114–16
Stone, Irving and Stephanie, 132
Stone, The, 13; Amanda Scherbenske on, 134–35, 140–41; closing night in Alphabet City, 173; Eitan Wilf and, 122, 143; ethos, 132, 140, 145; experimental music and, 122, 128, 138, 140, 142–44; finances, 134, 138–41; fundraiser, 141; hiding and seeking, 128–32; history, 122; inclusivity and exclusivity, 136, 137; jazz by default, 122–28; John Zorn and, 124, 126, 128–30, 132, 134, 143–45, 173; John Zorn on, 122, 141–42, 173; John Zorn's strategy for operating, 145; Monday night seminars, 123; moved to The New School, 122, 128, 132, 138–44, 173; music series, 139, 140; naming of, 132; opening, 122, 129–30, 132; original location, 122, 128–30, 132–39, 173; overview, 122; a purchase made with cultural capital, 137–42; reviews of, 126–27, 133–34; Richard Kessler

and, 140, 141, 144, 145; schedule, 122; serving music in the East Village, 132–37; serving through music at the New School's margins, 142–45; Teal at, 122–23; Tyshawn Sorey and, 123, 124; visibility, 122, 128–30, 132, 137–39, 143–45; website, 122, 132, 134–35; Whitney Museum of American Art and, 173
Stone Open House (SOH), 137
Stone Worship Orchestra, 137
"Stuttering" (Hersch), 40–43
Suhadolnik, Sarah, 161
Svigals, Alicia, 136
"sweet" music, 150, 151, 153
swing era, 150, 154, 155
swing music, 10, 26, 59, 81; Bill Evans and, 75–81; JALC and, 55, 59, 73–76, 83; Mary Lou Williams and, 68, 70, 72–74; SFJazz and, 87

Taylor, Billy, 52, 54, 83
Thinking in Jazz (Berliner), 94–95
Three Deuces, 1–2
tonic, 138, 139, 142
Toswell, M. J., 97
tourism, 9; New Orleans, 146–48, 170–71; Preservation Hall and, 146, 147, 157, 158, 162–63, 168, 170, 171; and The Stone, 139; Village Vanguard and, 18
transgression, 128; defined, 128; tradition of, 127
trio, jazz piano, 27–28. *See also specific trios*
Tristano, Lennie, 76
Turner, Mark, 19, 34
Tynan, John A., 74, 77

university jazz education programs, 96; local and global, 102–5; professionals on campus and students on the scene, 114–18; universities as places, 96–98
University of Nebraska (UNO), 104; Jazz Ensemble, 103–5; jazz studies program, 103–5
unmarked, the, 130; potential power of, 144; theory of, 129. *See also* visibility

Van Bebber, Mike, 106–8, 111, 113–14

Vereen, Ben, 65
Village Vanguard: anniversary celebrations, 21, 30, 37; becoming a jazz club, 23; cash-only policy, 33–34; characterizations of, 15, 16, 21; from experiment to landmark, 21–27; Fred Hersch and today's, 35–38; historical perspective on, 15–18; holding on and moving on, 30–36; John Coltrane and, 27, 30; live albums produced at, 28–30; Lorraine Gordon and, 24–25, 27, 28, 31–35, 37, 38, 47; mainstream jazz and, 16, 22, 24–27, 40–42; Max Gordon and, 21–25, 27, 28, 33, 34; opening, 21; overview and description of, 15–16; performers, 25; physical characteristics, 15–16; Preservation Hall and, 9, 149; redefinition (as a jazz club) and repetition, 27–30; Thelonious Monk at, 16, 23–25; tourism and, 18
visibility: vs. invisibility, 122, 128; John Zorn, The Stone, and, 122, 128–30, 132, 137–39, 143–45; Peggy Phelan on, 5, 129, 144; and power, 5, 129, 143–45; problematic nature of, 129. *See also* unmarked

Waits, Nasheet, 40
Waller, Thomas "Fats," 63–68, 90; aspects of and contributions to jazz, 65; Bill Evans and, 63, 66, 74, 75; characterizations of, 65; Judy Carmichael and, 65–68; persona and performance style, 65–68; physical description, 64, 65, 68
Waltz for Debby (Evans), 28
"Waltz for Debby" (Evans), 79, 80
Warren, Harry, 43
Watrous, Peter, 54
Wells, Christi Jay, 6
"What a Wonderful World" (Armstrong), 161
Whiteman, Paul, 151, 153
Whiting, Sam, 87
Whitney Museum of American Art, 173, 174
Wilf, Eitan Y., 122, 143
Williams, Cootie, 113
Williams, Martin, 4, 77

Williams, Mary Lou, 63, 64, 68–73, 75, 182n52; Billie Jean King and, 69–75, 182n52; *Black Christ of the Andes*, 72, 73; description, overview, and characterizations of, 68–70; feminism and, 71, 73–75; inducted into Hall of Fame, 68, 73; JALC and, 64, 68–69, 72–74, 88, 182n52; swing music and, 68, 70, 72–74; Thelonious Monk and, 70, 71
women's movement. *See* feminism

Yoshi's (Oakland, CA), 20, 21

Zorn, John, 127, 131, 139, 173; artistic standpoint, 122; aspirations, 128–29; background, 124–26; Benjamin Piekut on, 130–31; black musicians, race, and, 125–27; Dave Douglas and, 143, 144; description and characterizations of, 124–28, 143; experimental music and, 126–28, 130–31 (*see also* experimental music); finances, 140; influences on, 127–28; jazz and, 124–27; John Brackett and, 127, 128; lamp, 173, 174; music, 124, 125, 127, 130; musical poetics, 127; New School and, 139, 140, 143–45; Richard Kessler and, 140, 144, 145; transgression and, 127, 128; Whitney Museum of American Art and, 173; writings, 128. *See also under* Stone, The

Founded in 1893,
UNIVERSITY OF CALIFORNIA PRESS
publishes bold, progressive books and journals
on topics in the arts, humanities, social sciences,
and natural sciences—with a focus on social
justice issues—that inspire thought and action
among readers worldwide.

The UC PRESS FOUNDATION
raises funds to uphold the press's vital role
as an independent, nonprofit publisher, and
receives philanthropic support from a wide
range of individuals and institutions—and from
committed readers like you. To learn more, visit
ucpress.edu/supportus.

www.ingramcontent.com/pod-product-compliance
Lightning Source LLC
Chambersburg PA
CBHW020831230426
43666CB00007B/1177